Leading
WORSHIP

To John &
Sherry Street !
Bless you!

[handwritten signature]

TEXT BOOK SERIES

Leading WORSHIP

WHAT EVERY WORSHIP LEADER AND WORSHIP TEAM SHOULD KNOW

Shamblin Stone

LifeRich Publishing is a registered trademark of The Reader's Digest Association, Inc.

LifeRich Publishing books may be ordered through booksellers or by contacting:

LifeRich Publishing
1663 Liberty Drive
Bloomington, IN 47403
www.liferichpublishing.com
844-686-9607

Scripture taken from the King James Version of the Bible
Scripture taken from the New King James Version®. Copyright © 1982
by Thomas Nelson. Used by permission. All rights reserved.
Scripture quotations marked (NIV) are taken from the Holy Bible, New International Version®,
NIV®. Copyright © 1973, 1978, 1984, 2011 by Biblica, Inc.TM Used by permission of Zondervan.
All rights reserved worldwide. www.zondervan.com The "NIV" and "New International Version"
are trademarks registered in the United States Patent and Trademark Office by Biblica, Inc.TM
Scripture quotations taken from the Holy Bible, New Living Translation, Copyright © 1996, 2004.
Used by permission of Tyndale House Publishers, Inc., Wheaton, Illinois 60189. All rights reserved.
Scripture quotations taken from the Holy Bible, The Passion Translation®. Copyright © 2017,
2018, 2020 by Passion & Fire Ministries, Inc. Used by permission. All rights reserved.
Scripture quotations taken from the New American Standard Bible®, Copyright ©
1960, 1971, 1977, 1995 by The Lockman Foundation. All rights reserved.

Cover artwork by Larry DeTienne © 2022 Shamblin Stone. All rights reserved. This book was professionally edited by Joy Metcalf of Stet Editing Services, LLC. All photos, tables, charts, and graphics contained in this book are © 2022 Shamblin Stone. All rights reserved.

ISBN: 978-1-4897-3991-9 (sc)
ISBN: 978-1-4897-3990-2 (hc)
ISBN: 978-1-4897-3994-0 (e)

Library of Congress Control Number: 2022900522

Print information available on the last page.

LifeRich Publishing rev. date: 03/15/2022

DEDICATION

This book is Dedicated to
my grandson
Jesse David Gutierrez
Born December 5, 2017

According to doctors, both of Jesse's parents were unable to have children for different reasons. After prayer by several people, we experienced the birth of a miracle grandchild.

SPECIAL THANKS

Thank You to
Steve and Sheri Alexander
for your generous support,
making the editing of this book possible!

CONTENTS

Chapter Two

Examine Yourself

Chapter Three

Discovering Your Worship Ministry Philosophy

Chapter Seven
"Chain of Command"

Chapter Eight
"God's Praise Music"

Chapter Nine
"God's New Song"

Chapter Ten
"Music Conducting Skills"

Chapter Eleven
"Nonverbal Communication"

LIST OF PICTURES AND ILLUSTRATIONS

Chapter Sixteen

"The Worship Team Configuration"

Chapter Eighteen

"Practicalities"

LIST OF TABLES

Preface
LEARNING TO HEAR GOD'S VOICE

A WOUNDED HEART

When I was in elementary school, living in the town of Medicine Lodge, Kansas, I was given a puppy by one of the people in the town. The puppy was a true variety of breeds, a mutt, and was just barely old enough to be away from his mother. I was so excited when I brought that puppy home.

Also, there was a different family in town whose dog had birthed a litter of dachshund puppies. They had been able to sell all of their puppies except for the runt of the litter. Strangely, that same day they had given this runt to my sister.

My mother didn't know what hit her that day when both of her children came home from school carrying puppies. "We don't have dogs in this house!" she bristled.

Upon seeing our disappointment, my dad reasoned with my mom and after 30 minutes or so convinced her that it would be good to have a dog in the house.

"Fine," she eventually gave in, "but we're not having two dogs!"

That meant one of us was going to get to keep our dog, but which one? "Oh, let it be me," I prayed fervently.

"We're not keeping that one," my mother declared as she pointed at the puppy in my arms. I was devastated!

1

"Why not?" I burst into tears feeling like someone had just killed my best friend.

"Look at those paws," my mother pointed again. "They're huge! That dog's going to get as big as a horse!"

"So," I responded. "What's the matter with that?"

"We are not going to have any big dogs in this house!" she put her foot down again.

I looked to my dad to see if he would argue for my sake as he did a few minutes earlier, but he stayed silent. I know now that it was because he knew he would not be able to convince her to compromise on her new line in the sand, so he elected to stay quiet and be grateful for the compromise he had gotten.

I, on the other hand, was crushed and wounded in my emotions at a deeper level than I was capable of understanding at the time. Over the years, my hurt turned to anger toward my mother. Eventually, in my early 20s my anger turned to hatred for her. However, by that time I did not remember why I was angry with her, because I had suppressed the memory of that experience completely.

Out of my hatred and anger, I treated my mother terribly for many years. People would see me doing this and try to council me to respect her more. One pastor who was visiting our church as a guest speaker pulled me aside and read from the Ten Commandments *"Honor thy father and thy mother: that thy days may be long upon the land which the Lord thy God giveth thee."*[1] He tried to explained to me that if I did not start honoring my mother, I would not live long, according to that Scripture.

By that time, I had no idea why I treated my mother the way I did. My mother sought the council of others who told her it was just teenage rebellion on my part and that I would grow out of it. The problem was, I was still treating her like dirt well into my 20s. I hated her, but I didn't know why.

Every time I thought of her, I felt disgusted, angry, and hatred. I think I knew it was wrong to feel this way toward her, so I suppressed those feelings as best I could. However, the way I treated her revealed that my feelings were not buried very deep.

---

[1] Exodus 20:12 (KJV)

I know now it was the root of bitterness inside me toward her that had grown into an uncontrollable monster. I have learned that when we do not forgive someone when they hurt us, that unforgiveness destroys us—not them. Of course, my mother suffered from the way I treated her, but she never stopped praying for me.

TELLING MY MOTHER I WAS SORRY

I have told you in previous writings how I gave my life to Jesus in Danang, Vietnam, in 1970. It was not long after I invited Jesus to be the Lord of my life that He began working on things that were broken in me. One of the first things He convicted me of was the way I had always treated my mother with such disrespect and hatred for most of my life.

In Vietnam, I attended the chapel events every time they had something to attend. Not only did I go Sunday morning and Sunday evening, but I attended all the Bible studies throughout the week that the chapel sponsored. Also, because that was not enough for me, several of us got permission to use the chapel on our side of the airbase for daily prayer meetings.

Danang AFB Chapel #3

Chapel #3 consisted of two tiny prefab buildings side by side. On the left side is where the services were held, but on the right side was where we had our Bible studies and prayer meetings. It contained a very small library, tables, chairs, and a water cooler.

Our prayer meetings were not something structured. No one person led the prayer meeting. Sometimes we prayed quietly, and sometimes one of us would pray out loud for everyone to hear.

About three months after my conversion experience, on a Wednesday evening, several of us went to the little green Chapel #3 across the street from the aerial port at Danang to have a time of prayer together. Some sat in chairs, and some knelt at chairs. My heart was very burdened by the conviction of the Holy Spirit regarding the way I had treated my mother for many years, so I knelt down at a chair and draped my body over the seat.

I immediately began to repent again to the Lord for the way I treated my mother. With tears pouring out of my eyes, I told the Lord again how sorry I was for my heart attitude and my actions toward my mother.

"Lord," I prayed silently, "please tell my mother I'm sorry. I'm in a war zone, and I may not live long enough to tell her myself. I don't know if I will go home alive from this place. Please tell her that I love her and that I'm sorry for the way I have treated her!"

"Why don't you tell her yourself?" came the response from the Lord as clear as any voice I have ever heard.

When He said that to me, my mind questioned why He would say that. I was far across the Pacific Ocean, and she was in Raytown, Missouri, on the exact opposite side of the world. How was I supposed to tell her anything?

No sooner than I had thought that, I was "in the Spirit." For those of you who are not familiar with that phrase, it is used throughout the Bible. Here is a place where it is used in the New Testament.

> *I John, who also am your brother, and companion in tribulation, and in the kingdom and patience of Jesus Christ, was in the isle that is called Patmos, for the word of God, and for the testimony of Jesus Christ. I was **in the Spirit** on the Lord's day, and heard behind me a great voice, as of a trumpet, Saying, I am Alpha and Omega, the first and the last: and, What thou seest, write in a book, and send it unto the seven churches which are in Asia; unto*

Ephesus, and unto Smyrna, and unto Pergamos, and unto Thyatira, and unto Sardis, and unto Philadelphia, and unto Laodicea. Revelation 1:9–11 (KJV), emphasis added

As you read further in the book of Revelation, you understand that to be "In the spirit" is to be taken by the Spirit to another location. Some theologians call that being "translated." In John's case, he was taken into heaven by the Spirit.

Other places in the Bible, people were taken to various locations on earth. In the book of Acts, Philip was translated more than one day's journey by the Spirit after baptizing the Ethiopian Eunuch.

And when they were come up out of the water, the Spirit of the Lord caught away Philip, that the eunuch saw him no more: and he went on his way rejoicing. But Philip was found at Azotus: and passing through he preached in all the cities, till he came to Caesarea. Acts 8:39–40 (KJV)

Of course, I was brand new to the things of the Spirit and knew nothing about this Scripture or that this was even possible. But I suddenly found myself standing at the foot of my parents bed in Raytown, Missouri. It was nighttime there, and they were both asleep.

The Lord prompted me "Go ahead and tell her yourself. She will hear you."

Weeping, I began to struggle to say the words out loud. "Mom, I'm so sorry for the way I have treated you. I was so wrong! I wish there was a way I could make it up to you, but I can't. All I can do is tell you I'm sorry and hope that one day you will forgive me."

As quickly as I had gone into their dark bedroom, I was back in Danang draped over the chair in that little chapel office. The difference was the sense of being forgiven for my sins of treating my mother the way I had most of my life. I knew that, even if I did not make it home alive, I had made things right with my mother.

Mail was a lifeline to us in Vietnam. Because I wanted to receive mail, I wrote home every three or four days. I know I mentioned in a letter that I was sorry for the way I had treated my mother, and I know she wrote back telling me she forgave me. After that, my letters home were all about the great things God was doing in Danang. My mother's letters to me covered all the news from home. We never wrote about our strained relationship of the past many years. We communicated with each other as though nothing had ever happened.

After I had made it home alive, my mother and I spent hours talking to each other on the thirty-day leave I had before reporting to my next assignment. God used that time to heal all the wounds of the past between us.

One day as we were talking, I felt safe enough that I could tell her of my experience of being translated from Danang to Raytown. I had told no one of that experience, dismissing it as an emotional phenomenon, not a spiritual one.

"When did that happen?" she asked me in an anxious tone. "Do you know the exact date it happened?"

"I could figure it out," I responded. "Do you have a calendar?"

She went into the kitchen and retrieved her month-by-month calendar she had hanging on the wall and handed it to me. Flipping back through the months, I was able to pinpoint the exact day that God translated me to their bedroom. Strangely enough, my mother had circled the box of that day on her calendar.

When I told her the date and showed it to her on her calendar, she began to weep.

"While I was sleeping that night," she said through her tears, "I dreamed I went to Danang and saw you there. It was so real! That's why I circled that date."

She then went on to describe the Chapel #3 office building, inside and out, in detail. She told me in detail of our conversation that night, only she said she was standing outside the chapel building when I was talking to her.

"I have always thought that was just a very vivid dream," she told me, "but now I'm not sure."

"Mother," I explained, "you have described in detail a place I never told you about! I believe you were there, just like I believe I was here. God told me you would hear my words, and I know you did, because you have told me almost word for word what I said to you that night."

DISCOVERING WHEN BITTERNESS ENTERED ME

Never again did I treat my mother inappropriately. We had a wonderful relationship until she went to heaven in October 1999. The only disagreement we had in all that time was over speaking in tongues. Being a staunch Baptist, she believed that speaking in tongues was of the devil. I, on the other hand, discovered the wonderful gift this is to God's people.

Although she could never bring herself to accept this gift for herself, she did finally admit that I had not yielded myself to the devil. I share that in full disclosure so you understand we still had growing to do as individuals, yet even in our disagreement, our love for each other continued to grow stronger.

In 1973, God brought Chris to me as my wife. That is a completely different story that I won't get into right now, except to say I had told God I never wanted to get married. I wanted to focus on my relationship with God like Paul did. The Lord, on the other hand, had different ideas. After being married to Chris now for almost 50 years, I am very, very thankful He didn't listen to me!

Chris and I have had four children together who are all grown up now. We also have had many dogs over the years as pets. We have never owned cats because Chris is extremely allergic to them. When we first married, she could walk into a house where cats lived—they didn't have to be in the room with her—and her airways would close up in five or ten minutes, making it impossible for her to breathe.

She is not that bad now because we have prayed over her about this for as long as I have known her. However, she does not take unnecessary chances with cats. Most dogs she can handle as long as she keeps allergy medicine close. Here is a picture of Chris holding the dog we owned in the first two years we were married. We have not owned

Chris and Mickey

a lot of dogs, but every dog we have had weighed less than 25 pounds.

We were living in Prince George, British Colombia, Canada, in 1989.

I had been the music pastor at a church there since 1985. I was under a lot of stress, so Chris and I made arrangements for someone to watch the kids while we drove to the nearest town about an hour away to spend the night in a motel.

We got there on a Friday afternoon and decided to check out the town mall. Some of you will remember the large shopping malls of the 1980s. We went there just to walk indoors (it was January), kill time, and unwind. After seeing most of the mall, we came across a pet store, so we went in to browse.

Inside the store that day they had two little puppies for sale. There was a crowd gathered, and those puppies were being passed from person to person. Needless to say, they were very traumatized. We had walked up and stood among the people, so someone handed me one of the puppies.

When I took the puppy into my hands, it snuggled under my bearded chin and immediately stopped shaking. Every one of the group let out a collective sigh, and the store clerk remarked how that was the calmest they had ever seen that puppy.

"Looks like he found his owner," someone in the crowd spoke out.

We never intended to buy a puppy that day, but we did. Chris named our new family member Buddy, but I was the one Buddy chose as his master. He was mostly black with a few white spots on him, and when we first got him, he could fit into one of my hands.

The following week I made an appointment at the veterinarian for his next round of shots and an examination. The vet prided herself on being able to predict the adult size of puppies, and she told me Buddy would be between fifteen and twenty pounds. She also told me he would not get much taller than eight to ten inches.

I had taken buddy to two appointments in the first two months we had him. His growth in those two months matched her initial prediction, so she reiterated her initial prediction at the second visit. His final round of puppy shots we're scheduled for the three-month visit, then we could simply bring him back every year for his annual rabies shot.

Two weeks after his second visit, which was two weeks before his third visit, I was taking him for his morning walk. You have to know that Prince George, British Columbia, is over five hundred miles north of the American and Canadian border. In the winter, it snows all the time. In British Columbia, there is very little wind, therefore, when snow falls, it builds up in that place. It is common to see a fencepost with eight to ten inches of snow on top of it.

It had snowed the previous day, which made it very difficult for this tiny little dog to go for a walk. He would have to jump forward to make any progress at all. Every time he jumped, he disappeared inside the snow. I had on boots, so I could traverse the deep snow, but he was struggling to go anywhere with me.

To watch Buddy jump in and out of the snow struck me funny at first, and I laughed out loud. Then I felt sorry for Buddy, watching him struggle so hard. "If only he were a bigger dog," I thought to myself, "he wouldn't have so much trouble in the deep snow."

Then, for the first time since my childhood, God brought back the memory of the puppy I had been given as a child that my mother would not let me keep, because she said he would get too big. Opening up that memory file caused me to remember how hurt I was by my mother that day. Just as quickly as I remembered that event, God reviewed for me the memories of the two or three dogs we had owned since being married.

"Why do I always have to have little dogs?" I asked myself in anger. "Why can't I ever have a big dog?" I was voicing those questions inside my head out of the enormous amount of hurt associated with the memory which God had torn open from my childhood.

"Well, how big do you want this dog to be?" God asked me.

Embarrassed for complaining, I quickly told the Lord, "I guess I want this dog to be the size You want him to be."

"No!" God responded. "How big do YOU want this dog to be?"

"But God, that's not for me to decide," I tried to explain to God. "You are the one who decides the size of every living creature."

"How big," God spoke sternly and deliberately, "do you want this dog to be?"

From God's tone with me I realized He was seriously telling me to determine the size I wanted Buddy to be. I also understood that, by not answering His question, I was ticking God off, and I dared not argue with Him again.

"Well," I began slowly, "I'm really not sure." My mind was racing, trying to determine how to answer the Almighty God so I would not make him angrier with me. Holding my hand out to help me visualize different heights and the size of the animal it would take to reach those different heights, I finally extended my right arm at my side and put my palm parallel to the ground. "I suppose," I spoke out loud again, "that if I put my hand down like this I would like to be able to touch the top of his head."

"Then it will be so," God spoke one last time.

My heart was racing for several hours after that encounter. "I made God mad at me!" was all I could think about.

By the time I took buddy to his next veterinarian appointment, he had more than tripled in size. When the vet saw him, she was visibly shaken by the size he had become.

"Wow," she blurted out, "I sure misjudged this one! I told you he might get to be fifteen pounds, but he is over twenty-five pounds today."

I was too embarrassed to tell her why. I guess I was still ashamed for making God angry with me, and I didn't know how to tell her what happened without including that in the story.

One year later I took Buddy back to her for his annual rabies shot and checkup. By this time, he had grown to the height that I had told God I wanted him to be, and he weighed about 45 pounds. When I walked into the exam room with buddy, she immediately began to apologize to me again for her wrong prediction as to Buddy's adult size. When I could tell this bothered her so much, I knew I had to tell her what happened, so I did.

I was afraid she was going to think I was crazy, but she had no problems believing that God

Buddy, the Vet, and me

did that miracle for me. She even told me about a miracle that God had done for her as a child. She was more relieved to find out why her prediction concerning Buddy's size was so off.

Here's a picture of her, me, and Buddy at that visit. Buddy and I continued to see her every year until we left Prince George.

Through that experience with Buddy, God revealed to me the beginning of my anger and hatred toward my mother. Although I had forgiven my mother many years earlier, that experience allowed God to be able to heal me of that childhood hurt.

HEARING GOD'S VOICE

Whenever I use language like I did in telling the story I just told, I always have people ask me about hearing God's voice.

"How can you carry on a conversation with God?" is always the question.

"How can you NOT carry on conversations with God?" is always my response.

It took me several years to figure out that there are many Christians who do not know how to hear God's voice. I guess I was fortunate, because the man who led me to the Lord, Don Elliott, also discipled me. He taught me that prayer is talking with God the same way I would talk to him. Don also said that prayer is listening to God as much as, or more than, I talked and then doing what God said to do.

From the beginning, when I asked God a question, I would wait until I got an answer. At first it was difficult to decipher what the Lord was saying to me, but because I knew He was speaking to me, I knew that it was not His fault if I did not understand what He was saying to me. With that being settled, I could then go about the task of learning to hear and understand God's voice.

Many people will ask me, "How do you know that Jesus is speaking to you?"

My answer to that is simply, "Because He told me in the Bible that He would speak to us."

My sheep hear my voice, and I know them, and they follow me: John 10:27 (KJV)

11

If I am one of Jesus' sheep, this verse assures me that He will always talk to me.

Many people misquote this Scripture and say "My sheep know my voice." That is not what it says at all! It tells us that if we are His sheep, we all will hear His voice. It does not say that we will all know how to recognize His voice when we hear it. It takes a while to learn how to recognize His voice when He speaks to us.

It is Jesus in this Scripture who knows us, not us who knows His voice. Again, it takes a while to learn how to recognize His voice when He speaks to us.

The last statement of this phrase which Jesus declared says, *"and they follow me."* Not only is it important for us to learn how to hear His voice, but we must obey what He says! It is useless for us to hear Jesus' instructions and then not obey them.

If you are called to be a worship leader, then you MUST be able to hear God's Voice, and obey His leading in the moment of worship!

Just because you prayed and sought God all week long about the worship service does not satisfy this requirement of hearing and obeying God. You must be able to let God change directions of a worship service when He wants.

Leading worship requires being led by God's Spirit moment by moment. Of course, being a pastor requires that as well, but I am not trying to equip pastors with this book, just worship leaders.

There are unlimited reasons why we need to be able to hear from God in the moment and change directions at a moment's notice. Someone may have responded to God's Spirit and finally obeyed His prompting to come to church after a year of God calling them. Even if you know that person, you may not know what God used to get them to obey Him. It could have been a tragedy in their life. It may have been a word from an old friend. It may have been a memory of a loved one.

I am not advocating for seeker sensitive services. I am advocating for Spirit sensitive services. Of course, you may never know the reason why God directed you to change your worship plan for that service. God is not obligated to tell you why He has you do something out of the ordinary! Every worship leader MUST learn to hear and obey the voice of God without hesitation and without doubting.

JUDGE WHAT YOU HEAR BY THE BIBLE

It is important to know that God's Spirit will never say something to us which will violate, or go against, the written Word of God. Therefore, we must know what the Bible says if we are to judge what we are hearing with the Word of God.

Throughout history there have been many people say that God has told them to do something that was completely contrary to Scripture. The serial killer Son of Sam told police that God told him every time he was to kill someone. When we know God's law, we know God has commanded us not to murder or take someone's life. That means that killer was receiving instructions from a demonic spirit, not God's Spirit.

When we don't know the Bible, it is easy to think we are hearing from God, when in truth we are hearing from our enemy. That is why we must scrutinize everything we think we hear from God by the Word of God. That is also why we must spend time every day reading the Bible for as long as we are alive.

HEARING SPECIFIC INSTRUCTIONS FROM GOD

If you are being called by God to be a worship leader, He has already been training you how to hear His voice, so you will be able to receive specific instructions from Him when they are needed. Although the Lord will train you differently than He trained me how to hear and obey His voice, let me share with you a few of the experiences in my journey in hopes that they may encourage you in yours.

ANOINTING IN THE HANDS

One of the men I was stationed in Danang with, whom I have maintained contact with over the years, is my dear friend Bill English. Bill left Vietnam a week or so after I did. On his way home, he chose to stop by Raytown,

Bill English

13

Missouri, to spend a few days with me before spending the rest of his thirty-day leave at his home.

Bill taught me how to enjoy the presents of the Holy Spirit, and he taught me that speaking in tongues was not from the devil. Whenever Bill got lost in God's presence, his prayer language changed from an unidentified language into French. That's how we knew when he had gotten totally lost in the presence of God. By the way, Bill never learned to speak French, so he had no idea what he was praying in tongues.

One day Bill and I and our friend Rod Ellis were praying together in the youth room of my dad's church in Raytown. We had been praying for about forty-five minutes when the Lord spoke to me, as well as gave me a physical sign that it was him speaking. The sign was a sensation and the palms of my hands that power, like light, was streaming from them.

When I felt this sensation, I paused my prayer and silently asked God what it was I was feeling.

"That is the gift of healing," the Lord told me in a matter-of-fact way. "I want you to use it to lay your hands on Bill and say the words 'Be thou healed!'," God told me.

"I can't do that," I argued with God in my mind. "He would think I'm crazy!"

"Lay your hands on Bill, and pronounce 'Be thou healed!'" the Lord instructed me a second time.

"How do I know this is You talking to me?" I questioned. "How do I know I'm not just making this up in my mind? I will look really stupid if this is not You."

"You have to trust Me," the Lord answered. "Now reach out and lay your hands on Bill and declare, 'Be thou healed!'" the Lord instructed me for the third time.

I was so torn inside. I wanted to believe that I was hearing the voice of God, but I was afraid I had made the whole thing up in my mind. But then, what about this sensation in my hands? How could I make that up? Was I deceiving myself so much that I had made up this feeling in my hands?

"I'm scared, God," I told Him silently. "I don't want to do that."

I had no sooner said that in my mind when the sensation left my hands, and Bill stopped in the middle of his audible prayer, opened his eyes and stared at his hands, and declared out loud, "I feel a tingling in the palms of my hands."

When he said that, I knew I had missed God! God had given the sensation in my hands to show me that what He was saying to me was from Him, and I did not obey His instructions. He had asked me three times, and I said no to Almighty God, so God took the gift He had intended for me to use and had given it to Bill. My heart sank to the floor as I repented silently for my disobedience.

Bill stared at his hands, moving them slightly from side to side. "I wonder what this is," Bill asked out loud.

I knew, but I was too embarrassed to say anything.

"Uh oh," Bill spoke up again, "it's leaving."

No sooner had Bill said that, Rod pulled his palms up and began to stare at them. "It's in my hands now," Rod reported. "It feels like my hands are covered with oil," Rod went on. "Either that or a big bubble of mercury in the palm of my hands, and when I dump it out and turn my palm up again, it fills back up."

Rod turned his hands over three or four times as he was describing the sensation in his hands.

By this time, I was feeling terrible for telling God no. "If only I had said yes," I thought to myself. "Now God has taken the gift away that He wanted to give to me, and He is allowing Bill and Rod these experiences to show me what I have missed out on."

"Oh," Rod said, "it's leaving me now."

The next second I felt the sensation of the power of God enter the palms of my hands again. Bill felt tingling, Rod felt oil, but what I felt was radiating power shooting out of the palms of my hands as if it were an invisible light. It went out of my palms in the direction I pointed them.

"I feel it now," I audibly reported.

Once again God instructed me to lay hands on Bill and say, "Be thou healed," which I did without hesitation.

"How did you know I needed to be healed?" Bill asked me.

"I guess God told me," I responded.

GOD ANSWERS PRAYERS SPECIFICALLY

After my tour of duty in Danang and after my thirty-day leave, I reported to McConnell Air Force Base just south of Wichita, Kansas. Being single, I was housed in one of the barracks on the base. Here is a picture of my barracks there. I have circled the window of my room on the second floor. The only way to access the second floor was up the external stairway at the end of the barracks. Directly across the street from this end of the barracks was a baseball field used in off duty hours for recreation.

McConnel AFB barracks

In each of the rooms, there was one set of bunk beds, a desk, two chairs, and two built-in wardrobes with space for hanging close above and drawers below. Each floor of the barracks shared two common bathrooms with showers, one at each end of the floor. I was lucky enough to be in a room by myself.

One day after work hours, I was picking up my dry cleaning and laundry from the base laundry. The guy in line in front of me did not have enough cash to pay for his laundry, so I made up the difference for him. After I had grabbed my clothes and was walking out of the laundry door, the guy whom I had helped pay for his clothing was waiting for me. I thought he had waited just to thank me, but it turned out to be much more than that.

After talking to him for quite some time, he made the decision to give his life to Jesus. Then he asked me to help him become established as a Christian by allowing him to move into my room. Although I enjoyed not having a roommate, I felt the Spirit of God prompt me to agree to let him move into my room.

One day, after he had been there for a while, he woke up with the roof of his mouth swollen and pussy. When his work day was over, he came into the room and asked me what I thought he should do about it.

"Have you prayed about it?" I asked him. "What did God tell you to do?"

"I don't know," he responded.

"Well, let me pray for you," I said. "Lord, I ask that you dry up this pus in the roof of his mouth."

We went to bed and went to our respective jobs the next day. I was already in the room that evening sitting at the desk reading my Bible by the time he got there. When he spoke to me, he avoided pronouncing any consonants that required him to touch the roof of his mouth with his tongue.

Bill Miller, my roommate

"I _ont k_ow," he began, "maybe I hould_ go to the ER."

"Why?" I asked.

"I _an't touch the roof of ma mouth with ma tongue," he struggled to say.

"Why not?" I continued to ask him.

"Be_ause you praye_," he painfully answered.

"What do you mean?" I asked, trying my best to figure out what he was saying.

"You as_e_ Go_ to _ry up the pus," he explained, "an_ Go_ _id. Only _ow the roof of my mouth is _ried, wrinkle_ s_in that hurts horrib_y every time I tou__ it with my to__ue!"

I had forgotten that God is a literalist, which I learned from my episode of quitting smoking, and that He answers what we ask, not what we intended to ask.

"Before you do anything," I said, "let me pray a minute."

He bowed his head and closed his eyes while I did the same thing to seek God.

Before I could ask God anything, the sensation that I had experienced a few months earlier in Raytown came back into the palms of my hands. Then I heard God say to me, "Go touch him and say, 'Be thou healed!'"

"Lord, I can't do that!" I insisted. "He would think I'm crazy."

God repeated His instructions to me a second time. I stood up and walked across the room, stressing over God's directive. I had never been around anyone who operated in the gift of healing. I grew up in a Baptist Church, which believe that the gifts of the Spirit ceased when the apostles died. When they prayed for people to be healed in our church, it was always prefaced by the words, "If it be Thy will." I had never heard anyone command healing to take place. That was a completely foreign concept to me.

"I can't do it," I told the Lord.

Immediately the Lord repeated His instructions to me for the third time.

I was standing across the room facing my roommate who was standing in front of our bunk beds with his head bowed in prayer. As soon as I told the Lord "No" for the third time, the sensation in my hands left. When that happened, my heart sank. I had disobeyed God again, and once again He had taken the gift from me that He wanted me to use to bless someone else.

"Oh Lord," I began to weep and pray silently, "I am so sorry for being such a coward. I deserve for You to take this gift from me. But my roommate does not deserve to suffer from my disobedience. Please give me back the gift of healing, not for my sake, but for his. Please, don't let him suffer for my mistake!"

After that prayer, the sensation began slowly to come back into my hands as the Lord spoke to me. "Because you repented, and because of your unselfish prayer, I will give it back to you this time. However," God continued, "because of your disobedience, you will not be allowed to touch him, and you will be paralyzed from your waist down."

By this time the sensation in my hands was stronger than it had ever been. I was aware that the power of God was shooting out of my palms like invisible light rays. However, troubled by the last statement God had made, I tried to take a step or two but was unable to move my legs.

"Aim your hands toward your roommate," God instructed me, "and declare 'Be thou healed!'"

I slowly raised my hands and turned them toward my roommate whose eyes were still closed. When my palms turned towards him, he opened his eyes and looked at me. Falling backwards, then catching himself before he fell down, he opened his eyes very wide.

"Be healed!" I declared out loud.

When I said that, his eyes closed as he teetered back and forth on his feet. After a moment, he opened his eyes. With his mouth open, it was obvious he was touching the roof of his mouth with his tongue.

"It's gone!" he declared. "All the dried-up skin on the roof of my mouth is gone, and I can touch it without any pain at all!"

With that, he collapsed to the floor praising God for his healing.

I, however, continued to stand where I was, unable to move my legs. After a few moments, the Lord spoke to me again.

"Because you have been obedient to my instructions," the Lord said, "I will give you back your ability to walk."

Trying to move my legs, I successfully walked a few steps. Weeping, I began thanking the Lord for having mercy on me.

SIGNS IN THE SKY

To help my roommate get established in his faith, I began teaching Weekly Bible studies in our room every Tuesday night. That Bible study grew from just the two of us to more than twenty guys sitting on our beds, chairs, and floor. Because it continued to grow, we eventually had to move it to the base Service Center, where it grew to more than fifty in attendance. I was only a little over one year old in the Lord but was teaching a Bible study.

One Tuesday night while we were still meeting in our room, the Lord told me to take everyone outside onto the ball field. God had told me to tell them that he wanted to show them something when we got out there.

As we stood together in a group, yet facing every direction on that clear July night, God began to speak to me.

"Tell everybody to look at the sky in this direction," God told me as he indicated to me a specific point in the southwest sky.

Raising my hand pinpointing with my index finger, I told everyone, "God is telling me for us to look at this point in the sky, because he wants to show us something."

Everyone turned and I looked up to the direction I was pointing. We were all silent in anticipation. Nothing happened right away, but in three or four minutes of God telling me to have us all look, we all saw a shooting star in the exact place where God told us to look.

"Whoa," "wow," "awesome," and "praise the Lord" were heard randomly from everyone as we saw this phenomenon in the sky.

By the way, in case you're wondering, that week I called the National Weather Department at the Wichita airport to find out whether it was aware of a meteor shower on that night. The individual I spoke with told me there was no meteor shower that particular night and did not expect one for a couple of months.

We continued under-the-stars worship for a while, thanking God for His display in the heavens. Then I heard God speak to me again.

"Tell them to look at this point in the sky," God told me as he indicated a point much higher but in the opposite direction than He said to look the first time.

Every one eagerly turned and bent their heads back so they could look high in the sky. Nothing happened right away. As a matter of fact, we all stood in that uncomfortable position for more than ten minutes.

A couple of guys said to each other, "This is ridiculous! Let's just leave," and they turned their backs to walk away.

As soon as they turned, we saw the second shooting star streak across the sky in the exact position God told me to have us look. This reignited everyone's audible praise to Almighty God, which continued for quite some time. The ones who had looked away and missed the display felt bad enough on their own but were teased mercilessly by the rest of the guys.

After a few minutes, the Lord spoke to me a third time and gave me the exact position in the sky that he wanted us all to look at one last time. For the third time I pointed to a place in the western sky and told everyone to watch that place, because God said he was going to do something very unique this time in the sky.

We all stared intensely at the place where God said to look. After fifteen minutes of watching the sky, someone said, "Did I miss the shooting star?"

"No," several answered, "there has not been one yet."

Another guy spoke up, "I have been seeing something very strange in that point in the sky since Shamblin told us to look there."

"What do you see?" several of the guys asked.

"Well," he continued, "that is the planet Mars. It is not supposed to be pulsating the way it is. It always gives off a steady light."

There at the exact point in the sky where God told us to look was the red planet. Its light would take a second to get very bright, brighter than any star in the sky; then in the next second or two, it would get so dim that we barely could see it. That repeated itself over and over. It had been doing that for the previous fifteen to twenty minutes.

"Why did you point this out earlier?" someone asked him.

"I saw Mars was acting strange as soon as we looked at it," he answered, "but I thought we were waiting on another shooting star."

"Did God tell you we were to wait on another shooting star?" someone asked me.

"No," I answered. "He only said He would give us a sign in the sky."

The guy who had pointed out the pulsating of Mars spoke up, "Well, what we are seeing right now is a huge sign! I have been watching the sky all my life, and I have never seen any star or planet act like this."

As soon as he had said that, Mars stopped pulsating and once again gave out a steady red glow. We watched it for several more minutes, wondering if it would pulsate again for us, but it never did.

The Lord told me to tell everyone, "That's your lesson for tonight. With God all things are possible!"[2]

TURNING ON THE STREET LIGHTS

In addition to my Bible study on the base, I also attended and led worship for a Bible study in the home of a Boeing executive named Cliff Newberry. As best as I recall, their meetings took place on Thursday nights. It was at one of those meetings that I met Chris, my wife, for the first time.

Everyone who attended those meetings were single and looking for roommates to keep down their expenses. We had also heard about Christian community houses popping up all over the country. I had actually stopped in Los Angeles for a few days on my way back from Vietnam to spend time in a Christian commune out there. Having

---

[2] Matthew 19:26

experienced that lifestyle for about four days, I wanted to see that take place in Wichita. So, I begin asking God to provide a place where many of us could live in the same house.

On my way back to the Air Force base from the Newberry's one evening, the Lord told me he wanted to take me a different route. "Lead the way," I told him.

Instead of giving me a destination. He told me turn by turn where to go. I ended up on Murdoch Street, which was named for one of the early settlers of Wichita. Murdoch had started the *Wichita Eagle and Beacon* newspaper in the 1800s. On the corner of Murdoch and St. Francis streets stood an old two-story, Victorian-style home. It was huge! I didn't know at the time, but that was the house that Murdoch built and lived in. It was called by the Wichita historians "The Murdoch House."

"Check that out," the Lord said to me.

I pulled into the drive, which was gravel and had multiple places where cars could park off the street. When I parked on the side of the house, I could see there were no lights on inside or outside the house. I got out of my car and went up onto the front porch. There were no curtains at the windows, and from the light of the streetlights, I could see a bunch of medical equipment was being stored there.

"Is this the house you want us to have?" I asked the Lord.

God was strangely silent to my question. It was late, so I quickly drove to the Air Force base and went to bed. After all, I had to be at work at 8 a.m., and not only did they frown on us being late to work, they also wanted us to be alert at work.

I couldn't get that house out of my mind, so that weekend I took three or four of my friends from the Bible study to see the house. That time we went in the daylight, so we could see inside the picture window much better. We also walked around the house and imagined what it would be like on the inside.

That week I found out who owned that house. It belonged to a man who owned a medical supply store in Wichita. That explained all of the medical equipment we saw inside the house. I paid the man a visit at his store and asked if he would ever consider renting it to us. He told me he would rather sell it than rent it, but he agreed to show me the inside of the house.

Most of the people who were interested in living together were working during the day, so just myself and a couple other people went to see the inside of the house. It was awesome! The living room could have held over fifty young people comfortably. There were six or seven bedrooms upstairs. The dining room was huge and could serve as an overflow for the living room, holding at least twenty-five more people.

I wanted that house for a Christian commune, but God was not giving me clear direction concerning it. I started telling all my friends about it. Some asked me to see the house, so we would drive to it, walk around the outside, and end up on the front porch.

We were at the Newberry's one Thursday night in October 1972. I had told everyone about the house, and several of them wanted to see it.

At around 11 p.m. four or five cars arrived at the Murdoch house. We all parked along the south side of the house. Although it had been nice earlier in the day, it was dropping in temperature very fast, because there was no cloud cover to hold the earth's heat. None of us had worn jackets.

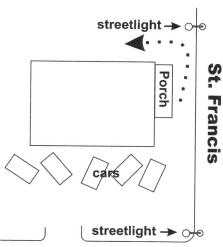

Murdock St.
The Murdock House corner

Here is a simple drawing of the corner where the Murdoch house sat. That night I was leading the group around the house in the direction of the dotted line.

We had gotten about midway along the north side of the house when the Lord told me to stop and have everyone turn around and watch the streetlight. I told them what the Lord said to me, and within a minute of us turning toward the streetlight, it went dark.

My first thought was that there was a power outage on that block, so I walked toward St. Francis Street to check out the other streetlights on the block. All the other streetlights were still burning bright. Just the one streetlight had gone out. We speculated among ourselves that the bulb had burned out and how remarkable it was that God had told us to look at the light at the moment it burned out.

"Tell them I am going to turn the light back on," the Lord instructed me.

"The Lord is telling me He is going to turn the light back on," I reported.

"Yeah, right," someone in the group jeered. "Like a burned-out bulb could ever give light! Besides," he continued, "that's the type of bulb that takes ten minutes to warm up once it is turned off."

"All I know," I responded, "is that I am learning not to doubt what God tells me. If He told me He is going to turn that light back on, then I believe Him!"

I had barely gotten those words out when that streetlight flickered, then came on immediately with its full brightness. The group responded with praises to the Lord.

We continued our walk around the house, and I asked everyone to join me on the front porch to pray about the house.

"It's too cold," someone said.

"I've got to work tomorrow," another spoke up.

More than half of the people who had come there that night got in their cars and left. There were only about eight who joined me for prayer on the porch that night. "They were right about one thing," I thought to myself. "I am freezing!"

On the porch we prayed that, if it were God's will, we would get the house. After prayer, someone started a worship song, so we all sang it through to the end. After that one or two more people left.

As they were driving off the lot, God spoke to me once again. "Tell everyone to watch the streetlight on the corner."

"God says to watch the streetlight on the corner," I declared, as I pointed to it.

As soon as we turned and looked at the corner streetlight, it flickered and went dark. There was not a lot of outward response to that light going dark, just some "Praise the Lords" but nothing overtly exuberant. A quick glance at all the other streetlights confirmed that the corner streetlight was the only one off.

"Tell them," the Lord instructed me, "that I am going to turn that light back on."

"God says He is going to turn that light back on," I announced.

Having just witnessed the Lord turn on the other streetlight less than an hour ago, nobody voiced any doubt out loud. Huddling together to try to stay warm on the porch of the Murdoch house, we commenced staring at the darkened corner streetlight.

After a half hour or so, one of the people broke the silence. "It's already 12:30 a.m. I have to be at work at 7:30. I'm sorry, but I just can't wait any longer."

As soon as they had disappeared down the street in their car, the corner streetlight flickered and came on, immediately as bright as it was before it went out.

"These people are missing what God is doing," someone commented.

"They have responsibilities tomorrow," someone spoke up in their defense.

"So do we," came the response.

"Tell them to watch both of the street lights at the same time," the Lord interrupted.

"God is telling me we need to watch both of the streetlights at the same time," I announced.

No sooner had I said that, then both streetlights flickered and went out at the exact same time.

Perhaps we were numb from the cold. Perhaps we were exhausted from the lateness of the hour and the heightened anticipation we had experience for the last hour and a half. Perhaps we were in shock from the display of power God was demonstrating, but there was only a slight collective gasp from our group when that happened.

"The Lord says He is going to turn both of these streetlights back on, one at a time, starting with the one furthest North, the one in the middle of the block," I reported to the ones who were standing on the porch with me.

I'm sorry to tell you that at this point I lost track of time. I cannot tell you how long we waited, staring at that darkened streetlight, waiting for God to turn it back on. I also cannot tell you when other people gave up and went home. All I know is that eventually that streetlight flickered and came on, immediately brighter than it was before it went out.

Once the first light came back on, we turned our attention to the street light on the corner. Again, it is hard for me to remember details at this point. All I remember is that we were down to only three or four people standing on the porch, huddling together to try to be warm.

The time between God turning on the light in the middle of the block and Him turning on the light on the corner was at least forty-five minutes. It was approximately 1:45 a.m. when I heard the Lord tell me, "Everybody watch!" I declared that to the two or three people standing there with me.

I have already told you that it was a clear, starry night. There was not a cloud in the sky! As soon as I declared out loud what God said, a lightning bolt came out of the sky and struck the corner streetlight, leaving it illuminated at least ten times brighter than normal. When that happened, I fell to my knees worshiping God. It took about ten minutes for that light too slowly dim to the brightness of the other streetlights. Slowly my legs regained enough strength for me to walk, and I could drive back to the Air Force base.

"The tragedy," I thought to myself as I drove home, "is that only three people stayed long enough to witness that miracle." For the others, the price was too much for them to pay.

By the way, for those of you who cannot handle having loose ends, the Lord never allowed us to get that house.

THE BIBLICAL WORSHIP TEXTBOOK SERIES

You are reading the fourth book in a series of four books I wrote that contain what God has taught me about Christian worship. These books are as follows:

Biblical Worship: God Has Always Had a Way He wants to Be Worshiped—this book covers general aspects about worship and establishes that God has the right to tell us how, when, and where He wants us to worship Him.

Portrait of a Worshiper: How God Designed and Created Us to Fulfill Our Purpose—this book shows that the way God designed and created us as human beings makes it possible for us to accomplish the purpose for which He created us, which is to worship Him. It is about worship from an individual perspective.

The Importance of Worshiping Together: Vital Biblical Dynamics for Unified Worship—this book introduces the biblical reasons for group worship and addresses some of the major threats against unity in worship. It is about worship from a sociological perspective.

Leading Worship: What Every Worship Leader and Worship Team Should Know—this book outlines the biblical qualifications for worship leaders, because God has made it clear that the gatherings of the church must always have leadership. It also introduces the biblical patterns of worship and applies them to the various practical aspects of leading worship.

When the Lord began teaching me about worship back in the late 1970s, He made it clear that He would only reveal to me about ten percent of what He wanted His church to know about worship. These books are my attempt to be obedient to God to share the revelation knowledge I have received from Him about worship. I am also anxious to learn the other ninety percent from others whom God has given revelation about worship!

The prefaces of these books are pieces of my story or testimony, designed to introduce you to me.

Chapter One

DETERMINING YOUR CALL
TO LEAD WORSHIP

ARE YOU CALLED TO LEAD WORSHIP?

Because worship leaders are so visible in the body of Christ, many people whom God does not call aspire to this ministry. Immature Christians will sometimes be more attracted to the more visible ministries in a local church. Cleaning the toilets or attending the nursery does not have the same potential to be appreciated by as many people as being a worship leader.

Even if God has called you to lead worship, you need to find out if He has called you to be a primary worship leader or a secondary worship leader. Not everyone who wants to lead worship is called to lead worship. Likewise, not everyone called to lead worship is called to do so in large gatherings or as a primary worship leader.

How would you feel if you were told by God, or someone else, that you are not called to lead worship? Could you lay it down and walk away from it? Would you worship with all your heart as a member of the congregation, or do you have to have people looking at you to worship with high praise?

Everyone is called to be a worshiper. Only some are called to be a primary or secondary worship leader! It is not a question of whether you are called to be a worshiper. Every Christian is called to be a worshiper. We know that by reading the Bible.

> *This people I have formed for Myself; They shall declare My praise. Isaiah 43:21(NKJV)*

EVERY CHRISTIAN IS CALLED INTO MINISTRY

Every person who has given their life to the Lord is also chosen by God for a specific ministry calling. I did not say that every person will be called by God to make their living through their ministry.

Only some worshipers are called to function as a Levite did in the Old Testament and receive offerings from the others for their sustenance. Also, those who are called to make their living by their ministry do not have a more important ministries than those who are not called into full-time ministry. It is simply God's choice who does "what" and how they do it in His church. Remember, no ministry is more important than another in the kingdom of God.

If you do not know the ministry God has called you to do, then it is important that you find that out as soon as possible. It is not wise to go through life not knowing God's call on your life.

> *Wherefore be ye not unwise, but understanding what the will of the Lord is. Ephesians 5:17 (KJV)*

I assume you may be just as frustrated as I am when someone tells me what to do but does not tell me how to do it. Permit me to take a few minutes to talk about what the Bible has to say about determining God's will for our lives.

WHAT MOTIVATES YOU?

The first question you need to ask yourself is, "What do I enjoy doing?" Another way to ask that question would be, "What type of ministry am I motivated toward?"

In Romans 12, Paul explained to us that God has created all of mankind with seven distinct Ministry motivations. These have been called "motivational gifts" by several different Bible teachers. God has given every person varying degrees of those seven motivational gifts. If you can discover which of those seven gifts God has put a desire in your heart to do, you are well on your way to discovering God's will for your life.

There are extensive studies available concerning Romans 12's list of seven motivational gifts. If you have not taken a test to discover your motivational gift, please look up one online and take it. Determining which motivational gift is strongest in you is a great first step to take to know God's will for your life. Here is the Scripture this teaching is taken from.

> *For by the grace given me I say to every one of you: Do not think of yourself more highly than you ought, but rather think of yourself with sober judgment, in accordance with the measure of faith God has given you. Just as each of us has one body with many members, and these members do not all have the same function, so in Christ we who are many form one body, and each member belongs to all the others. We have **different gifts**, according to the grace given us. If a man's gift is **prophesying**, let him use it in proportion to his faith. If it is **serving**, let him serve; if it is **teaching**, let him teach; if it is **encouraging**, let him encourage; if it is **contributing** to the needs of others, let him give generously; if it is **leadership**, let him govern diligently; if it is showing **mercy**, let him do it cheerfully. Romans 12:3–8 (NKJV)*

Here is a short explanation of the type of person who has each of these motivational gifts operating in their life.

Prophetic

If you are prophetic, you can be intolerant of sin. You are prone to be impatient with sinners and tend to be a bit of a perfectionist in spiritual and natural matters. Until you mature, you can be pushy and expect more from other people than sometimes they expect of themselves. You see the potential in others, not just their present state or abilities.

Server

If you are a server, or helper, you are most fulfilled when you are helping someone else realize their goals and dreams. You are most creative in coming up with ways to improve someone else's vision. You, many times, are capable of giving great attention to detail, and you don't mind doing the jobs nobody else want to do. No responsibility is too small for you.

Teacher

If you are motivated by teaching, you are always teaching in everything you do. You are not satisfied with surface-level knowledge about areas of interest. You investigate the depths of what interests you. Life is extremely organized in some areas, usually not all areas. You take joy in seeing those you teach succeed.

Encourager

You are positive and optimistic, a "glass is half full" kind of person. Other people enjoy being around you, because they always feel better after being with you. When you walk into a room, the atmosphere changes noticeably. When you are absent, it is also noticed. You cheer people without even trying. Many encouragers don't even realize what they do.

Giver

Whereas all are expected to give, a giver receives an incredible "high" or adrenalin rush when they are able to meet someone's need. It is the most fun a giver can have on the earth, to supply the needs of others. Some givers like to remain anonymous; others prefer the recognition for what they give. A true giver will give even when they have very little to give. They can become addicted to giving.

Leader

You can spot a leader even when they are a child. They are the ones who are always telling the other children what to do. They organize, they delegate, they make things happen. They expect everybody around them to do as they say, and are shocked when someone doesn't do what they are told. They are always coming up with a better way of doing something. They are visionaries, not detail people. They do not do well with repetitive jobs.

Mercy Motivated

Those who give mercy frustrate the leaders and the prophetic people. Giving people more than one or two chances to succeed does not make any sense to them. To the mercy giver, every person deserves as many chances as it takes for them to be successful. We never give up on anyone, as long as they are alive. A mercy person makes the best listener. Likewise, a person with mercy can find it difficult to establish boundaries or to say no.

It is not my intention to give you an extensive teaching on these motivational gifts. I would like for you to research this on your own and find out which motivational gifts are strongest in your life. Once you have determined that, you will have a better idea of the category of ministry God wants you involved in.

However, to learn your specific calling, you will need to explore one or more of the following Biblical ways.

DETERMINING GOD'S CALL #1—THE DESIRES OF OUR HEART

> *Delight thyself also in the LORD; and he shall give thee the desires of thine heart. Commit thy way unto the LORD; trust also in him; and he shall bring it to pass. Psalms 37:4–5 (KJV)*

The word "heart" in this Scripture is the Strong's concordance Hebrew word number 3820.[3] It is defined as "the soul, heart (of man)." It goes on to define it as the "mind, knowledge, thinking, reflection, memory, inclination, resolution, determination (of will), the conscience, the center of our moral character; as in the seat of appetites, the seat of emotions, and passions, and the seat of courage." If you have read *Portrait of a Worshiper*, you will recognize this "heart" as the soul of each person.

The first instruction in this Scripture is for us to "delight" ourselves in the Lord. What does it mean to delight ourselves in anything? I believe it has to do with choosing to find pleasure and delight in whatever object of delight we choose. In this case, we are choosing the relationship with our Lord to be our focus. That means we delight in getting to know the Lord, we delight in worshiping the Lord, and we delight in learning more about the Lord. It means the totality of our enjoyment and pleasure in life is found in the Lord.

When the Lord is indeed our entire focus, our heart begins to change to desire what He desires. No longer are the selfish, ego-driven desires of our flesh important to us. Our desires begin to change to want what God wants for us more than what we want.

When our desires begin to line up with God's desires for us, that is when we will begin to realize the desires of our heart.

> Now this is the confidence that we have in Him, that if we ask anything according to His will, He hears us. And if we know that He hears us, whatever we ask, we know that we have the petitions that we have asked of Him. 1 John 5:14–15 (NJKV)

Here is the way Paul wrote about this principle of receiving from God what God has put within our heart to desire.

> ... for it is God who works in you both to will and to do for His good pleasure. Do all things without complaining and disputing, Philippians 2:13–14 (NKJV)

---

[3] Strong, J. *Strong's Exhaustive Concordance of the Bible.* (Peabody: Hendrickson Publishers, 2007).

Here is the way John wrote about this principle of God putting His will in our hearts. This Scripture is referring to God putting His will into the hearts of evil men.

> For God hath put in their hearts to fulfil His will, and to agree, and give their kingdom unto the beast, until the words of God shall be fulfilled. Revelation 17:17 (KJV)

Therefore, the way we can determine God's specific will for our lives is to look deep into our hearts. We ask ourselves what we desire most in our heart. What has God put in us to want more than anything else?

The phrase "to will" in Philippians 2 means "to desire or want more than anything else." We are not trying to determine the fleshly desires of our pride and ego; we are wanting to determine the deep desires of the God-implanted dreams for our life. When we discover what Godly calling has been implanted deep in our heart by God, we then have discovered God's specific will for our lives.

BE CAREFUL, OUR HEART CAN DECEIVE US

This is not a fail-safe way to determine God's will for our lives, because we all have the potential of being deceived.

> And the Lord smelled a sweet savour; and the Lord said in His heart, I will not again curse the ground any more for man's sake; for the imagination of **man's heart is evil** from his youth; neither will I again smite any more everything living, as I have done. Genesis 8:21 (KJV), emphasis added

> There are many devices in a man's heart; nevertheless the counsel of the Lord, that shall stand. Proverbs 19:21 (KJV)

We never rely on looking into our heart only, because of the potential it has to deceive us. By the way, when we are deceived, we are always the last person to find out about it. That is the very definition of deception. To guard against undetected deception in our lives, we must remain teachable and accountable.

There is no place for lone-ranger Christians in the body of Christ. It is the straggling sheep that the wolf kills. A wolf never runs into the middle of the flock, because he would get trampled to death by the frightened, stampeding sheep. Instead, the wolf waits until he can get between a sheep and the rest of the flock. In that lonely place, no sheep will survive. We all need other people to examine what we are thinking on a weekly basis!

How does a sheep get drawn away from the rest of the flock? No sheep in their right mind willfully rebels against their Sheppard/flock and willfully places themselves in harm's way. Sheep have to be led astray by deception. One way deception can come to us is we can be led into deception by not worshiping God with our whole heart.

> *This people draweth nigh unto me with their mouth, and honoureth me with their lips; but their heart is far from me. But in vain they do worship me... Matthew 15:8–9a (KJV)*

Worshiping God with outward motions may fool everyone else around you, but God always knows the truth.

> *The heart is deceitful above all things, and desperately wicked: who can know it? I the LORD search the heart, I try the reins, even to give every man according to his ways, and according to the fruit of his doings. Jeremiah 17:9–10 (KJV)*

HOW IS OUR HEART PURIFIED?

Every potential and present worship leader needs to memorize this Scripture. Again, if you are called to be a primary or secondary worship leader in the body of Christ, then this following Scripture will apply to you, God will see to that.

*Sorrow is better than laughter: for by the sadness of
the countenance the heart is made better. Ecclesiastes
7:3 (KJV)*

So you want to be a worship leader, do you? Well, get ready, because this Scripture is your destiny, until God is satisfied that He can trust you to lead His people into His presence.

Do not say, "I am not proud, therefore I will not go through this breaking process." Every Spirit-led worship leader I know has gone through this maturing process. If it does not happen early in life, it will happen later. You will want it to happen as early in life as possible. Many worship leaders who obtained a level of notoriety early in life have not survived this process when they went through it later in life. By "not survived," I mean that many are not leading worship today, many are not walking with the Lord to this day. They simply could not allow God to break their hearts, so now they sit on the "bench." The saddest cases, however, are those who have refused to go through this breaking process yet are still in positions of worship leadership today. They are worshiping with their lips, but their heart is far from God. Their worship has become only a performance—a form of Godliness with no power.

King David messed up in ways that most of us will never sin. Still he is called a man after God's own heart by God. The reason David received this glowing report from God Himself was because of this lifelong prayer and attitude depicted in Psalms 51.

*Create in me a clean heart, O God, and renew a
steadfast spirit within me. Psalms 51:10 (NKJV)*

David understood something that no other Jew of his day understood. God was not after the legal burnt sacrifices for sins committed that Moses wrote down for the people as law. God was after a right heart from us.

*For You do not desire sacrifice, or else I would give it;
You do not delight in burnt offering. The sacrifices of God
are a broken spirit, A broken and a contrite heart — These,
O God, You will not despise. Psalms 51:16–17 (NKJV)*

Do you want to be a worship leader like David? Then get ready to have your heart broken—over and over. That's what God wants in His worship leaders. Until you learn to worship God with a broken heart, you are not qualified to be a worship leader!

HOW TO DETERMINE GOD'S CALL #2 – GOD'S PEACE

In the 1970s, I once heard a Bible teacher state, "The Devil can duplicate and counterfeit everything God has except for God's peace." I have found that to be true in my life. Once you have known God's peace, there is no way you will settle for a counterfeit.

> **Until you learn to worship God with a broken heart, you are not qualified to be a worship leader!**

True Godly peace is one of the nine fruits of the Holy Spirit. Here is where Paul the Apostle listed these fruits for us.

> But the fruit of the Spirit is love, joy, **peace**, longsuffering, kindness, goodness, faithfulness, gentleness, self-control. Against such there is no law. Galatians 5:22–23 (NKJV), emphasis added

Those characteristics of the Holy Spirit are proof that the Holy Spirit is present and operating in our lives. In addition to peace being one of the validations of the presence of the Holy Spirit in our personal lives, peace is also one of the three traits of the kingdom of God.

> For the kingdom of God is not eating and drinking, but righteousness and **peace** and joy in the Holy Spirit. Romans 14:17 (NKJV)

Wherever the kingdom of God is, you will have those three attributes as verifications that you indeed have encountered the kingdom of God. Now God has told us that He wants to dwell with us.

*And I heard a great voice out of heaven saying, Behold, the tabernacle of God is **with** men, and he will dwell **with** them, and they shall be His people, and God Himself shall be **with** them, and be their God. Revelation 21:3 (KJV), emphasis added*

Although this Scripture does not use the word "kingdom," wherever God is, He is in charge. In other words, God wants to rule and reign in our lives. At closer examination, the Kingdom of God is not only verified by God's peace, God actually wants to rule our lives *by* His peace.

*And let the **peace** of God **rule** in your hearts, to which also you were called in one body; and be thankful. Colossians 3:15 (NKJV), emphasis added*

How this works is simple. Whenever we have a decision to make in our lives, we ask God to show us which decision He wants us to make. Then we wait until we are able to detect which decision carries with it the peace of Almighty God.

If you have never known God's peace before this time of decision, this process will not work. Prepare for times of decision before they come by asking God to pour out His peace upon you in times of worship. Spend time in His peace. Let God speak to you through His peace and love. Remember, God's peace comes as verification of His Holy Spirit and Lordship over your life. Determining God's call by God's peace is easy if you have spent time in the presence of God by worshiping Him.

Remember, it is too late to use this biblical method of determining God's will if you have never known God's peace before in your life.

*Whose mouth is full of cursing and bitterness: Their feet are swift to shed blood: Destruction and misery are in their ways: And **the way of peace** have they not known: Romans 3:14–17 (KJV), emphasis added*

When seeking God's will through peace, the favorite attack of the enemy against us will be confusion. Keep that in mind when seeking God's will.

> For God is not the author of confusion, but of **peace**, as in all churches of the saints. 1 Corinthians 14:33 (KJV), emphasis added

If God is not the author of confusion, that means our enemy is confusion's author. In determining God's will through peace, we must always attribute confusion to our enemy and flee from it as fast as possible. No amount of confusion should be tolerated by us at any time! If we follow after God's peace, we will find that it brings with it a whole list of benefits.

> Now the God of **hope** fill you with all **joy** and **peace** in **believing**, that ye may **abound** in **hope**, through the **power** of the Holy Ghost. Romans 15:13 (KJV), emphasis added

Another word for "believing" is faith. Notice that when you are filled with joy and peace, it comes with a dose of "believing," or an increase in faith. The result of being able to believe God more is that we will increase in hope a little more. The object of our hope is the God of Hope who continues to fill us with more joy and peace when we seek Him. That results in more faith to believe God for greater things. We repeat this cycle over and over in our life until we "abound in hope." To the degree we know the God of hope, we will abound in hope. And all that happens by the power of the Holy Spirit.

Not only will we abound in faith and hope in our Christian

The Hope Cycle

walk, but we will have a level of God's peace, which will not make sense to the world's way of thinking.

> *And the peace of God, which surpasses all understanding, will guard your hearts and minds through Christ Jesus. Philippians 4:7 (NKJV)*

God's peace, through Christ Jesus, or the lack of God's peace, will guard us from making wrong decisions by a deceived heart or a carnal mind.

HOW TO DETERMINE GOD'S CALL #3–PROPHETIC CONFIRMATION

For those of you who are not accustomed to hearing words like "prophesy" or "prophetic," let me give you a brief introduction to this terminology. Different traditions and different Christian denominations develop varying definitions to those words, and some Christians do not use those words in reference to current church activity at all.

Prophesy or prophesying is simply speaking on behalf of God. Peter referred to it like this.

> *If any man speak, let him speak as the oracles of God; if any man minister, let him do it as of the ability which God giveth: that God in all things may be glorified through Jesus Christ, to whom be praise and dominion for ever and ever. Amen. 1 Peter 4:11 (KJV)*

When someone in the church is struggling with knowing God's will for their life, that is not the time for us to spout off our own ideas. If we do that, we will only bring that person into more to only say the things that God wants to say to people. Remember, even Jesus said He only said the things He heard the Father say.[4] Are we better than Jesus? If Jesus did not speak his own opinion while on earth, who are we to give someone our opinion when they are seeking God's will?

Prophesying is simply speaking on behalf of God. This practice of

---

[4] John 12:49–50

letting God speak through us is very much encouraged in the Bible to be a present-day activity in the church.

> *For you can all prophesy one by one, that all may learn and all may be encouraged. 1 Corinthians 14:31 (NKJV)*

Do not think that prophesy is for only an elite, special few? Every Christian can learn to speak for God. The key is to learn how to recognize the voice of God when He is talking to us. Every Christian hears God's voice.

> *My sheep **hear** My voice, and I know them, and they follow Me. John 10:27 (NKJV), emphasis added*

As I have said in my previous books and in this book's preface, this is one of the most misquoted Scriptures of the Bible. I usually hear it quoted like this. "My sheep know my voice ..." What it says is that God's sheep, all of us, hear God's voice, whether we know it or not. If you don't think God speaks to you, the problem is that you simply have not learned how to recognize God's voice yet. The problem is not that God does not speak to you, because this Scripture tells us that His sheep hear His voice. God is talking to us whether we recognize His voice or not.

The first way we learn how to recognize God's voice is to spend as much time as possible reading the Bible. God's Word teaches us how God speaks, so we can begin to recognize when He speaks to us.

What is incredible about the gift of prophesy from the Holy Spirit is when you are listening to the Spirit of God and He tells you something that you could not know without Him telling you. This is also called a prophetic "word of knowledge." It is usually something that the person you are ministering to will recognize that only God could have revealed. I have seen this happen hundreds of times throughout my ministry, and it still amazes me how much God loves His people that He would go to such great lengths to prove His love to His children in this way.

Let me share just one example of a true event that happened several years ago. I will not tell you the name of the town where I was or the names of the people this story involves to protect their privacy. Much of my ministry over the years has been in a trans-local vein. This event took place on one of the many trips I have made to a town I had never been to, in a church I had never attended before, in front of people I had never seen.

I was ministering for several evenings in a church in northern Saskatchewan. On Wednesday evening, there was a middle-aged couple sitting on the second row in the center section of the church. To look at them, they seemed happily married and gave the appearance of mature Christians. However, I found out later that they had told each other earlier that day that they would go to church one last time. If they did not hear from God that day, they would proceed with their plans to divorce.

I finished teaching from the Bible, and God began telling me things about different people in the congregation. If the people were sitting toward the back of the church, I asked them to come down the aisle a ways so I could hold the mic and still stand close to them while I prophesied over them. After ministering to several different people, God told me He wanted to tell this couple something. Since they were close to the front, I simply went and stood in front of them, in front of the first pew. I asked if I could minister to them, and they both nodded yes.

God then told me everything that had happened between them that day and that they were at church that night as a last resort before divorcing. Then God told me to pray that He would restore their love for each other, which I did aloud. I received a letter from them a few weeks later telling me that they had fallen in love all over again. God had restored their marriage.

There is no way I could have known what was going on between that couple from natural knowledge. It took the supernatural power of the Holy Spirit operating His gift of prophesy through me to give that couple the answer to their desperate, last-ditch prayer. God is also wanting to speak through you as well, so He can rescue many more lives as well.

When we start taking on the responsibility of speaking for God, we must realize how potentially dangerous it is to misrepresent God. Therefore, God has instructed us that all prophesies should be judged by established, proven ministries.

> *Let two or three prophets speak, and let the others judge. 1 Corinthians 14:29 (NKJV)*

Never give a prophesy, and never receive a prophesy, without a proven prophetic minister having the opportunity to judge what is said. Never speak a prophetic word to somebody unless you are willing to be told you missed God. This is for your protection and the safety of those that you speak to for God. Prophesy is not an infallible thing. We are all humans, and we all can make mistakes.

> *For we know in part and we prophesy in part. 1 Corinthians 13:9 (NKJV)*

There is not one human, living or dead, who has known everything there is to know on any given subject. Just like we all only know part knowledge; at best we can only prophesy partially correctly. That is why every prophetic word must be judged.

However, just because we will never get it totally correct is no reason for us to not try to develop the ability to speak on God's behalf. We are actually commanded to desire to be used prophetically in other people's lives.

> *Pursue love, and desire spiritual gifts, but especially that you may prophesy. But he who prophesies speaks edification and exhortation and comfort to men. 1 Corinthians 14:1, 3 (NKJV)*

There have only been a few recorded times in history where God's voice was heard from heaven audibly. But there are multiple thousands of documented events where God has spoken through one human to another. Our entire Bible is an example of this. That is one of the reasons people go to church— to hear God speak to them through a sermon or a prayer.

Prophetic confirmation of God's call is a powerfully important way to know God's will. Even Timothy in the Bible received some of his call to ministry through prophesy.

*Do not neglect the gift that is in you, which was given to you **by prophecy** with the laying on of the hands of the eldership. Meditate on these things; give yourself entirely to them, that your progress may be evident to all. 1 Timothy 4:14–15 (NKJV), emphasis added*

Just because you receive a prophetic word that you are called into a particular ministry does not mean you are simply to sit around waiting for it to happen. In this Scripture, Paul gives Timothy some explicit instructions of what to do about the gift or call of God on his life that was given to him through prophecy.

Here is what Paul instructed Timothy to do:

1. Meditate on those gifts or calling. In other words, think about these gifts and callings all the time. Daydream about them. Visualize yourself doing them.
2. Give yourself completely to them. Don't just think about doing these callings and operating within these gifts, but do something about them as well. If you need to go to school, go to school. If your school requires one hour of homework for every in-class hour, then put in two hours, an hour extra. Give yourself 100% to being ready to do what God has called you to do.

If you do those two things, I assure you that your progress will be evident to everyone.

HOW TO DETERMINE GOD'S CALL #4–NATURAL TALENT AND GIFTINGS

Another way to determine God's call and will for your life is to look at the natural gifts and abilities you have. I am not talking about the desires you have. We already discussed those in How to Determine God's Call #1. I am talking about looking at the skills and abilities you have developed over your life. Those are skills you can function in right now. Those are the things you may enjoy doing or the things you are good at right now. For instance, through tragedy you may have learned some coping skills. You may not enjoy doing that, but at least you may be good at it.

Please make a list of all your skills and abilities. After you finish your list, copy it over into a prioritized list, starting with your most skillful ability, and go to your least skillful ability. Then make a third list of the same items starting with your most favorite activity to your least-favorite activity. Then prioritize this list from the oldest to the most recently acquired skill or talent.

Each of those lists will tell you different things about God's call for your life. Then ask yourself this question: What have I learned about myself, my callings, and my giftings from this exercise?

The reason our life skills and developed talents indicate God's call for us is found in this Scripture.

> *The steps of a good man are ordered by the Lord,*
> *And He delights in his way. Though he fall, he shall not*
> *be utterly cast down; For the Lord upholds him with His*
> *hand. Psalms 37:23–24 (NKJV)*

The phrase "good man" is only one word in the original Hebrew. According to the Strong's concordance, "good man" is this: "Strong's Hebrew Number 1397 1) man, strong man, warrior (emphasizing strength or ability to fight)"[5]

If you haven't figured it out yet, let me inform you—life on earth as a human being is a fight to the finish. Scientists tell us that the sperm that fertilized the egg, which produced your body, was one out of hundreds of thousands. You were a fighter from the beginning. All of those potential sperm simply died in their fight for life, except you.

No one who gives up the fight for life lives very long. If you are alive and reading this, you have fought to survive and succeeded. Although you have been knocked down, you have not been knocked out. Although you have fallen, you have not been destroyed. There are two reasons for your survival. First, you are a fighter. Second, God holds you up when life's struggles get too difficult.

---

[5] Strong, J. *Strong's Exhaustive Concordance of the Bible.* (Peabody: Hendrickson Publishers, 2007).

*The steps of a good man are ordered by the Lord: and
he delighteth in his way. Though he fall, he shall not be
utterly cast down: for the Lord upholdeth him with His
hand. Psalms 37:23–24 (KJV)*

That Scripture applies to you and me, because we are fighters. We will not give up, no matter what life throws at us! Therefore, every step we take in life has been ordered by our God. No experience we have had is an exception.

Am I saying that the innocent child being abused or the helpless person diagnosed with cancer is in God's will? No, I am not saying that at all! Please understand the difference between these two experiences. The steps we take are the choices we make, not the events that happen to us. Life happens. It is how we respond to life that determines whether we "overcome" life or life overcomes us. Go back and read the stories of Joseph and Job for examples of bad life experiences happening to innocent people. The choices Joseph made in the hard years qualified him for the promotion he received to second in command over the most influential nation in the world.

As I look back over my life, I can see how God has used every life skill and talent He has directed me to develop to fulfill the call he has placed on my life. Even when I thought God was sending me on a detour, there has always been a redeemable purpose in every step He has led me to take.

The skills and talents I have developed in one phase of my life have prepared me for the following challenges and God's progressive call on my life. Solomon wrote about this experience as well.

*A man's gift makes room for him, And brings him
before great men. Proverbs 18:16 (NKJV)*

God will use the natural gifts he has given us, the talents He has caused us to develop throughout our lives, to help us function in our calling and ministry. Therefore, to understand God's call to ministry for us, we can look at our natural gifts, skills, or talents as well.

HOW TO DETERMINE GOD'S CALL #5–SPIRITUAL VISITATIONS

The Bible is full of stories about people who had spiritual encounters of all kinds. Some had God talk to them in dreams. Others saw visions. Some had angelic visitations. Some heard the audible voice of God. A few were physically translated from one place to another. Some were spiritually transported. Some experienced incredible miracles of life-saving and life-changing proportions. Another saw two entire armies raised from the dead. Some experienced a Christophany or Theophany (where God or Jesus actually appeared to them). Some witnessed Jesus' natural body being transfigured into His spiritual body. Those and hundreds of others witnessed the visitation of saints who had passed away appear to them in their spiritual bodies.

> *[32] And what more shall I say? For the time would fail me to tell of Gideon and Barak and Samson and Jephthah, also of David and Samuel and the prophets: [33] who through faith subdued kingdoms, worked righteousness, obtained promises, stopped the mouths of lions, [34] quenched the violence of fire, escaped the edge of the sword, out of weakness were made strong, became valiant in battle, turned to flight the armies of the aliens. [35] Women received their dead raised to life again.*
>
> *Others were tortured, not accepting deliverance, that they might obtain a better resurrection. [36] Still others had trial of mockings and scourgings, yes, and of chains and imprisonment. [37] They were stoned, they were sawn in two, were tempted, were slain with the sword. They wandered about in sheepskins and goatskins, being destitute, afflicted, tormented—[38] of whom the world was not worthy. They wandered in deserts and mountains, in dens and caves of the earth.*
>
> *[39] And all these, having obtained a good testimony through faith, did not receive the promise, [40] God having provided something better for us, that they should not be made perfect apart from us. Hebrews 11:32–40 (NKJV)*

The world was not worthy of these people who followed after God with their whole hearts—who obeyed God even when it cost them their lives. Some received miracles at their time of testing; others chose not to receive miracles of deliverance.

Whatever we face in life or in death, we have this promise that the Lord will go through it with us.

> *Yea, though I walk through the valley of the shadow of death, I will fear no evil; For You are with me; Psalms 23:4 (NKJV)*

By the way, do you know what the "something better for us" is that is being referred to in Hebrews 11? The "promise" we receive that the Old Testament saints could not receive was this.

> *the mystery which has been hidden from ages and from generations, but now has been revealed to His saints. To them God willed to make known what are the riches of the glory of this mystery among the Gentiles: which is* **Christ in you, the hope of glory.** *Colossians 1:26–27 (NKJV), emphasis added*

So, in this sense, you and I have received a bigger miracle of God's visitation than the Old Testament saints received. If we can just learn to hear His voice, He is with us always and will always guide us, if we let him.

HOW TO DETERMINE GOD'S CALL #6 – GOD'S GRACE

The grace of God is God's ability to do what He wants us to do. If God wants us to not fear, God's grace becomes our courage. If He wants us to believe, God's grace becomes our faith. If God wants us to worship Him in extraordinarily difficult circumstances, God's grace becomes our song. God will never call

> **God will never call on us to do something that He will not give us the grace to complete.**

49

on us to do something that He will not give us the grace to complete. Here's how the conversation between Jesus and Paul ended when God was trying to get Paul to do something Paul did not have the strength to do on his own.

> And He (Jesus) *said to me, "My **grace** is sufficient for you, for My **strength** is made perfect in weakness." Therefore, most gladly I will rather boast in my infirmities, that the **power** of Christ may rest upon me. 2 Corinthians 12:9 (NKJV), emphasis added*

In this case, God's grace became Paul's strength. Whatever God is calling you to do, He will always give you the grace to do it.

> *Faithful is he that calleth you, who also will do it. 1 Thessalonians 5:24 (KJV)*

Likewise, it becomes equally easy to determine when God does not want you to do something. There is simply no grace from God present in your life to accomplish what you are trying to do.

However, there is a caution that goes along with this method. Anything God wants you to do, your enemy does not want you to do. Immaturity will cause us to interpret the enemy's resistance as lack of God's grace. Before making changes in our life based on this method, make sure it is truly a lack of God's grace you sense, not the resistance of the devil.

HOW TO REALIZE GOD'S CALL #1–MEDITATION

Please permit me to revisit this Scripture.

> *Do not neglect the gift that is in you, which was given to you by prophecy with the laying on of the hands of the eldership. Meditate on these things; give yourself entirely to them, that your progress may be evident to all. 1 Timothy 4:14–15 (NKJV)*

Once you have determined God's will, do not assume it will automatically come to pass. We have responsibilities in the process of bringing God's calling into reality. The first instruction Paul gave Timothy was to **not neglect** the gift of God's call on his life. In the busyness of our lives, it is easy to unintentionally neglect God's call on our lives. Paul is reminding us here to make sure we do not do that.

Paul's first clarification of how not to neglect this gift or call is to "meditate" on these things. Meditation is simply to muse or to think about something **all** the time. That practice is much more important than most Christians realize. What we think about determines what we become.

> For as he thinks in his heart, so is he. "Eat and drink!"
> he says to you, But his heart is not with you. Proverbs
> 23:7 (NKJV)

Those of you who have read my book *The Importance of Worshiping Together* know that I discussed this Scripture in length in that book. For those of you who have not read that book, let me give you a quick review.

This is a physical law that God designed into the physical universe. Just like centrifugal force is a physical law and will always work, so this law always works. Whatever you think, you become.

For centuries non-Christians have discovered this physical law and used it to produce great wealth and fame—yet without establishing a relationship with the God of the universe. In the 1960s, Earl Nightingale recorded one of the bestselling "personal development/success" LP albums of all time entitled *The Strangest Secret*. On the vinyl LP, Nightingale defined the strangest secret as, "You become what you think about most of the time."

He became rich selling that album, and his followers tapped into this physical law with him and experienced the measure of success that God intended for people to enjoy who obey this law.

Sometimes we Christians read the Bible as if it is filled with suggestions or good ideas from God that are optional. We need to take the Bible much more seriously than we do. Most of God's instructions are based on physical laws that He built into the world; and when we obey them, we reap benefits automatically, because that is the way God designed it to work.

HOW TO REALIZE GOD'S CALL #2–INVOLVEMENT

Paul's next instruction of how not to neglect your call or gift was to "give yourself entirely to them." In other words, get some training and spend time doing. The word "entirely" indicates that every available minute is given to developing the knowledge and skills you will need to accomplish God's call on your life. Don't be a "couch potato" Christian, just sitting around waiting on God to bring His call on your life to pass. It will never happen that way! Give yourself completely to what God has called you to.

HOW TO REALIZE GOD'S CALL #3–THE PRAYER AND PROPHETIC PRINCIPLES

Prophetic Principle: God will do nothing without telling us first. I talked about that in the preface of my book *The Importance of Worshiping Together.* Here is a brief review of this principle.

*Behold, the former things are come to pass, and new things do I **declare**: before they spring forth **I tell you of them**. Isaiah 42:9 (KJV), emphasis added*

God has chosen to tell us about everything He wants to do in our lives before He does it. He will tell us in the various ways I have outlined for you here in this chapter. One of His favorite ways of revealing his intentions is through prophetic revelation.

Surely the Lord GOD will do nothing, but He revealeth His secret unto His servants the prophets. Amos 3:7 (KJV)

God will not do anything unless He tells us about it first. That is His promise, according to these Scriptures. The reason God does things this way is found in this Scripture.

> *I have even from the beginning **declared** it to thee;*
> ***before it came to pass** I shewed it thee: lest thou shouldest*
> *say, Mine idol hath done them, and my graven image,*
> *and my molten image, hath commanded them. Isaiah*
> *48:5 (KJV), emphasis added*

God chooses to operate by His prophetic principle to guard against any man thinking or saying that what took place was the result of any god other than the true and living God. Even a person's own skills and abilities can become an idol or god to them. God always tells us something before it happens so He will get the glory for it.

Prayer Principle: God will do nothing unless someone asks Him to do it. He established that principle to encourage us to maintain a relationship with Him.

> *You desire but do not have, so you kill. You covet but*
> *you cannot get what you want, so you quarrel and fight.*
> ***You do not have because you do not ask God**. James 4:2*
> *(NIV), emphasis added*

If God automatically protected the innocent or took care of every need we have without us asking Him for it, we would not bother seeking Him and calling on Him for mercy and help. If that was the way things were, we could enjoy God's goodness without having any type of relationship with Him. But that's not what God wants. He wants a relationship with us based on love.

To love someone, you have two get to know them. To get to know someone, you must communicate with them. We need to understand that God wants to do good things for His people more than we want Him to do them, but He has chosen to limit Himself to only do what He is asked to do.

As you read this next Scripture, discern the heart of Jesus begging us to ask the Father for whatever would bring us joy. This statement Jesus made shows how much God wants to give us whatever we ask Him for. Jesus wants us to be full of Joy.

*And in that day you will ask Me nothing. Most assuredly, I say to you, **whatever** you ask the Father in My name He will give you. Until now you have asked nothing in My name. **Ask, and you will receive**, that your joy may be full. John 16:23–24 (NKJV), emphasis added*

Because God gave man free will, God must wait until we ask for His help before He can act. Otherwise, God's intervention in our lives would be a violation of the free will He gave us. If we do not ask, God will never violate our free will and do something without our asking or inviting Him into the situation to be Lord of it.

The only biblical reason that God would not answer our requests is found in this Scripture, which is a continuation of the Scripture we were reading previously.

You ask and do not receive, because you ask amiss, that you may spend it on your pleasures. James 4:3 (NKJV)

What the Lord is trying to teach us here is that there is a difference between Godly joy and physical pleasures. If we are asking God for something out of selfish ambitions or to feed our pride, we will not receive what we ask Him for. Or if we ask God for something in a way that tries to manipulate Him, that is asking the wrong way or asking amiss. God is the Lord, and He will not allow anyone to manipulate Him.

There is a way that we can be guaranteed to receive everything we ask God for. That secret is found in this scripture.

*And this is the confidence that we have in Him, that, **if we ask any thing according to His will**, He heareth us: And if we know that He hear us, whatsoever we ask, we **know** that we have the petitions that we desired of Him. 1 John 5:14–15 (KJV), emphasis added*

If you want to guarantee that you will receive everything you ask for from God, then simply only ask Him what He wants you to ask Him. Because this is the only way to be sure that God will answer our prayer, our first prayer concerning any situation should be, "Lord, what do You want me to ask You for?"

The prophetic and prayer principles are always intended to work together. In other words, we need to always ask God what He wants us to ask for. Then we can ask Him for it with confidence that we will receive it.

Here is a scripture that shows exactly how God intended for those two principles to work together.

> *Thus says the Lord God, This also I will let the house of Israel ask Me to do for them: I will increase their men like a flock. Ezekiel 36:37 (NASB)*

Because of wars and other events, Israel found itself with fewer men than women. That was a very perplexing situation for the Israelites. Through this prophetic word, God was letting them know that He was aware of their dilemma, and God encouraged Israel with a prophetic promise. He promised to increase their men like a flock.

However, worded carefully with this prophetic promise, was the condition that **every** prophetic word from God comes with.

> *This also I will let the house of Israel ask Me to do for them:..." Ezekiel 36:37 (NASB)*

Whatever God has shown you, promised you, or called you to do by whatever means He has used is God saying to you, "This is what I want you to ask me to do in or for or through you." Remember, if we do not ask for it, God cannot do it! We can pray whatever we want to pray, but the "effectual" prayer is the one we pray according to God's will.

> *Confess your faults one to another, and pray one for another, that ye may be healed. The effectual fervent*

prayer of a righteous man availeth much. James 5:16 (KJV)

The prayer that will be effectual is the prayer that God told us to ask Him. We can then pray that prayer with fervor and passion because we know we are praying according to God's will.

If, then, God has called you to be a worship leader and that has been confirmed to you in one or more of the ways I have gone over in this chapter, you need to be asking God every day to establish you in that ministry. God can't do that unless you ask Him to do it, according to the prayer principal.

KNOW THE POTENTIAL OF YOUR CALL

Just like God wants us to understand His will for our lives, He also wants us to know the extent of the call He has for us in the various ministries He has called us into.

Because God will be true to His prophetic principle, He will show us early in our journey where He wants to take us in our callings. However, just like Joseph didn't know when to keep quiet about what God showed him about his brothers bowing down to him in the future, our immaturity can cause problems along our journey as well. How do we avoid disqualifying ourselves and prolonging our journey to the completion of God's will for us? Here are a few tips I have learned along my journey. Maybe they will help you avoid some pitfalls.

JOURNEY PRINCIPLE #1–THINK SOBERLY ABOUT YOUR CALL

This Scripture has helped keep things in in perspective for me throughout my life.

> *For I say, through the grace given to me, to everyone who is among you, not to think of himself more highly than he ought to think, but to **think soberly**, as God has dealt to each one a measure of faith. For as we have many*

members in one body, but all the members do not have the same function Romans, 12:3–4 (NKJV), emphasis added

If you are a thespian, you are familiar with this statement: "There are no small parts, only small actors." What makes a roll in a script seem small to one actor and a great opportunity or challenge to another is the attitude with which they approach that part.

We must think soberly concerning the scope of our ministry. God may have a worldwide ministry for you, but that will never happen if you do not humble yourself first. There is no place for stars on a worship team! No one has a more important job than another.

JOURNEY PRINCIPLE #2–CONSIDER EVERYONE BETTER THAN YOURSELF

I have known people who would not take a supporting role on a worship team. If they could not be the primary worship leader, they would not be involved at all. Others have adopted the attitude that unless they could play their particular instrument on the worship team, they would not be involved at all.

If you are a drummer, maybe even the best drummer your church has, you still need to be willing to let others take their turn on the drums and support the whole worship team by singing or playing percussion traps, etc., while giving someone else a chance to develop. Our attitude must be to raise up others to do what we do, not to protect our position on the team. Always have the attitude that others are better or have more potential than yourself.

Let nothing be done through strife or vainglory; but in lowliness of mind let each esteem other better than themselves. Look not every man on his own things, but every man also on the things of others. Philippians 2:3–4 (KJV)

JOURNEY PRINCIPLE #3–DON'T PROMOTE YOURSELF

Be willing to take a lower seat and be content there so God can promote you in His time.

> *But when you are invited, go and sit down in the lowest place, so that when he who invited you comes he may say to you, 'Friend, go up higher.' Then you will have glory in the presence of those who sit at the table with you. For whoever exalts himself will be humbled, and he who humbles himself will be exalted." Luke 14:10–11 (NKJV)*

JOURNEY PRINCIPLE #4–THINK CHRIST-LIKE THOUGHTS

Even if you have been told by God that there are great things in your future, don't be like young Joseph and run around telling everybody. Stay humble. Avoid the "star syndrome!" Anyone who receives recognition for their ministry calling here on earth probably will not receive any further reward in heaven. Of course, that depends on our attitude here on earth when we are receiving recognition.

Think about this. Jesus was God Himself come to earth in the flesh. To say that Jesus is God is fully correct. Or to say Jesus is the Son of God is also correct, because Jesus was born of Mary. Therefore, to say that Jesus is equal with God is correct as well. But even though Jesus is God, take a look at the attitude Jesus had when he came to earth.

> *Let this mind be in you which was also in Christ Jesus, who, being in the form of God, did not consider it robbery to be equal with God, **but** made Himself of no reputation, taking the form of a bondservant, and coming in the likeness of men. And being found in appearance as a man, He humbled Himself and became obedient to the point of death, even the death of the cross. Therefore God also has highly exalted Him and given Him the name which is above every name Philippians 2:5–8 (NKJV)*

The way Jesus thought is the way we are supposed to think. Jesus *is* God, yet His attitude positioned Him to be exalted by the Father. Here is how Jesus thought which qualified Him to be exalted in the Kingdom of God.

1. Didn't build His reputation
2. Took the form of a bondservant
3. Embraced the likeness of a man—humanity
4. Continued to humble Himself
5. Became totally obedient to the Father
6. Was obedient unto death
7. Was obedient to die in the worst possible way—on the cross

We are instructed to have this same mental attitude, which Christ has, that enabled Him to accomplish all of those things. Unfortunately, most of us are still struggling with the first item on the list. Until we stop being concerned about our reputation, it is impossible for God to promote us to the full extent of His call for our lives.

JOURNEY PRINCIPLE #5—DO EVERYTHING THE BEST YOU CAN

We had a saying when I was in the U.S. Air Force that one of my supervisors taught me: "That's close enough for government work." Good enough is not good enough for kingdom work. Whatever we do should be done as well as we can possibly do it, as unto the Lord. What caused Daniel to be noticed by leadership and promoted?

> *It pleased Darius to set over the kingdom one hundred and twenty satraps, to be over the whole kingdom; and over these, three governors, of whom Daniel was one, that the satraps might give account to them, so that the king would suffer no loss. Then this Daniel distinguished himself above the governors and satraps, because **an excellent spirit** was in him; and the king gave thought to setting him over the whole realm. Daniel 6:1–3 (NKJV), emphasis added*

There needs to be a balance in us. We need to do everything we do as excellently as we can but not judge ourselves and other's too harshly when we or they do not achieve the goals.

JOURNEY PRINCIPLE #6—PROMOTION COMES FROM THE LORD

For promotion cometh neither from the east, nor from the west, nor from the south. But God is the judge: He putteth down one, and setteth up another. Psalms 75:6-7 (KJV)

The way to get ahead in God's kingdom is never to promote ourselves but to realize that our God will promote us when it is time for us to be promoted. Look at Moses for an example of waiting on God's promotion. He waited for eighty years. Forty of those years were on the back side of the desert. Joseph is also a tremendous example of God's promotion in the right season. Promotion does not come by you manipulating circumstances to make sure you are in the right place for promotion—the "east or west." In God's kingdom, promotion only comes from God.

Chapter Two

EXAMINE YOURSELF

A WORSHIP LEADER MUST FIRST BE A WORSHIPER

If at this time you feel that God has called you to be a worship leader, then you are ready for an extensive time of self-reflection to determine whether there are areas of pride or self-centeredness that will need to die before you can be an effective worship leader.

I would like to ask you several questions about your worship life. When I taught this course in a classroom setting, I always assigned these questions as homework to be handed in. The truth is, I never read any of this homework, because I felt that it was none of my business. Each student got full credit for this assignment just for handing it in.

These questions are simply to facilitate the potential worship leader's self-reflection. They are designed to help us discover our attitude about worship, because if we are not worshipers, we have no business trying to lead others in worship.

If you are married, you could benefit by discussing your answers to these questions with your spouse at some point. If you are not married, you may choose to discuss your answers with a mentor or pastor. If you discover something through this exercise that needs to change in your life, the best place to start is always repentance in prayer.

HAVE YOU BEEN BIRTHED INTO WORSHIP?

Do you worship God in private or only in a group setting? If you worship God privately, most likely you are a worshiper. If you worship God only when you are around other people, you probably need to have worship birthed within you at the least, and you could need to repent for being more interested in what men think then what God thinks.

Having worship and praise birthed within us is a phrase I have heard used sense the 1980s. Here is the scripture this concept comes from.

> *And of Zion it shall be said, This and that man was born in her: and the Highest Himself shall establish her. The Lord shall count, when he writeth up the people, that this man was born there. Selah. As well the singers as the players on instruments shall be there: all my springs are in thee. Psalm 87:5–7 (KJV)*

Zion represents the presence of God, which is only brought to earth by God's people praising Him.[6] This verse also mentions the "singers" and the "players on instruments" will be birthed in Zion or the place of God's presence. This is confirmed for us in Psalms 100 where we are commanded to come before God's presence with singing.[7]

If worship has been birthed within you, you will want to worship God all the time. If that has not happened to you yet, I suggest you fast and seek God, asking Him to birth you into worship.

If you do not worship God in private, then you need to figure out why. Are you simply not making time to worship God in your private life? If that is the case, prioritize your time. Set aside time every day to spend with God. That time should include both times of worship and reading the word of God.

The worst-case scenario if you answered no to this question is that you are only worshiping in front of people to show them how spiritual you are, but you truly do not have a worship life. If that is the case, simply repent and ask God to birth worship in you.

---

[6] Psalm 22:3
[7] Psalm 100:2

HOW IS YOUR PERSONAL WORSHIP LIFE?

Do you express your worship to God differently in private than in a group setting? If you answered yes to this question, there could be a couple of reasons for that. Some people are more liberated in their private worship and feel they are unable to express themselves freely to the Lord in a group setting. Others worship more liberated or animated in the group setting than in private.

There is not one way that is right and another way that is wrong. The purpose for this question is for you to find out if this is happening in your worship life. If it isn't, then you don't need to worry about it. If it is, then you need to find out why and fix it.

If you are not as liberated in your worship in a group setting as you are in your bedroom at home, ask the Lord if you have fear of men that needs to be repented of. If you are more expressive in worship around other people than you are when you are alone, ask the Lord if your worship is nothing but a show for the people you are with and not for Him.

DO YOU HAVE THE HEART OF A SHEPHERD?

During worship in a group setting, are you oblivious or aware of how others are expressing their worship to God? The purpose of this question is simply to bring attention to what you do when you worship. It is not a bad thing to be aware of how others are expressing their worship in the group setting, especially for one who is called to lead worship. A worship leader who only gets lost in the presence of God and leaves the congregation to fend for themselves is not approaching their responsibilities with a shepherd's heart.

A shepherd leads the sheep by going before them—that is true. However, a shepherd who is not aware of where the sheep are can be dangerous for the sheep. A shepherd must always know whether the sheep are with him. A shepherd should lead the sheep in such a way as to minimize stragglers from being left behind in worship.

If you are not the primary or secondary worship leader in a group setting, then, by all means, lose yourself in the presence of the Lord as you worship, and pay no attention to how others around you are expressing themselves in worship.

DO YOU HAVE THE HEART OF A WORSHIPER?

Would you say you have a passion for spending time in God's presence? If you don't, you are not a true worshiper.[8] If you are not a worshiper, you are disqualified from being a worship leader. If you desire to be a true worshiper, begin to seek God, asking him to birth worship within you.

DO YOU HAVE A HEART FOR OTHERS?

Would you say you have a passion for seeing others released into liberty in their private and group worship? That question applies mainly to those who are called to be primary worship leaders. A primary worship leader needs to have a shepherd's heart. Shepherds are more concerned about the sheep than themselves.

If you do not have a passion to help others become worshipers yet, that does not mean God will not birth that in you one day. Becoming a worship leader is more about the journey than the destination. If you know God has called you to lead worship, you have this to look forward to. You will become more excited about people who become worshipers than you are about yourself being a worshiper.

DO YOU HAVE PRIDE?

When you do something in the public eye, how important is it to you to be recognized and appreciated for what you have done? That question speaks to your maturity. Every one of us wants to be recognized when we do something good or right. The more mature we become as Christians, however, the less we depend upon recognition from men and the more we depend upon the validation we receive from God. We want to get to

---

[8] John 4:23

the place where we do not desire any recognition from men, and we do all we do to the glory of God.[9]

DO YOU EXPERIENCE WORSHIP DISTRACTIONS?

During worship in a group setting, do you sometimes see fellow worshipers as a distraction to your intimacy with God? That is one of the enemy's tactics. He tries to use anything to distract us from our purpose as worshipers. He is doubly successful when he can use someone who is worshiping God to distract us from our worship of God. Left unchecked, that attitude can result in us despising worship itself, which is the real goal of Satan's attack.

As a worship leader, we must never allow any feelings of frustration to settle in our hearts. Frustration always comes from a judgmental attitude. There is no place for that type of self-centered attitude in a worship leader. A worship leader should be more excited about someone else's worship life than their own. That can only take place when you are secure and settled in your own worship life.

ARE YOU SENSITIVE TO THE PROPHETIC?

In group worship when you are not leading, does your heart confirm the direction the worship leader is going or show you when the worship leader may have missed God's direction for the meeting?

Every worship time will be unique if the leader is following the Holy Spirit's leading. Also, God will change the direction of a planned worship service based upon who exercised their free will and came to church that day. God knows the needs of each person and will redirect a service to minister to someone who is there.

A worship leader must plan the service earlier in the week based on the Holy Spirit's leading. However, a worship leader must also lead the worship service based on the Holy Spirit's leadership in real time. That requires that every worship leader is capable of hearing from God and immediately obeying God without hesitation. That is a practical

---

[9] 1 Corinthians 10:31

application in the church of the spiritual prophetic gifts of the Spirit listed for us in 1 Corinthians 12.

Being prophetic is much more than standing up in the congregation and declaring, "Thus saith the Lord!" It is the ability to know God's heart for any given situation. That is why, to be a primary worship leader, you must be called to be one of the fivefold ministries mentioned in Ephesians 4.

> *And he gave some, apostles; and some, **prophets**; and some, evangelists; and some, pastors and teachers; For the perfecting of the saints, for the work of the ministry, for the edifying of the body of Christ: Till we all come in the unity of the faith, and of the knowledge of the Son of God, unto a perfect man, unto the measure of the stature of the fulness of Christ: Ephesians 4:11–13 (KJV), emphasis added*

Throughout the Old Testament, being prophetic is associated with worship. Worship is also what ushers in a spirit of prophecy. Prophecy and worship go hand in hand. An unidentified author in an article on the website gotquestions.org has this to say about prophets in the Old Testament. "*During these times, prophets were often associated with musicians who sang praise to God.*"

Here is a scripture where the prophet Samuel is telling Saul about a future event that would happen to him.

> *After that thou shalt come to the hill of God, where is the garrison of the Philistines: and it shall come to pass, when thou art come thither to the city, that thou shalt meet **a company of prophets** coming down from the high place with a psaltery, and a tabret, and a pipe, and a harp, before them; and they shall prophesy: And the Spirit of the Lord will come upon thee, and thou shalt prophesy with them, and shalt be turned into another man. 1 Samuel 10:5–6 (KJV), emphasis added*

If you are a primary worship leader, you must be prophetic! You must be able to hear and sense God's direction for a corporate gathering. One of the ways God develops that in a potential worship leader, before He releases them into that ministry, is to reveal the spiritual and musical direction a warship gathering should be going as they are experiencing it as part of the congregation.

No human does everything right all the time. That seems to be the definition of a human being. Even seasoned, prophetic worship leaders will miss God sometimes. The important thing when we miss God and lead the meeting in a wrong direction is to get back on track as quickly as possible. The general population of a church service will usually never know when the worship leader takes the worship in the wrong direction. However, someone who is being call into worship leading will pick up on those types of mistakes in other worship leaders.

That is one way that God trains future worship leaders to know when they are being led by the Holy Spirit. Therefore, that is a great validation of one's call to lead worship.

Be careful, however, because Satan will try to use that Godly training exercise against you. He will try to interject a judgmental spirit against that worship leader, or a spirit of pride, telling you, "you could do better than them."

ANOTHER PRIDE QUESTION

Which is more important: leading worship in a home Bible study or for a Sunday morning service? Both are equally important. Just because there may be more people in attendance on Sunday morning does not make it more important than a lesser-attended home Bible study. The worship leader's responsibility is to bring the people of God into His presence and to bring God's presence to the people of God. Whether you are doing that for ten people or one hundred people is irrelevant. The goal is still the same.

Because mistakes in front of more people seem to have greater consequences than mistakes in front of a few people, we will usually think that leading worship in front of a larger crowd carries more weight. That idea has its roots in pride.

WHAT IS YOUR NATURAL EXPRESSION OF WORSHIP?

What is your God-given natural expression of worship, and how would you express worship if you lost your ability to express yourself in that way?

In chapter seven of *Portrait of a Worshiper*, I introduced the concept of God-given expressions of worship. Please read chapters six and seven of that book to gain a more complete understanding of this concept. Once you have read those chapters, answer the above question. If you have not discovered your natural, God-given expression of worship, please seek the Lord to tell you what it is. Then go on to ask yourself how comfortable you are in expressing your worship to God in all thirty-four Biblical ways I listed in that book.

TELL ME WHY

Why do you want to be a worship leader? I hope it is because you feel God has called you to be a worship leader. I hope it is because you have a passion for God's presence. I hope it is because you have a burning desire to help others experience God's presence. I hope it is not because you desire recognition or position. I hope it is not because you think it is a great opportunity to sing and play music. I hope it is not because you think it is cool.

Chapter Three

DISCOVERING YOUR WORSHIP
MINISTRY PHILOSOPHY

WORSHIP MINISTRY PHILOSOPHY

There are two basic components, or goals, most churches desire for their worship ministries. They desire music quality in the worship, and hopefully they also desire spiritual anointing in the worship. "Spiritual anointing" is a phrase meaning "to be led by the Holy Spirit."[10] Both components can be extremely important for various reasons. Some of those reasons are good, and some of them are carnal yet seem spiritual at first glance.

How important you believe those two components are to your worship ministry will determine your worship ministry philosophy. This philosophy will influence every decision you make in your worship ministry.

The reason it is vital for you to address your worship ministry philosophy is because it will never work for a worship leader and a senior pastor to have extremely different philosophies of worship ministry. Therefore, for the sake of the church, any differences in philosophy need to be worked out well before someone is installed into a leadership position. My goal here is to help church leadership come into a balanced

---

[10] Romans 8:14

and unified philosophy of worship ministry before a lack of unity in that area does damage to the church.

Because a church's worship ministry philosophy is influenced by the two goals I just talked about, most churches will gravitate to either the consumer-driven model of worship ministry or the presence-of-God-driven model. A simple way of explaining the differences between those two philosophies is this: The consumer-driven model tends to be most concerned about the quality of music the worship team produces; the presence-of-God model is more concerned about having the presence of God inhabit the praise[11] than anything else.

Most of us would say we want both of those very important aspects to grace our worship ministry in our local church. However, the real definition of this part of our ministry philosophy will come when we are forced to answer questions like these:

1. Which one of those two qualities or components do we want first?
2. If we absolutely have to give up one of them, which one would it be?"

Please do not answer those two questions quickly in your mind. Take the time to think through the ramifications of each scenario and how they would affect the health and growth of your church, both in the short and long term. Ask yourself how visitors would perceive your church if either one of those qualities was missing from your worship. Also, consider how your current church members would respond to those scenarios. If your worship team sounds terrible but seems to be anointed to usher in God's presence, would you be able to trust God that your visitors or current members would be sensitive enough to the Spirit of God to endure the bad sound for very long?

Perhaps you are thinking that your worship team is indeed lacking in one of those areas right now. Maybe your team is very skilled but has no clue how to invoke the presence of God in its worship. Or maybe your

---

[11] Psalm 22:3

team knows how to enter the presence of God but is totally lacking in skill. Or maybe you are seeing grave challenges in your worship team in both areas.

In the exercise to follow, I am not asking for your assessment of the current state of your worship team. What I want you to consider is where is the point that you would be willing to compromise on each of those components, and at which point you are not willing to cross the line with compromising those two worship components.

DISCOVERING YOUR WORSHIP MINISTRY PHILOSOPHY

If you are a worship leader, you should take this test/questionnaire with your current or potential senior pastor. Each of you should go through it privately first, marking your answers in pencil, so they can be erased later if necessary.

After you have both gone through the test privately and individually marked your answers, then schedule a time together to discuss the results with each other. If there are places where you are more than ten percentage points different from each other, discuss the reasons why you marked your answer the way you did and see whether you can come to a compromise between the two of you.

In preparing for this meeting to discuss this test, you have the following homework. Ask yourself if your position on each graph is a conviction or a preference. If it is a conviction, be prepared to present your reasons for that conviction. A conviction should only be based on the Bible. No other points of reason are allowed when discussing a conviction! If your position on a graph is a preference, be prepared to share your reasons for that preference. Personal experience or non-Biblical reasons may be presented to defend your preferences.

When you meet to discuss this test, allow yourselves plenty of time. You may need to continue the discussion on another day or on several days; but do not rush this process!

Another ground rule that is important, DO NOT withhold your opinions or convictions as you go through this process. If you are a worship leader, do not hold back for fear you may not get selected for a position. If you are a pastor, do not hide your convictions or opinions for fear you may not have a worship leader. Both parties must be totally honest with the other in this process, or it will not work!

When you do meet, discuss each graph thoroughly before going to the next graph. If on any point you cannot arrive at a compromise in your convictions or preferences, the discussion is over. At that point, you should pray for each other to have God's best in each other's life, give each other a hug or handshake, and part as brothers and sisters in Christ. If you ignore this advice and try to make your ministry relationship work, then you could cause your church a lot of pain. Some churches never recover from these types of wounds. Remember, God holds the leadership responsible for what happens to the flock.[12]

Here is the test for you to take. Make sure you think through, and pray through, each graph before you mark the graph! There are no right or wrong answers to this test, so mark each graph honestly from your heart. By the way, frequently people have made their initial mark on a graph, yet when they did their research to prepare for the discussion meetings, they had to change their position before getting to the meeting. Also, many people have come to the meetings convinced they were established in their position only to change their position once they heard the case presented by the other person.

The important thing to remember in this process is to be teachable and willing to change. After all, none of us have all the answers about anything.

> For what if some did not believe? shall their unbelief make the faith of God without effect? God forbid: yea, **let God be true, but every man a liar**; as it is written, That thou mightest be justified in thy sayings, and mightest overcome when thou art judged. Romans 3:3-4 (KJV), emphasis added

Can we handle it when our position is judged, or do we always have to be right? Are we teachable, or have we got it all figured out? God is the only one who is true all the time!

---

[12] Jeremiah 23:1

WORSHIP MINISTRY PHILOSOPHY TEST/QUESTIONNAIRE

Final Instructions

In a perfect world, we can have everything that makes for a wonderful worship and music ministry in our church. However, we do not live in a perfect world. Therefore, we all have to make compromises in our worship ministry. Where do you place the ideal compromise between the two things listed on the top and bottom of each graph below. Please do not mark your answers hastily, but think through the ramifications each scenario would have on your church and upon your visitors. Then mark your answer IN PENCIL with a single X along the graph.

The way to find out where you would place each X is to first ask yourself where your tolerance level is for each item listed on the left, then on the right. Keep those points in your mind. After you answer that question for each side, ask yourself whether the percentage balance between the two items truly represents your heart for both ends of the graph. If it doesn't, compromise the positions of the X's in your mind until you find the one spot along the graph representing your ideal compromise between each of the two components, and mark your X there as pictured here.

0% 10% 20% 30% 40% 50% 60% 70% 80% 90%100%
100%90% 80% 70% 60% 50% 40% 30% 20% 10% 0%

Example Answer

Graph #1

Which would you rather have on your worship team: a professional musician or an anointed worshiper?

0% 10% 20% 30% 40% 50% 60% 70% 80% 90%100%
100%90% 80% 70% 60% 50% 40% 30% 20% 10% 0%

Graph #2

Which would you rather have in your worship service: polished (well-rehearsed) worship music or God's presence?

0% 10% 20% 30% 40% 50% 60% 70% 80% 90%100%
100%90% 80% 70% 60% 50% 40% 30% 20% 10% 0%

Graph #3

Which would you rather have in your worship service: the latest worship songs or worship music that reflects the spiritual level of your church?

0% 10% 20% 30% 40% 50% 60% 70% 80% 90%100%
100%90% 80% 70% 60% 50% 40% 30% 20% 10% 0%

Graph #4

Which would you rather have in your worship service: professionally written and published hymns and songs or local church-birthed worship songs reflecting the teaching?

0% 10% 20% 30% 40% 50% 60% 70% 80% 90%100%
100%90% 80% 70% 60% 50% 40% 30% 20% 10% 0%

Graph #5

Which would you rather have in your worship service: an in-tune worship singer or an anointed worship singer?

0% 10% 20% 30% 40% 50% 60% 70% 80% 90%100%
100%90% 80% 70% 60% 50% 40% 30% 20% 10% 0%

Graph #6

Which would you rather have in your worship service: coordinated dress on the worship team appearing unified or unity in the Spirit?

0% 10% 20% 30% 40% 50% 60% 70% 80% 90%100%
100%90% 80% 70% 60% 50% 40% 30% 20% 10% 0%

Graph #7

Which would you rather have in your worship service: following and finishing the song list or worship service plan or a spontaneous "song of the Lord" delivered by a well-meaning, off-key member?

0% 10% 20% 30% 40% 50% 60% 70% 80% 90%100%
100%90% 80% 70% 60% 50% 40% 30% 20% 10% 0%

Graph #8

Which would you rather have in your worship service: anointed special music that ministers or spontaneous congregational worship?

0% 10% 20% 30% 40% 50% 60% 70% 80% 90%100%
100%90% 80% 70% 60% 50% 40% 30% 20% 10% 0%

Graph #9

Which would you rather have in your worship service: an anointed sermon or an anointed worship time?

0% 10% 20% 30% 40% 50% 60% 70% 80% 90%100%
100%90% 80% 70% 60% 50% 40% 30% 20% 10% 0%

Graph #10

Which would you rather have in your worship team: musical skill and training or faithfulness?

0% 10% 20% 30% 40% 50% 60% 70% 80% 90%100%
100%90% 80% 70% 60% 50% 40% 30% 20% 10% 0%

Graph #11

Which would you rather have in your worship service: the best worship leaders always leading or unskilled worship leaders leading at times for the sake of training them and giving them experience?

0% 10% 20% 30% 40% 50% 60% 70% 80% 90%100%
100%90% 80% 70% 60% 50% 40% 30% 20% 10% 0%

Graph #12
Which would you rather have on your worship team: only the best instrumentalists and singers or those whom God has given you to equip and develop?

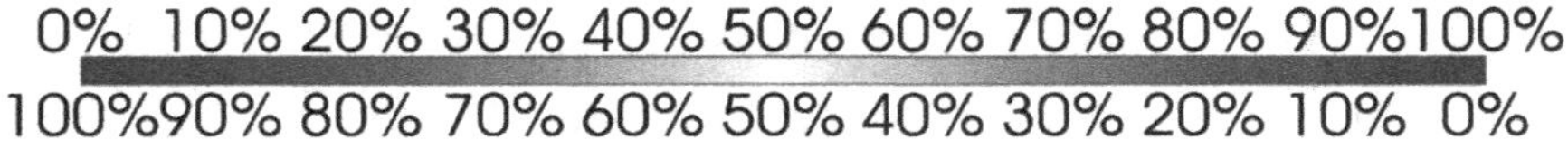

0% 10% 20% 30% 40% 50% 60% 70% 80% 90%100%
100%90% 80% 70% 60% 50% 40% 30% 20% 10% 0%

Graph #13
Which would you rather have on your worship team: a pursuit of musical excellence at all cost or a celebration of a lack of skill joined to the presence of God?

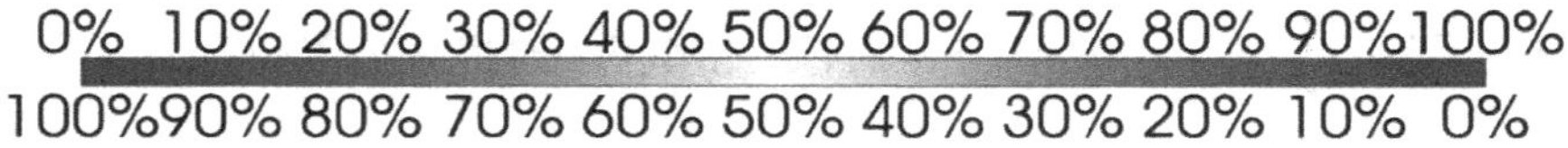

0% 10% 20% 30% 40% 50% 60% 70% 80% 90%100%
100%90% 80% 70% 60% 50% 40% 30% 20% 10% 0%

Chapter Four
BIBLICAL QUALIFICATIONS OF ALL CHURCH LEADERS

BIBLICAL LEADERSHIP QUALIFICATIONS

Are there qualifications for leadership in the Body of Christ? Of course, there are! The Old Testament is full of examples of godly leadership, and in the New Testament Paul systematically outlined for us in 1 Timothy 3 the qualifications for church leadership. Worship Leaders, including all secondary worship leaders, should meet these New Testament leadership qualifications, because they are in a highly visible ministry in the church. Here is Paul's instructions to Timothy concerning church leadership.

> *[1]This is a true saying, If a man desire the office of a **bishop**, he desireth a good work. [2]A bishop then must be blameless, the husband of one wife, vigilant, sober, of good behavior, given to hospitality, apt to teach; [3]Not given to wine, no striker, not greedy of filthy lucre; but patient, not a brawler, not covetous; [4]One that ruleth well his own house, having his children in subjection with all gravity; [5](For if a man know not how to rule his own house, how shall he take care of the church of God?)*

⁶Not a novice, lest being lifted up with pride he fall into the condemnation of the devil. ⁷Moreover he must have a good report of them which are without; lest he fall into reproach and the snare of the devil.

*⁸Likewise must the **deacons** be grave, not double-tongued, not given to much wine, not greedy of filthy lucre; ⁹Holding the mystery of the faith in a pure conscience. ¹⁰And let these also first be proved; then let them use the office of a deacon, being found blameless. ¹¹Even so must **their wives** be grave, not slanderers, sober, faithful in all things. ¹²Let the deacons be the husbands of one wife, ruling their children and their own houses well. ¹³For they that have used the office of a deacon well purchase to themselves a good degree, and great boldness in the faith which is in Christ Jesus. 1 Timothy 3:1–13 (KJV), emphasis added*

A synonym of the word "bishop" in those Scriptures is the word "elder." The words "elder" and "deacon" indicate ranks or chain of command ministry positions in the body of Christ. Those positions, Paul is telling us here, are to be filled with people of true Biblical character who are firmly grounded in the Word of truth.

I am a visual learner, and I like to build charts to help me visualize what I am learning. Here is a chart of the leadership qualifications of the three groups of ministry leadership that Paul mentioned in the above scripture. Please study this chart, taking time to note which qualifications are duplicated in each column.

Table 1. Biblical Church Leadership Qualifications

Bishop/Elder	Deacon	Leader's Wife
blameless	found blameless	
the husband of one wife	the husband of one wife	
not given to wine	not given to much wine	
not greedy of filthy lucre	not greedy of filthy lucre	
rules well his own house	rules their own houses well	
children in subjection with all gravity	rules their children well	
Not a novice	first be proved	
sober		sober
	be grave	be grave
vigilant		faithful in all things
	not double-tongued	not a slanderer
of good behavior	Holding the mystery of the faith in a pure conscience	
given to hospitality		
apt to teach		
has a good report of them which are without		
not covetous		
patient		
not a brawler		
no striker		
	great boldness in the faith	

As we progress up the ranks of church leadership, the more scrutiny our lives are under. Notice in Paul's list of qualifications for a bishop or elder are to not be a brawler or a striker. However, those qualifications do not appear in the list for a deacon or spouse. You may wonder whether that means it is all right for a deacon ranked minister to settle disputes by brawling or striking another individual? No, it is not! However, should a deacon lose their cool bad enough to strike someone, the deacon should not be automatically disqualified for ministry for doing that. His possible disqualification would need to be determined by the type of ministry he is involved in. If his ministry is people oriented and more visible in the church, discipline should be more severe than if his ministry is more things oriented.

Most who function at the eldership level of ministry within a local church have people-oriented ministries and are much more visible within the local church. For them to strike someone and experience no public consequences from the church could hurt the church in a huge way. Therefore, Paul makes sure we understand it is important for people of higher rank within the chain of command of a local church to be held to the highest standard.

It is equally important for those functioning at a lower rank of ministry within the local church to desire and strive to live and function at the highest level of standards so they are qualified to be promoted, should God desire to promote them.

In Paul's lists of qualifications for church leadership, we see that a deacon and his spouse should watch their tongues. Paul says deacons are not to be "double-tongued," meaning they are not to say one thing to one person and a different thing to another.

Consistency of truth is the issue here. Of all the character flaws a Christian leader can display, this is the easiest to fall into and justify. We can do that from a heart of not wanting to hurt a person. Rest assured that practice will always be discovered sooner or later. Then, once truth comes out, it is virtually impossible to explain to a congregational member why you lied. You can't say, "I was trying to protect you." That does not work at that moment. Then, once trust is broken, it is impossible for them to receive ministry from you again, and it can cause that person to find it difficult to ever trust another church leader.

Paul instructs the spouses of leaders to not be slanderers. When you think about it, that is the same instruction Paul gave to the deacons (to not be double-tongued) but with a more specific application. To slander someone, we have to never tell the person to their face what we are saying to others about them—hence the phrase "to talk behind their back." That means that we are double-tongued with that person, but it implies a malicious motive as well. The results are always the same, however. This practice of a church leader or their spouse becomes yet another proof to the offended church member that they can never trust a church leader or a church leader's spouse. Unfortunately, these character flaws are found within many church leaders today because those leaders were promoted before this part of their character could be developed.

The reason controlling the tongue is not mentioned in the qualifications for bishops is because that character trait should have already been established well before their release into ministry, and that practice should continue throughout the rest of their lives.

Anyone desiring to function in any level of Christian ministry should desire to meet all the qualifications for all levels of ministry. One example of this is the qualification for a bishop to be able to teach. Because this qualification does not occur in the list for deacons, does that mean that a person is not permitted to teach until promoted to an elder? Of course not! How does a person learn to teach if the individual does not teach? It simply means that by the time a person is promoted to elder level of ministry, the person should also be able to teach and prepare others for that level of ministry as well.

THE FIVEFOLD MINISTRY OFFICES

Every elder in a church is considered to be one of the "ascension ministry gifts" or ministry offices listed for us in Ephesians 4.

> And He Himself gave some to be **apostles,** some **prophets,** some **evangelists,** and some **pastors** and **teachers,** for the equipping of the saints for the work of

ministry, for the edifying of the body of Christ, Ephesians 4:11-12 (NKJV) emphasis added

Every church elder will be one of these five types of ministry callings: apostle, prophet, evangelist, pastor, or teacher. Most ministers will have a combination of at least two or more of these fivefold ministry callings. One of those five will usually be predominant in every elder's ministry. Here are the short definitions of each.

Apostle

An apostle is an overseer of multiple ministries. Using today's vocabulary, an apostle would be called a senior pastor. Some apostles oversee more than one church. An apostle can also be a starter of ministries, a church planter, and a missionary.

Prophet

A prophet is an elder who functions in the prophetic gifts of the Holy Spirit on behalf of the church and the individuals in the church. Of the nine gifts of the Spirit listed for us in 1 Corinthians 12, the prophetic gifts are: a word of knowledge, prophecy, and discerning of spirits.

Evangelist

An evangelist is one whose primary ministry is to win people to Jesus Christ.

Pastor

A pastor is a spiritual parent who raises spiritual children.

Teacher

A teacher in the body of Christ will teach both the Word of God and what will equip the saints to do their ministry. For instance, a teacher is required to instruct the nursery workers how to do their job or the Sunday school teachers how to do their job as well. A minister of music would be required to teach those in the worship department how to sing, play instruments, and worship and lead worship.

Chapter Five

BIBLICAL QUALIFICATIONS FOR ALL WORSHIP LEADERS

BIBLICAL WORSHIP LEADERSHIP QUALIFICATIONS

To determine the Biblical qualifications for worship leaders/worship team members, let's look at the lives of David, the Levites, and Asaph in 1 Chronicles. We know that David is known for being a worshiper, but for this study, we also need to look at the history of the Levites and a particular Levite named Asaph. Asaph began as one of the brethren on the large worship team that David put together and was eventually promoted from within the ranks to take Chenaniah's position as chief musician.

Let's examine what qualifications every worship leader and every worship team member should have by looking at these people in scripture.

CALLED BY GOD

The Levites were chosen (called by God) to carry the presence of God (the ark of the covenant) before the people.

> *Then David said, "No one may carry the ark of God but the Levites, for **the LORD has chosen them** to carry*

the ark of God and to minister before Him forever." 1
Chronicles 15:2 (NKJV), emphasis added

According to *Nelson's Illustrated Bible Dictionary*, a Levite is defined like this:

> *LEVITES: [LEE vites] – descendants of Levi who*
> *served as assistants to the PRIESTS in the* **worship**
> **system** *of the nation of Israel. As a Levite, AARON and*
> *his sons and their descendants were charged with the*
> *responsibility of the priesthood – offering burnt offerings*
> *and* **leading the people in worship** *and confession.*
> *(Numbers 8:6) The designation of a tribe for special*
> *service to God grew out of an unusual concept of the*
> *Hebrew people known as the firstfruits. Because the*
> *Levites were the ones who voluntarily returned to their*
> *Lord after worshipping the golden image, they were*
> *chosen for service to the sanctuary, thus replacing the*
> *firstborn as* **God's representatives of the holiness** *of His*
> *people. (Numbers 3:12–13,41)*[13] *emphasis added*

The most important qualification for a worship leader is that God must have called you into that ministry. If you are functioning as a worship leader and yet have not been called by God to do that ministry, it will affect the church negatively in at least two ways.

First, it examples for the congregation that receiving a call from God into a particular ministry is not necessary to function in that ministry. Let me simply say: This is a dangerous precedent to establish in your church.

Second, as long as someone is in a position of ministry where God did not call them to function, that keeps the person whom God has called into that ministry position from being able to function in their ministry.

Also, keep this in mind: You may have been called to a particular ministry in the past, but is it God's will for you to do that ministry now? It may be time to raise up others to do that ministry.

---

[13] *Nelson's Illustrated Bible Dictionary* (Thomas Nelson Publishing, 1986).

BE QUICK TO REPENT

A worship leader must be quick to repent of sins, especially concerning worship. As we just learned, the Levites were quick to repent after Aaron led the entire congregation to worship a golden calf. Here is the scripture talking about that event:

> *Then Moses stood in the gate of the camp, and said, Who is on the Lord's side? let him come unto me. And all the sons of Levi gathered themselves together unto him.*
> *And the children of Levi did according to the word of Moses: and there fell of the people that day about three thousand men. Exodus 32:26, 28 (KJV)*

In the scripture before this one (1 Chronicles 15:2) about David's revelation concerning who should be leading worship, David was quick to repent when he realized he was allowing the leading of worship, or the carrying of the ark of God's presence, in ways with which God was not pleased.

Here's a quick review of the back story of David's repentance. Before David had become king, King Saul took the Ark of the Covenant into battle against the Philistines, hoping that gesture would cause the Israelites to win the battle. Because God had not instructed Saul to do that, they lost the battle and the Ark of the Covenant was captured.

It is a very funny story of what happened next when the Philistines put the ark in their temple beside their god Dagon. Dagon is a merman god, half fish and half man.

When the Philistines returned to their temple the next morning, the heavy stone statue of Dagon was on its face before the Ark of the Covenant. Although the people could not figure out how such a heavy statue could fall over, they stood it up and went about their day worshiping Dagon. The next morning, they found the statue of Dagon on its face before the Ark once again, but this time Dagon's hand was broken off.

Not only were those strange events happening, everyone in the

Philistine nation were stricken with hemorrhoids. When they finally figured out that the reason all those things were happening was because of the ark, they removed the Ark of the Covenant and put it in storage in Abinadab's house. They did not return it to Israel.

When David became king, his burden was to bring the Ark of the Covenant back home. To do that, David came up with a good plan. He knew the ark was sacred, so he didn't want to haul it back on a cart that had been used to hall manure and hay, so he ordered a new cart to be built.

The Israelites located the ark, and the Philistines were more than happy to get rid of it, so the Israelites took the cart to pick up the ark. On the way home, they met with tragedy.

> *7So they carried the ark of God on a new cart from the house of Abinadab, and Uzza and Ahio drove the cart. 8Then David and all Israel played* music *before God with all their might, with singing, on harps, on stringed instruments, on tambourines, on cymbals, and with trumpets.*
>
> *9 And when they came to Chidon's threshing floor, Uzza put out his hand to hold the ark, for the oxen stumbled 10Then the anger of the Lord was aroused against Uzza, and He struck him because he put his hand to the ark; and he died there before God. 1 Chronicles 13:7–10 (NKJV)*

It can be a very costly lesson to learn that God will not receive worship when we do it our way, not His. Because Uzza died, David left the ark with a man named Obed-Edom for three months and went back home to seek the Lord.

After several days, God showed David what he did wrong. That is the revelation from God that David received found in the 1 Chronicles 15, which we read previously.

> *Then David said, "**No one may carry the ark of God but the Levites**, for the LORD has chosen them to carry*

*the ark of God and to minister before Him forever." 1
Chronicles 15:2 (NKJV), emphasis added*

Uzza was not a Levite; therefore, he was not permitted to carry the
presents of God represented by the Ark of the Covenant. Once God
showed David that, David was quick to repent and change his actions.
Because of that, the ark was successfully brought back on the Israelites'
next attempt.

Let me just make a couple of observations here. First, if you are
functioning as a worship leader but you are not a spiritual Levite (called
by God to be a worship leader), you are probably experiencing death in
your life in some way. Second, if you are trying to lead worship following
man's ideas, even your own good ideas, you are trying to carry the
presence of God on a new cart. It always works much better when we
lead worship according to God's patterns found in the Word of God. We
will discuss those patterns later in this book.

By the way, I've heard it said
that a new cart is nothing more
than a board with a couple of big
wheels. It is my conviction that
churches should never be run by a
board and committees. That is not
a Biblical pattern at all, especially

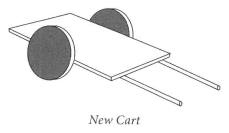

New Cart

when it comes to worship. Spiritual oversight must only be given to
ministries by the fivefold[14] ministers and the church elders.

Now let's go back to the point of being quick to repent. As a worship
leader, we will make many mistakes. Sometimes we will lead the people
according to our flesh and not the Spirit, like David did when trying to
use a new cart. It is easy to do that. When it happens, it is very important
that we are not full of pride, which makes us afraid to admit we made
a mistake. The devil will tell us that, if we admit we were wrong, those
following us will not trust us again. However, if we are quick to admit
when we do wrong, that will cause those following us to trust us even
more.

---

[14] Ephesians 4:11

SANCTIFY YOURSELF

Worship leaders represent God's holiness; therefore, they must continually sanctify themselves, especially in preparing to carry the presence of God, which is to lead worship.

> *He said to them, "You are the heads of the fathers' houses of the Levites; sanctify yourselves, you and your brethren, that you may bring up the ark of the LORD God of Israel to the place I have prepared for it. 1 Chronicles 15:12 (NKJV), emphasis added*

Notice the language that David used to instruct the Levites to prepare themselves to bring the ark back home. His instruction was to *"sanctify yourselves,"* not to "be sanctified by the Lord." That tells us that sanctification is something we must do. That begs the question: What is sanctification? Let's turn again to the *Nelson's Illustrated Bible Dictionary* to define it for us. This is the main part of that definition.

> *SANCTIFICATION: ... as separation from the world and setting apart for God's service is a concept found throughout the Bible. Spoken of as "holy" or "set apart" in the Old Testament ...*[15]

Separating ourselves from the world and setting ourselves apart for God's calling is something we must do by our choices. If we find ourselves in a weakened state, of course we can call out to God for help. However, God will not override our free will and sanctify us without us asking for help. We must sanctify ourselves. Also, sanctification is not a one-time experience. It is a lifelong pursuit of holiness and righteousness.

As worship leaders, every time we are to lead worship, we must go through the process of sanctifying ourselves. Here's the prayer that David prayed for God's help to do this.

---

[15] *Nelson's Illustrated Bible Dictionary*

Search me, O God, and know my heart: try me, and know my thoughts: And see if there be any wicked way in me, and lead me in the way everlasting. Psalm 139:23–24 (KJV)

David instructed the worship team, who were of the Levites, to sanctify themselves. Their response to his instructions was recorded in Scripture.

So the priests and the Levites sanctified themselves to bring up the ark of the LORD God of Israel 1 Chronicles 15:14(NKJV)

As worship leaders we must come prepared spiritually for the task. We should never wait till we are at church to begin to prepare ourselves but rather begin days before by seeking God and reading His word.

BE APPOINTED BY THOSE IN AUTHORITY

Chain of command originated with God. In this story found in 1 Chronicles 15, David is king.

Then David spoke to the leaders of the Levites to appoint their brethren to be the singers accompanied by instruments of music, stringed instruments, harps, and cymbals, by raising the voice with resounding joy. 1 Chronicles 15:16 (NKJV)

That is a wonderful example of how chain of command is supposed to work. Worship leaders should never be self-appointed. They also should not be appointed by someone who has no real spiritual authority in the church. Notice that the appointments of this worship team in 1 Chronicles chapter fifteen could be traced all the way up to the king, who gave authorization for the leaders of the Levites to appoint from among their brethren the worship leaders, singers, and instrumentalists.

It is also worth noting that David did not micromanage the leaders of the Levites by telling them who to appoint. David knew that his leaders could be trusted to choose the right people. In today's church life, senior pastors need to stop micromanaging those underneath their covering. When you give authority to someone, do not keep taking that authority back by specifically instructing them what to do. Tell them what to do in general terms. That forces them to seek God for themselves for the details. That allows them to own their responsibilities as well as their mistakes.

However, in the New Testament church of today, appointments to worship leadership positions should always be approved by the pastor or bishop and pastoral team of the church before anyone is appointed. It is always possible for one person to be blinded concerning someone's character. Therefore, exercise percussion, and do not appoint leaders quickly. In the New Testament, any leadership was installed in front of the entire church. A symbolic ceremony of those in authority laying their hands upon the new appointee demonstrated for the entire church this person's new leadership Authority. That's why Paul cautioned not to appoint leaders quickly.

Lay hands suddenly on no man, neither be partaker of other men's sins: keep thyself pure. 1 Timothy 5:22 (KJV)

In other words, if you as a leader appoint someone into the leadership before their character is established, then you will be seen to condone the sin in their life.

SUBMIT TO MUSICAL TRAINING

In the book *The Importance of Worshiping Together*, I established that music is to group worship what prayer is to individual worship. If you have not yet read that book, it would be advisable for you to do so to understand how important music is to worshiping together.

Because God gave us music as the most powerful expression of worship for our gatherings, anyone called into worship leading needs to be trained in music. Here is the Scripture that establishes that principle.

> *And Chenaniah, chief of the Levites, was for song: he instructed about the song, because he was skillful. 1 Chronicles 15:22 (KJV)*

Chenaniah trained all of the Levites in music. He was skillful in music; therefore, he trained the rest of the Levites to also be skillful. If you want God to use you as a worship leader, you need to have skill regarding music.

Here are the minimum musical skill requirements for all worship leaders and worship team members. Primary worship leaders should have all of those skills established before they are appointed into positions of authority. Worship team members can be developing those skills as they participate in worship leading.

Singing

Every worship team member needs to know the fundamental techniques of singing. The Worship College, found at www.theworshipcollege.com, offers a six-session video course entitled *The Fundamentals of Singing*. That course will teach you the correct way to sing. It even has a session to help those who do not know how to match pitches yet.

Every worship team member, even instrumentalists, must sing. The Bible makes it clear that we come before God's presence with singing.[16] The purpose for musical instruments is to support and accompany the singing.

Music Theory

Music is made up of the three components of melody, harmony, and rhythm. A worship leader needs to have a basic understanding of the fundamentals of music. Understanding melody and harmony involves these basic concepts:

a. the major and minor scale patterns of steps and half steps
b. the grand staff

---

[16] Psalm 100:2

c. the key signatures of all major and minor key centers
d. the piano keyboard
e. the circle of fifths
f. the intervals between any two notes
g. the triads for every major and minor key center
h. the variations of these triads: major, minor, diminished, augmented, 7th, 9th, 13th, sus, 2nd, the use of the "/," etc.

Understanding rhythm involves these basic concepts:

a. a measure of music
b. note and rest symbols and values
c. time signatures
d. counting measures and divided beats
e. duplets and triplets
f. simple and compound rhythms
g. dotted notes/rests and ties
h. the music feels: straight rhythms, dotted rhythms, waltz rhythms, and syncopated rhythms
i. music conducting skills

It is the rhythm of music that permits multiple instrumentalists and singers to be able to perform music together. Without the rhythm's structure, we have no way of performing a song with others at the same time. It is the melody and harmony part of music that enables us to sound good together, even though we may not be singing the same notes. That is why music was created—to enable us to speak the same things at the same time.

Over the years, I have known many worship leaders who have chosen not to be trained in music themselves but to rely on their instrumentalists' music knowledge. Those are worship leaders who have someone else tell them when they are to sing a musical phrase, what key a song is in, what the rhythm of the song should feel like, etc. When that happens, the one who should be leading musically is actually being led by a subordinate.

In Scripture, that is a demonic practice attributed to Jezebel's spirit. It is when a figurehead leader is being led by someone else, making it appear that the figurehead is in charge, when in truth they are not. This practice is referred to as the pattern, way, or spirit of Jezebel, based on this Scripture.

*But there was none like unto (King) Ahab, which did sell himself to work wickedness in the sight of the LORD, whom **Jezebel** his wife **stirred up**. 1 King 21:25 (KJV), emphasis added*

Although Ahab was king, Jezebel manipulated him or stirred him up to do whatever she wanted him to do. That means that Jezebel was actually running the kingdom from her secondary position, not her husband Ahab.

Patterns and principles are very important. Throughout the word of God, there is a distinction drawn between a Godly pattern and an ungodly pattern. We are told that when we do things the way God tells us to do them, we experience the blessing of the Almighty God. However, when we do things after the pattern of the world, we receive the consequences. And one step beyond that, when we follow demonic patterns, that opens us up to those demonic influences in our lives.

If a worship leader does not know enough about music to lead their musical ensemble or worship team and are relying upon those in their team who know more than them about music, they are leading their worship team according to a demonic pattern. Whenever we do something the way demons do them, that gives those demons the legal right to inhabit and influence everyone's life who is involved. That means, if you are leading worship according to the pattern of Jezebel, you are inviting the spirit of Jezebel into your church.

To guard against that, simply make sure every worship leader who is appointed in your church has had adequate musical training. If you are a secondary worship leader and you find yourself on a worship team that is following this jezebel pattern, here are some things you can do, to help you make sure you are not participating in this demonic pattern and thus inviting a curse upon yourself and your church.

1. Offer musical suggestions privately to the worship leader, not in front of the other members of the team.

2. Never agree to lead in any way from your secondary worship leadership position.
3. If you must, teach the worship leader something to equip them to be able to lead, do it in private, then let them lead it in the team setting. However, be careful that this does not become a habit where they depend upon you to cover their lack of training.
4. In the worship service, avoid the temptation to come to the worship leader's rescue when their lack of musical skill or knowledge gets them into trouble. They need to become acutely aware of their need for musical training, and that will not happen if you keep covering for them.
5. If you are running sound, never try to cover the worship leader's mistakes with the way you mix the sound. Let their mistakes be heard so they can correct their mistakes themselves.

DEMONSTRATE AN APTITUDE FOR MUSIC

A worship leader and all worship team members should demonstrate an aptitude and/or talent for music and should be skilled in both singing and playing a musical instrument.

When David first tried to bring the Ark of the Covenant back to Jerusalem, the Bible tells us that there were many Israelites playing musical instruments and singing as they brought the ark back on the new cart.

> So they carried the ark of God on a new cart from the house of Abinadab, and Uzza and Ahio drove the cart. Then David and all Israel played music before God with all their might, with singing, on harps, on stringed instruments, on tambourines, on cymbals, and with trumpets. 1 Chronicles 13:7-8 (NKJV)

After what happened to Uzza on that first attempt to bring the Ark of the Covenant back, David and the Israelites wanted the second attempt to be successful. That is shown by their extremely organized celebration through music for that event.

For their first attempt, they simply said, "Anyone who wants to play an instrument can do so." However, after the tragedy where Uzza died, David was very careful to do everything according to God's will.

When building a worship team for your church, never do it the first way! Never simply send out an appeal for anyone and everyone to join the worship team. Anyone who is on the worship team in your church needs to be appointed to that position after the church leadership considers their character and skill.

David's establishment of the worship team for the second attempt to bring the ark back was much more structured and organized than the first attempt. The most important instruction God gave David was this.

> Then David spoke to the leaders of the Levites to appoint their brethren to be the singers accompanied by instruments of music, stringed instruments, harps, and cymbals, by raising the voice with resounding joy. 1 Chronicles 15:16 (NKJV)

The most important part of every worship team is the singers! The Levites were appointed to be a large choir of singers. There were hundreds of Levites, so this choir David appointed would be massive by today's standards. This large choir was to be accompanied by instruments of music. But it is important to note that even the instrumentalists were supposed to sing as they played their instruments. Singing is the most important musical expression of worship to God![17] The only exception in Scripture to instrumentalists singing were the trumpeters. That is why they were listed separately from the other instrumentalists in this passage of Scripture. Here is the orchestra that David had the Levites appoint from among their brethren.

> [19]So the singers, Heman, Asaph, and Ethan, were appointed to sound with cymbals of brass;
> [20]And Zechariah, and Aziel, and Shemiramoth, and Jehiel, and Unni, and Eliab, and Maaseiah, and Benaiah, with psalteries on Alamoth;

---

[17] Psalm 100:2

²¹And Mattithiah, and Elipheleh, and Mikneiah, and Obededom, and Jeiel, and Azaziah, with harps on the Sheminith to excel.

²²And Chenaniah, chief of the Levites, was for song: he instructed about the song, because he was skilful.

²³And Berechiah and Elkanah were doorkeepers for the ark.

²⁴And Shebaniah, and Jehoshaphat, and Nethaneel, and Amasai, and Zechariah, and Benaiah, and Eliezer, the priests, did blow with the trumpets before the ark of God: and Obededom and Jehiah were doorkeepers for the ark. 1 Chronicles 15:19–24 (KJV)

I know these are a lot of hard-to-pronounce names, but it is important to see that this large choir of singers was being accompanied by a twenty-four-piece orchestra as they brought the Ark of the Covenant back home. All of those instrumentalists are referred to as singers, except for those playing the trumpets. When your lips are busy with a trumpet, you cannot sing.

The instruments that accompanied the large choir are listed as these: cymbals of brass, psalteries, harps, and trumpets.

Here are the members of this orchestra:

Table 2. David's Orchestra

Brass Cymbals	Psalteries	Harps	Trumpets
Heman	Zechariah	Mattithiah	Shebaniah
Asaph	Aziel	Elipheleh	Jehoshaphat
Ethan	Shemiramoth	Mikneiah	Nethaneel
	Jehiel	Obededom	Amasai
	Unni	Jeiel	Zechariah
	Eliab	Azaziah	Benaiah
	Maaseiah		Eliezer
	Benaiah		

I find it interesting to note that on their first attempt to bring the ark back home, they had all of those instruments plus an additional instrument. The additional instrument was the tambourine. The first attempt to bring back the ark was where everyone was doing their own thing. The second attempt was organized and structured.

If you play the tambourine for worship, don't just show up with it and play along. First, ask to be invited onto the worship team. Second, attend all rehearsals of the worship team. Third, be teachable. Do not play all the time! A tambourine is a specific percussion trap instrument that should only be used at specific times in music. Fourth, be willing to sing in the choir when it is not appropriate to play the tambourine. Fifth, be willing to learn how and when to play other percussion trap instruments. Please do not carry on the tradition of tambourines being synonymous with doing your own thing, which began at the first attempt to bring the Ark of the Covenant back to Jerusalem.

There are three words in this orchestra description that need some definition. The first is psaltery. What is that? We don't use that term today, so to understand, we must do some investigating to find out what is meant by that word. Thank God for the Strong's concordance.

This is Strong's Hebrew word number 5035 "nebel," translated "psaltery," which is a musical instrument—either a portable harp or a lute or guitar (with bulging resonance-body at lower end).[18] In other words, a psaltery is a stringed instrument.

The second word that needs to be investigated comes in this phrase.

"… with psalteries on Alamoth." 1 Chronicles 15:20 (KJV)

The word "Alamoth" is not used in the English language. Therefore, it is a mystery to me why the translators did not translate it for us. It is Strong's Hebrew word number 5961 "Alamoth" meaning (soprano voices of) young women.[19] In case you think David only used men in

---

[18] "5035. nebel," Bible Hub, accessed November 1, 2020, https://biblehub.com/hebrew/5035.htm.

[19] "5961. alamoth," Bible Hub, accessed November 1, 2020, https://biblehub.com/strongs/hebrew/5961.htm.

his choir and orchestra, the translation of this word should settle that for you. Here are just a few Scriptures that mention that God wants both men and women to sing to Him: 1 Samuel 18:6, 2 Chronicles 35:25, Ezra 2:65, Nehemiah 7:67, 2 Samuel 19:35, Isaiah 54:1, and Ecclesiastes 2:8. The last word we need to define is found in this phrase:

"... with harps on the Sheminith to excel." 1 Chronicles 15:21 (KJV)

Again, Sheminith is not found in the English language. It is Strong's Hebrew word number 8067 "Sheminith": an eight-stringed lyre.[20] A Sheminith was a smaller version of the harp that could be carried and played, rather than sat down at to play.

The most important point we should take away from these Scriptures is that to advance as a worship leader, you should be able to both sing and play a musical instrument of some kind.

One last thing we should note about David's orchestra is that he utilized all three families of musical instruments, just like we do today. The three categories of acoustical musical instruments are percussion instruments, string instruments, and wind instruments.

Table 3. Three Types of Musical Instruments

Brass Cymbals	Psalteries	Harps/Sheminith	Trumpets
Percussion	Strings		Wind

Additionally, there are four people listed with the orchestra whose job was not to play a musical instrument but to be a door keeper. Those four individuals are named as Berechiah, Elkanah, Obededom, and Jehiah.

In the tabernacle of Moses, the Ark of the Covenant was hidden behind a thick veil and was not available to the general public. When David brought back the ark, he placed it in a tent where everyone could see it. That was a prophetic act that pointed to Jesus, where the presence

---

[20] "8067. sheminith," Bible Hub, accessed November 1, 2020, https://biblehub.com/hebrew/8067.htm.

of God is available to all of us, not just to a select few. The ark was placed on a hill so everyone could look at it. We are also told that David put it in a tent. But tents have sides that close if they are not being held open. To ensure that the ark was visible from all sides, four men were appointed for the purpose of holding open the four doors of the tent, one on each side.

In today's church, the door keepers are called the ushers. Based on this Scripture, I consider all ushers to be the gateway to worship. For that reason, I believe an usher should meet the requirements of a deacon outlined in 1 Timothy. The congregation's worship experience can be greatly enhanced or hindered by the church ushers. Let me be clear, however, an usher is a watchman, not a worshiper. Of course, I believe every Christian is called to be a worshiper, but when you are functioning as a door keeper, you are to be watching out for the worshipers.

DEMONSTRATE COMMITMENT IN OTHER MINISTRIES

We have already established that the Levites were to carry the presence of God. When we look into the *Nelson's Illustrated Bible Dictionary*, we find this as part of the definition for the word "Levites."

> *LEVITES: ... But all the other Levites who were not descended directly from Aaron were to serve as priestly assistants, taking care of the tabernacle and the Temple and performing other **menial duties** <Num. 8:6>*[21]

Many musicians suffer from what I call a "star syndrome," which means they find it beneath their station to do menial tasks. I believe every worship team member should be assigned a menial task, one they will not receive any recognition for, to test their character. We do not need stars in the kingdom of God; we need servants.

> *Yet it shall not be so among you; but whoever desires to become great among you shall be your servant. Mark 10:43 (NKJV)*

---

[21] *Nelson's Illustrated Bible Dictionary* (Thomas Nelson Publishing, 1986).

A person who will not humble themself to do menial service has no business being in a highly visible ministry like the worship team.

BE ABLE TO PLAN AND LEAD A LARGE PRODUCTION

In Chapter four of *Biblical Worship,* I went over several of the Greek and Hebrew words that are translated into the synonyms of the word "worship" in the Bible. One of the words we looked at extensively was the word "halal." Halal is the Hebrew word for praise. It is also the root of the universal word "hallelujah."

According to Strong's concordance, there are eleven different definitions of the word "halal." One of those definitions is "to make a show."[22] That means one of two things. It can either be used to call someone a show off, or it can mean a large musical and artistic production.

When David and the children of Israel brought back the Ark of the Covenant the second time, they did it with a large, well planned, well-rehearsed musical processional or parade, a performing arts production. Not only did that processional involve a large choir and an orchestra, it also included dancers.

Not everyone who is on your worship team will be able to plan, direct, and produce a large musical production, but for those who want to advance to the position of chief musician like Chenaniah in 1 Chronicles 15:22 and Asaph in 1 Chronicles 16:5, you need to develop the skills it takes to head up an extravaganza type of show for the Lord.

That means you will need to take a music conducting course. To conduct or direct music, you need to be able to read music. Therefore, all of the music theory requirements that I listed above you must know and understand thoroughly. In addition to music theory, the music conducting course that you take must cover these music conducting skills:

a. all music conducting beat patterns with both hands, including measures of 2, 3, 4, 5, slow 6, fast 6, 7, 9, and 12

---

[22] Shamblin Stone, *Biblical Worship* (Westbow Press, 2012), 56.

b. divided beat patterns for measures of 2, 3, and 4
c. breath beats for every beat and divided beats
d. cutoffs for every beat and divided beats
e. music conducting priorities
f. choosing music for your ensemble
g. conducting a rehearsal
h. preparing for the rehearsal
i. conducting musical dynamics, holds, and musical interpretation
j. the use of the face, eyes, and mouth when conducting

For this huge production, Chenaniah was the leader. Here is the description of that major production found in the Scripture.

> So David, the elders of Israel, and the captains over thousands went to bring up the ark of the covenant of the LORD from the house of Obed-Edom with joy. And so it was, when God helped the Levites who bore the ark of the covenant of the LORD, that they offered seven bulls and seven rams. David was clothed with a robe of fine linen, as were all the Levites who bore the ark, the singers, and **Chenaniah the music master** with the singers. David also wore a linen ephod. Thus, all Israel brought up the ark of the covenant of the LORD with shouting and with the sound of the horn, with trumpets and with cymbals, making music with stringed instruments and harps. 1 Chronicles 15:25–28 (NKJV), emphasis added

I would like to point out something from this Scripture that I feel is very important for any worship team. It is this.

> And David was clothed with a robe of fine linen, and all the Levites that bare the ark, and the singers, and Chenaniah the master of the song with the singers: David also had upon him an ephod of linen. 1 Chronicles 15:27 (KJV)

How your worship team dresses is as important as how they play and sing. I believe worship teams should be clothed in coordinated dress, as you see here in this Scripture. All of the worship team had on robes of fine linen. The color of fine linen is defined for us on the website http://www.magiclinen.com.

> *The color of natural, undyed linen fiber is often referred to as "linen gray." However, it is not the typical gray you would imagine ... and can range between ivory, ecru, oatmeal, and taupe.*[23]

So, the entire worship team was dressed in off-white robes. The only exception to this dress code was for the king, who also had on an ephod. This colorful outer garment identified David as the king, even though he was participating as one of the worship team. The leadership participating in worship is a precedence that all pastors and church leaders should follow. If you want your congregation to be worshipers, then you must be a worshiper first.

Why is it important to have coordinated dress on the worship team? Coordinated dress lets there be no visual standouts from the rest of the team. In music, the first purpose of a choir is to sing with "one voice." For an orchestra, it is to make "one sound." What that means is that in a musical ensemble, the only time one singer or one instrumentalist should stand out from the rest of the group is when the person has a solo line

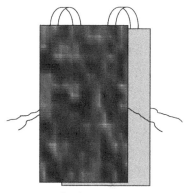

An ephod outer garment

in a song. To feature that person for the moment is done by having them step forward out of the group. Once the individual's solo is done, the person should step back into the group and visually and musically blend so the ensemble appears and sounds as one again.

---

[23] "What Color Is Linen? The Natural Linen Color Explained," Magic Linen, accessed November 6, 2020, https://magiclinen.com/blog/what-color-is-linen.

SUPPORT THE VISION OF THE CHURCH LEADER(S)

David received God's vision of how this worship extravaganza should look. Of course, David could not execute that vision without the help of Chenaniah, or the music minister, and the worship team, the Levites.

As king, David received the vision from God for the directions this worship event should take. David then shared that vision with those he had placed in authority so they could to help him bring the vision into reality.

If you are a pastor of the church, you are the one responsible to receive vision from God concerning every part of the church. However, you are not expected to implement the vision. God will give you people to bring that vision to pass.

If you are a chief musician or worship team member, God will also give you vision for your church's worship. However, make sure your pastor approves your vision, because the pastor is held responsible before God for everything in the church.

If you are the pastor, be open to what God has given to those you have placed in charge of the worship. If you are not, they will become frustrated, and you will possibly lose them to a pastor who will listen to them. Make sure you're ministry philosophies are compatible before you start sharing ministry vision with each other.

If you are a chief musician or worship team member and your pastor does not share your vision for worship, be patient. Do not abandon ship! Give God time to speak to your pastor. Be willing to defer to the pastor's decisions until you can come to a consensus concerning the church's worship.

ADMINISTRATIVE SKILLS

Any time you are putting on this type of worship event, it requires a lot of administration. Throughout 1 Chronicles 15–16, we see how every aspect of this event had to be administered by the leaders of the Levites. If you serve on a worship team, you will also find yourself doing administrative duties from time to time. Simply embrace this as a part of your responsibilities, as part of what makes it possible for you to lead the congregation in worship.

FOOD HANDLING AND DISTRIBUTION

Part of this worship extravaganza involved feeding those who were there to worship.

> *And when David had finished offering the burnt offerings and the peace offerings, he blessed the people in the name of the LORD. Then he distributed to everyone of Israel, both man and woman, to everyone a loaf of bread, a piece of meat, and a cake of raisins. 1 Chronicles 16:2–3 (NKJV)*

Obviously, not every time we gather to worship will we share a meal, but when we do, the worship team is not exempt from the kitchen duties. This Scripture says David distributed the food. However, we know from other Scriptures in those chapters that the way David got things done was by delegation.

FAITHFUL

The number one requirement for anyone called into ministry of any kind is to be found faithful.

> *And I thank Christ Jesus our Lord, who hath enabled me, for that he counted me faithful, putting me into the ministry; 1 Timothy 1:12 (KJV)*

Asaph was faithful in all he was assigned to do. Therefore, he was promoted to be Chenaniah's replacement as chief musician under David.

> *And he appointed some of the Levites to minister before the ark of the LORD, to commemorate, to thank, and to praise the LORD God of Israel: **Asaph the chief**,*

and next to him Zechariah, then Jeiel, Shemiramoth, Jehiel, Mattithiah, Eliab, Benaiah, and Obed-Edom: Jeiel with stringed instruments and harps, but Asaph made music with cymbals; 1 Chronicles 16:4–5 (NKJV), emphasis added

ARRANGE, REHEARSE, AND LEAD MUSIC

When we were first introduced to Chenaniah, we learned three things about him.

> *And Chenaniah, chief of the Levites, was for song: he instructed about the song, because he was skillful. 1 Chronicles 15:22 (KJV)*

He was a music instructor, he was skillful at music, and he was in charge. When Asaph took his place, we assume that he too was skillful in music and was able to lead and teach music. We know he was able to arrange music for the choir and orchestra, because the Scriptures tell us that David gave his new song to Asaph to arrange for the musical worship ensemble.

> *And on that day David first delivered this psalm into the hand of Asaph and his brethren, to thank the LORD:*
> *"Oh, give thanks to the LORD!*
> *Call upon His name; make known His deeds among the peoples!*
> *Sing to Him, sing psalms to Him; talk of all His wondrous works!*
> *Glory in His holy name; let the hearts of those rejoice who seek the LORD! 1 Chronicles 16:7–10 (NKJV)*

David wrote the song, but Asaph arranged it for his brethren. He also led the rehearsals of the song, which meant that he also directed the song in the performance.

BE PROPHETIC

Asaph carried a prophetic edge in his ministry, his music, and his worship, which was recognized and released by David, who was his spiritual authority and covering. Asaph also passed on this prophetic mantle to those he trained in music ministry.

> *Moreover David and the captains of the army separated for the service some of the sons of Asaph, of Heman, and of Jeduthun, who should* **prophesy with harps, stringed instruments, and cymbals**. *... Of the sons of Asaph: Zaccur, Joseph, Nethaniah, and Asharelah; the sons of Asaph were under the direction of Asaph, who* **prophesied according to the order of the king**. *...., who* **prophesied with a harp** *to give thanks and to praise the LORD. 1 Chronicles 25:1-3 (NKJV), emphasis added*

I believe every worship leader, and every worship team member MUST operate in the prophetic realm. It is not an option!

David told them to prophesy on their instruments, and they did—without hesitation. Worship leaders need to be so in tune with God that those in authority can point to anyone of the team at any time to ask them to prophesy on their instrument or by singing, and they do so without any hesitation whatsoever.

That is the most vital qualification for any worship leader! If you do not know how to hear God's voice, you have no business leading worship!

In the book *Portrait of a Worshiper,* I established Biblically that the Spirit of God within us initiates all Biblical worship. If God's Spirit initiates our worship as individuals, He also initiates our joint worship as well. It is the worship leader's responsibility to know at any given moment within a group worship experience which direction the Spirit of God is leading.

You may say, "Isn't the planning time for the service when the leader is supposed to hear from God about the direction of a service?"

The answer is "yes and no." Yes, a worship leader needs to seek God all the time the leader is planning a service. However, for any number of reasons, God may choose to change directions when it comes time for the worship service to take place.

"Why would God do that?" you may ask. "Doesn't God know what he wants days and even weeks before the time comes for the service to take place?"

Of course, He does. But humanity is not a bunch of robots. God gave us free will. Depending on who chose to attend the service that day, God may want to "call an audible." He knows just what every one of us needs and the best way we will respond to Him in our intimate time with Him. The service you've planned as a worship leader may have been designed by God to minister to someone who did not attend that day.

A worship leader and worship team must be prepared to completely abandon their preplanned agenda and be completely led by the Holy Spirit in the songs they do and in prophetic, spontaneous worship.

Again, to be a worship leader requires that you hear from God concerning the direction of every worship time you lead! That means spending time with God in preparation for worship. It also means developing the sensitivity and obedience to God's Spirit that will allow Him to change directions of a worship service at a moment's notice.

CATEGORIZING THESE QUALIFICATIONS

All of these worship-leading qualifications fall into one of three categories: ministry and spirituality, character and humility, and musicianship. Here are the qualifications listed under the category they belong to.

Ministry and Spirituality
    Called by God
    Sanctify yourself
    Faithful
    Prophetic

Character and Humility
    Quick to repent
    Appointed by those in authority
    Demonstrate commitment in other ministries first
    Support the vision of the church leader(s)
    Administrative skills
    Food handling

Musicianship
    Aptitude for music
    Musical training
    Sing
    Lead a large production
    Arrange, rehearse, and lead music

A WORSHIP LEADER'S SELF-CHECK EXAM

How do you measure up with David, Asaph, and the Levites in your qualifications to be a worship leader? Here is a test to help you figure that out. Once you have taken this test, I suggest you share your answers with your spouse or a close friend for the purpose of praying together regarding the results.

This self-exam is designed to help you do the following:

1. Determine whether God has called you to be a worship leader.
2. Identify areas of lack that you should work on so God can use you as a worship leader.
3. Solidify your call to be a worship leader to yourself and others.

SELF-EXAM FOR WORSHIP LEADERS

Name: _____

Date started: _____ Date completed: _____

INSTRUCTIONS: Before you begin, pray this prayer. "Lord, please reveal to me the truth about myself as I contemplate my answers to these questions." Be honest with yourself in answering these questions. Write down what is truth, not what you want to be truth.

Ministry and Spirituality Section

1. How confident are you that God has called you to be an elder or a fivefold minister in the body of Christ?
    (circle one)
    not confident   1   2   3   4   5   very confident

2. What do you base that on? (Write your answer on a separate piece of paper or in a Word document.)

3. How confident are you that God has called you to be a worship leader?
    (circle one)
    not confident   1   2   3   4   5   very confident

4. What do you base that on? (Write your answer on a separate piece of paper or in a Word document.)

5. Are you called to be a primary worship leader like Asaph, or is your calling to be a worship team member like the Levites? (circle one)
    a. primary worship leader
    b. worship team member
    c. not sure what God has for me

6. What do you base that on? (Write your answer on a separate piece of paper or in a Word document.)

7. How much time do you spend each week studying your Bible?

8. How much time do you spend each week in prayer and personal worship?

9. How important is it to you to live a holy lifestyle before God and in front of your fellow man?

    (circle one)

    not important   1   2   3   4   5   very important

10. Is the Bible your standard for holiness or righteousness?

11. Do you believe that the Bible is the flawless, inerrant Word of God?

12. How important is it for you to be faithful to your commitments and ministries?

    (circle one)

    not important   1   2   3   4   5   very important

13. Do you hear the voice of God when He speaks to you in your spirit?
    a. yes
    b. no
    c. sometimes

14. If no, does God speak to you in a unique way, such as an impression, a feeling, a thought, a physical sensation, etc.?
    a. yes
    b. no
    c. sometimes

15. If yes, how does he speak to you?

16. If no, how do you discern God's will and heart in any given moment?

17. Have you ever prophesied verbally with words?
    a. yes
    b. no

18. Have you ever prophesied vocally with singing?
    a. yes
    b. no

19. Have you ever prophesied using a musical instrument?
    a. yes
    b. no

20. Have you ever operated the spiritual gift of a word of knowledge before?
    a. yes
    b. no

21. Have you ever been present when someone else has operated the spiritual gift of a word of knowledge?
    a. yes
    b. no

22. Have you ever experienced the discerning of spirits before in yourself or someone else?
    a. yes
    b. no

23. When you are a member of a worshiping congregation, are you able to tell when the worship leader misses God? That means that God's Spirit wants the warship to go in one direction, but the worship leader goes in a different direction.
    a. yes
    b. no
    c. sometimes

24. hen you are a member of a worshiping congregation, are you able to confirm in your heart when the worship leader is following God's direction for that service?
    a. yes
    b. no
    c. sometimes

25. Have you ever been present when God has released the prophetic song of the Lord/new song[24] within a worship service?
    a. yes
    b. no

26. Have you ever been used of God to sing a prophetic song of the Lord/ new song in a worship service?
    a. yes
    b. no

Character and Humility Section

27. Do you repent to God quickly when you sin?
    a. yes
    b. no
    c. sometimes

28. If you are functioning as a worship leader presently, who installed you into that position?

29. (#29–32) List all ministries you have been involved with since becoming a Christian. Once you have made your list, write a number beside each ministry to show which ones gave you the most satisfaction or sense of accomplishment. Number one indicates the most satisfaction.

30. Were you faithful in these ministries? Write yes or no beside each ministry on your list.

31. How long were you involved in each ministry? Write that beside each ministry you listed.

32. Did you raise up a replacement to take your place in those ministries when you left? Write yes or no beside each ministry on your list.

---

[24] Isaiah 42:10, Psalms 40:3

Here's the way your list should look.

Table 4. #29–32 Ministries List

Ministry	Order #	Faithful	Duration	Replacement
		Yes no		Yes no

33. Do you support the vision and direction of your church's leadership?
    a. yes
    b. mostly
    c. somewhat
    d. no

34. Are you organized in your personal life?
    a. yes, extremely organized
    b. mostly organized
    c. somewhat organized
    d. not really organized

35. From the list you made of ministries you have been involved with, which ones did you help to administer?

36. Have you ever helped in the kitchen for church meals?
    a. yes
    b. no

Musicianship Section

37. Do you have an aptitude for music, as well as a desire to play and sing music to glorify God?
    a. yes
    b. no

38. What musical instruments do you play, **including singing**? How long have you played each instrument? Did you take lessons, or were you self-taught? What is your skill level on those instruments? Here's what your list should look like.

Table 5. Musical Instruments List

Instrument	How Long	Training	Skill Level
		__ Lessons __ Self-taught	__ Beginner __ Intermediate __ Advanced

39. If you sing but do not play a musical instrument, which instrument are you drawn to learn?

40. What is your plan to learn to play that instrument?

41. If you play an instrument but do not sing, what is your plan to remedy that?

42. In addition to the applied musical skills of playing instruments and singing, have you had any additional training in any of the following musical subjects? Please indicate how much training you have had and where you received that training.

Table 6. Musical Training List

Subject	How Much	Where	When
Music Theory			
Sight Singing			
Music History			
Music Arranging for Voices			
Music Arranging for Instruments			
Music Conducting/Directing			
Song Writing			

43. Have you ever been part of a large-scale production as a vocalist; instrumentalist; dancer; drama troop member; flag/banner bearer; and/or by doing things behind the scenes like costumes, makeup, props, set design, sound, lights, promotion, and front of house?
   a. yes; if yes, what?
   b. no

44. Have you ever helped plan and/or administer a large-scale production?
    a. yes; if yes, what did you help plan?
    b. no

45. Have you ever planned and directed a rehearsal for worship or a large-scale production?
    a. yes
    b. no

Chapter Six
"THE FIRST WORSHIP LEADER"

THE LIGHT BEARER

Everything God does on Earth has its beginnings in heaven. That is true of worship as well. Because that is the case, the first worship leader was the worship leader of heaven before God developed the earth.

In this chapter, I want to introduce you to the very first worship leader. He was created for that job. His name indicates what he was assigned to do in heaven. The design of his physical body was given to him for the purpose of leading worship in heaven.

Who was that very first worship leader? It was one of the archangels. His name is Lucifer.

In Latin, the name "Lucifer" means "light bearer." In other words, Lucifer's Latin name represents what his responsibility was in heaven. He was to bear the light or glory of God.

It is important to know that the light did not originate with Lucifer, but he was just the bearer of that light. Another way to think of it is that Lucifer was the reflector of God's glory or light in the same way we are described to be the reflectors of God's glory in Isaiah 60.

> *Arise, shine; for thy light is come, and the glory of the LORD is risen upon thee. For, behold, the darkness shall cover the earth, and gross darkness the people: but the*

*LORD shall arise upon thee, and **his glory shall be seen
upon thee**. And the Gentiles shall come to thy light, and
kings to the brightness of thy rising. Isaiah 60:1–3 (KJV),
emphasis added*

God's glory will be seen upon us. It is not our glory but God's glory shining through or from us.

Before we were created as the human race, God created all types of angelic beings to worship him. He created Lucifer to lead the hosts of Heaven in the worship of Himself. While leading the hosts of heaven in worship, Lucifer was to reflect and show forth God's glory. When Lucifer rebelled, God created mankind to reflect His glory.

Lucifer's name is the Strong's Hebrew word number 1966 "helel." Here is the definition of his name.

> *Strong's Hebrew: 1966 (helel) – a shining one, lucifer.
> From "halal" (in the sense of brightness); the morning-
> star – lucifer.*[25]

"Helel" is a variation of the Strong's Hebrew word number 1984 "halal." That word was translated into the English word "praise." For a more complete study of this word, go to page 51 in *Biblical worship.*[26]

"Halal" is the root from which we have the universal declaration of praise to the Almighty God, "Hallelujah," which is used by every earthly language.

Lucifer's name in Hebrew declares his original responsibilities in heaven, which was to bear the glory of God or to show forth God's praise by leading the heavenly hosts in praise and adoration of God.

The way God created Lucifer also reveals the purpose God created him for. Here's the way Ezekiel described the way Lucifer looks.

> *Thou hast been in Eden the garden of God; every
> precious stone was **thy covering**, the sardius, topaz, and*

---

[25] "1966. helel," Bible Hub, accessed December 11, 2020, https://biblehub.com/hebrew/1966.htm.
[26] Shamblin Stone, *Biblical Worship* (Westbow Press, 2012)

the diamond, the beryl, the onyx, and the jasper, the sapphire, the emerald, and the carbuncle, and gold: the workmanship of thy tabrets and of thy pipes was prepared in thee in the day that thou wast created. Ezekiel 28:13 (KJV), emphasis added

According to Biblical records, there were only four persons in the garden of Eden. They were Adam, Eve, God, and Lucifer—who is now called Satan, or the devil. In this Scripture above, God is doing the talking, so we know it is not God being talked about or described. Both Adam and Eve are human and have skin or flesh as their covering. So, the only personage this Scripture could be describing is Lucifer.

Lucifer's covering is not skin. It is *"every precious stone,"* especially the ones listed in this Scripture. When the glory of God was on Lucifer, the precious stones glistened and gleamed, making Lucifer the most beautiful creation of God. However, without the light and glory of God to illuminate him, Lucifer is dark, cold, and stony.

LUCIFER, THE ONE-MAN-BAND

Not only was Lucifer created to reflect the glory of God, we are also told in this Scripture that he was created with musical instruments within his body for the purpose of leading the heavenly choir in worship of the Almighty God.

*... the workmanship of thy **tabrets** and of thy **pipes** was prepared **in** thee in the day that thou wast created Ezekiel 28:13b (KJV), emphasis added*

The most important thing found in this Scripture is that Lucifer is a created being. Lucifer is not a God; he was created like all of the rest of God's creation, like every other living being which exists.

The next thing we need to understand from this Scripture is that God created musical instruments in Lucifer's body. The two instruments that are listed here are tabrets and pipes. Tabrets are a type of tambourine, which is a percussion instrument, providing rhythm for the worship of heaven. For more information as to why rhythm is important in group worship, go to page 66 in *The Importance of Worshiping Together.*[27]

Pipes are a wind instrument used to play melodies and harmonies for both leading and accompanying vocal worship. The human voice is actually a wind instrument. We even use that word as a slang term when referring to someone's voice, as in "They sure have a good set of pipes!" The scripture here is not referring to Lucifer's voice, however, but rather to the additional wind instrument(s) built into his body.

These are not the only musical instruments God built into Lucifer's body. In Isaiah, we are told of a third type of instrument that Lucifer was created with.

> *Thy pomp is brought down to the grave, and the noise of thy **viols**: the worm is spread under thee, and the worms cover thee. Isaiah 14:11 (KJV), emphasis added*

It is the very next verse that identifies whom Isaiah is speaking of in this chapter. Here is that verse:

> *How art thou fallen from heaven, O **Lucifer**, son of the morning! How art thou cut down to the ground, which didst weaken the nations! Isaiah 14:12 (KJV), emphasis added*

There is no question that Isaiah is writing about the archangel Lucifer, who became Satan. Although this verse does not use the word "in," it is a safe interpretation to assume that the viols mentioned here are also inside Lucifer's body, based on the scripture in Ezekiel.

The old English word "viol" represents the musical string instrument family, in which we find the violin. Some people feel that Lucifer had more than one stringed instrument in his body, because the word "viol" is plural in this scripture. If that is the case, then Lucifer also had more than one tabret and more than one wind instrument as well. The number of musical instruments found in Lucifer's body is not important

---

[27] Shamblin Stone, *The Importance of Worshiping Together* (LifeRich Publishing, 2020).

to speculate. What is important, however, is that all three types of acoustical musical Instruments known to mankind are represented within Lucifers body.

Table 7. Acoustical Musical Instrument Families and Musical Instruments in Lucifer's Body

Percussion	Wind	Stringed
Musical Instruments in Lucifer's Body		
Tabrets	Pipes	Viols

With these musical instruments built into Lucifer's being, he led the hosts of heaven into grandiose (pomp) celebrations of worship of the Almighty God.

Pomp is the majestic lifting up of praise. It can also refer to pageantry, or a proud celebration of a king. God created pomp for worshiping Himself and assigned Lucifer to lead the celebrations as part of Lucifer's responsibilities. However, once Lucifer sinned, he was never allowed to lead worship in heaven again, and even the sound of his stringed instruments was silenced, according to the Scriptures.

THE ANOINTED CHERUB THAT COVERETH

Let's return to Ezekiel 28 to see whether there is anything else we can learn about Lucifer.

> *[14]Thou art the anointed cherub that covereth; and I have set thee so: thou wast upon the holy mountain of God; thou hast walked up and down in the midst of the stones of fire. [15]Thou wast perfect in thy ways from the day that thou wast created, till iniquity was found in thee.*
> *[16]By the multitude of thy merchandise they have filled the midst of thee with violence, and thou hast sinned: therefore I will cast thee as profane out of the mountain of God: and I will destroy thee, O covering cherub, from the midst of the stones of fire. [17]Thine heart was lifted up*

because of thy beauty, thou hast corrupted thy wisdom
by reason of thy brightness: I will cast thee to the ground,
I will lay thee before kings, that they may behold thee.
Ezekiel 28:14–17 (KJV)

In this Scripture, Lucifer is called the "anointed cherub that covereth." We understand that being anointed is to be set apart for a purpose. God has anointed every person who is called a Christian for a specific task. If you do not know what that purpose is for your life, you need to be spending time seeking God about that.[28]

Right now, we are studying the original purpose God had for Lucifer. The key to understanding that purpose is the word "covereth." In today's English, we would use the word "covers." Here is the Strong's concordance definition of that word.

Strong's Hebrew 5526: 1) to hedge, fence about, shut in 2) to block, overshadow, screen, stop the approach, shut off, cover 2a) (2a1) to screen, cover (2a2) to cover oneself (2a3) protector 2b) (2b1) to screen, cover (2b2) to cover, defecate 3) to cover, lay over 4) to weave together (4a) to weave together (4b) to weave, weave together[29]

Everyone knows that a dictionary definition has multiple meanings listed, and it is up to the reader to determine which definitions apply in the current use of the word. With that in mind, I believe it is safe to declare that definition 2b2 above does not apply in this case. Lucifer's responsibilities in heaven did not include "pooping" in front of God's thrown or covering it with poop.

From the Scriptures, we can see that the definitions that apply to Lucifer's responsibilities in heaven are 2b1 and 4. Why was it important for Lucifer to screen heaven from the throne of God? Left uncovered, God's glory is too intense for any created being to look at. God even told Moses

---

[28] Ephesians 5:17
[29] "Ezekiel 28:14," Bible Hub, accessed December 15, 2020, https://biblehub.com/parallel/ezekiel/28-14.htm.

that no one can't look at God's glory directly and live.[30] Hebrews chapter 12 talks about when God allowed His glory to rest on Mount Sinai. It was a terrifying experience for the children of Israel. Moses himself was paralyzed with fear. The people knew not to approach the mountain, but it says when animals got too close to it, they immediately died.[31]

Lucifer's responsibilities in heaven included to cover the glory of God, thereby protecting the rest of God's creation from the destruction that would be imminent without any covering. For Lucifer to cover God's glory, he was allowed to be on the mountain of God with God. He had freedom to walk up and down in the middle of the alter or "stones of fire."

Isaiah, who was permitted to visit heaven and wrote about it in Isaiah 6, also spoke of seeing the alter and having an angel touch his lips with a live coal from the alter of God.[32]

By Jesus coming to earth and dying for our sins, His blood is now our covering. Jesus' blood covers us so we can approach our holy God in worship.

As worship leaders, part of our responsibilities includes allowing the glory of God to be seen on us. We now have direct access to God and his glory because of the blood of Jesus, which covers us. Just as Lucifer was created to show the glory of God, so now have we been created to show forth God's glory.[33]

The last part of this definition says that the word "covereth" means "to weave together." That is a key part of any worship leader's responsibility. Think about that with me. In every gathering of believers, you will have all different types of worshipers. You will have those who are young in the Lord, and you will have those who have walked with God for many years. You will have those who spend many hours each day reading the word of God and those who never crack the Bible open except on Sunday mornings. You will have those who spend a lot of time in personal prayer and worship of God and those who never think about God all week long.

As I outlined for you in *The Importance of Worshiping Together*, the goal of every worship gathering is unity in worship. That maximizes

---

[30] Exodus: 33:20
[31] Hebrews 12:18–21
[32] Isaiah 6:6
[33] Isaiah 60:1

the effectiveness of our worship. Therefore, as a worship leader, I must be sensitive to every person who is gathered with us to worship God. I do not want to get so lost in the presence of God that I ignore everyone there. I want to bring everyone gathered into a unity of worship before the throne of God. In that regard, I must weave together everyone's heart as we approach the throne of God.

Remember, when Christian's hearts are in unity, that's when God "commands a blessing."[34]

> *This heavenly harmony can be compared to the dew dripping down from the skies upon Mount Hermon, refreshing the mountain slopes of Israel. For from this realm of sweet harmony God will release his eternal blessing, the promise of life forever! Psalms 133:3 (TPT)*

LUCIFER WAS APPOINTED TO HIS POSITION

Lucifer was set in place as the worship leader of heaven by God Almighty. Ezekiel 28:14 declares that God appointed Lucifer to the position he had in heaven. God said, "I have set thee so." Let's compare the way several different versions of Biblical translations state this phrase.

> *... I have set thee so...(KJV)*
> *... I established you ...(NKJV)*
> *... for so I ordained you ...(NIV)*
> *I appointed you ...(TLB)*
> *... and I placed you there ...(NAS)*

No matter which version of the Bible you read, it is clear that Lucifer did not appoint himself to his position in heaven. All positions of authority must be given by God through someone He has placed in authority.

To be a biblical worship leader, you must have been appointed by someone in authority in your church! Being self-appointed is not God's way.

---

[34] Psalms 133:3 KJV

LUCIFER'S RESPONSIBILITIES WERE IN HEAVEN

Where did Lucifer lead worship? The clear answer to that question is in heaven.

> How art thou fallen **from heaven**, O Lucifer, son of the morning! how art thou cut down to the ground, which didst weaken the nations! Isaiah 14:12 (KJV), emphasis added

Lucifer performed his duties in heaven until he sinned. Where Lucifer was banished to was "the ground." This is Strong's concordance Hebrew word number 776 "erets," which means "the earth."[35] The contrast is that Lucifer was removed from his position in heaven and thrown to the earth. Jesus even spoke to his disciples about seeing that happen before mankind was created.

> And he (Jesus) said unto them, I beheld Satan as lightning fall from heaven. Luke 10:18 (KJV)

A worship leader must have a place where they lead worship. If you tell me you are a worship leader and I ask you where you lead worship, you need to be able to tell me the place where you lead worship.

With God, it is always all about the local church. In the Scriptures, even the apostles and profits were sent out from the local churches. You have no authority in the body of Christ unless you are connected with a local church and submitted to that leadership.

LUCIFER WAS PERFECT IN ALL HIS WAYS

We don't know how long Lucifer functioned in the position of worship leader in heaven before pride destroyed his ministry. God even declared that Lucifer was the poster child of perfection. Lucifer had great wisdom and was the epitome of beauty God said that everything Lucifer did, in all his ways, was perfect.

---

[35] "776. erets," Bible Hub, accessed December 22, 2020, https://biblehub.com/hebrew/776.htm.

"You were the seal of perfection,
Full of wisdom and perfect in beauty.
[15] You were perfect in your ways from the day you
were created,
Till iniquity was found in you. Ezekiel 28:12b, 15
(NKJV)

In *Portrait of a Worshiper* Chapter one,[36] starting on page 18, I talked about how God declared every part of his earthly creation to be "good" or perfect on the evening of the day in which He created it, except for mankind. God has chosen to wait until the end of this age before he declares that any one of us humans are "good."

At that final judgment, God will declare one of two things over every person who has ever lived. The first of these two declarations is this:

His lord said unto him, **Well done, thou GOOD and**
faithful servant: *thou hast been faithful over a few things,*
I will make thee ruler over many things: enter thou into
the joy of thy lord. Matthew 25:21 (KJV), emphasis added

The second thing God might say to us is this:

His lord answered and said unto him, Thou **wicked**
and slothful servant*, thou knewest that I reap where I*
sowed not, and gather where I have not strawed: And
cast ye the unprofitable servant into outer darkness: there
shall be weeping and gnashing of teeth. Matthew 25:26,
30 (KJV), emphasis added

It was God's custom, after he created something, to stand back and watch to see if what he made was working properly. The pronouncement that something was "good" by God meant that it was "functioning the way it was designed to function." This habit started long before God's development of the earth. We know this because God had already pronounced Lucifer to be "perfect."

---

[36] Shamblin Stone, *Portrait of a Worshiper* (Westbow Press, 2018).

The reason God didn't declare that mankind was "good" when we were created is because we were created to worship God. God chooses to wait to see whether we will worship Him throughout our lifetime before he declares we functioned the way we were designed to function.

I personally believe that the reason God waits to declare whether mankind is good is because Lucifer rebelled and stopped functioning the way he was designed to function. The free will that God gave to all spiritual beings, which are humans and angels, leaves the opportunity for us, like Lucifer, to choose not to function the way we were designed to function. That is why this determination must be done after we have lived our lives on earth.

So, if Lucifer, the picture of perfection, could fall into the iniquity of pride, how much more easily can we fall into the very same sin and disqualify ourselves from worship ministry as well? We must rely on God's grace to keep us from the sin of pride, which is the greatest temptation for all musicians and worship leaders.

MANKIND WAS CREATED TO TAKE LUCIFER'S PLACE

Because Lucifer sinned, God created the human race to worship Him. For more on this topic, explore *Biblical Worship* Chapter eight and *The Importance of Worshiping Together* Chapters two, three, and five. Those chapters will help you understand the timeline and purpose God has for the human race in regard to worship.

Because the worship leader Lucifer was cast out of heaven onto the earth, there is a correlation between his heavenly purpose and our purpose as worship leaders here on earth. Here is a brief comparison to show you how God wanted humanity to take over the responsibilities of worship in the universe.

1. Lucifer was called a light bearer.
    As a worship leader, we are called to carry the light of God's glory.

Arise, shine; for thy light is come, and the glory
of the Lord is risen upon thee. Isaiah 60:1 (KJV)

2. Lucifer was created for his purpose.
   As worshipers and worship leaders, we were created by God for the express purpose of praising Him.

   > *This people I have formed for Myself; They shall declare My praise. Isaiah 43:21 (NKJV)*

3. Lucifer was created with three different musical instruments in him. We are created as a living vocal or wind musical instrument, and we are commanded to use that instrument in approaching the presence of Almighty God.

   > *Serve the Lord with gladness: come before his presence with* **singing**. *Psalms 100:2 (KJV), emphasis added*

   > **Sing** *unto the Lord a new song, and his praise from the end of the earth,… Isaiah 42:10a (KJV), emphasis added*

   By giving us two hands, we also have a built-in percussion instrument.

   > *O* **clap your hands**, *all ye people; shout unto God with the voice of triumph. Psalms 47:1 (KJV), emphasis added*

4. Lucifer was anointed for his responsibilities "the anointed cherub that covereth".
   Anointing has a couple of meanings. It can mean to be appointed, like Lucifer was appointed to the worship leading position of heaven. However, in our case as human beings, to be anointed by God's Holy Spirit is also to be empowered to do what He has chosen us to do.

   > *But the anointing which you have received from Him abides in you, and you do not need*

that anyone teach you; but as the same anointing teaches you concerning all things, and is true, and is not a lie, and just as it (He) has taught you, you will abide in Him. 1 John 2:27 (NKJV)

5. Lucifer's responsibility in heaven involved weaving together the worship of the heavenly hosts.
   Our responsibilities as worship leaders include bringing together every congregational member into a dynamic, unifying worship experience.

   Who shall not fear thee, O Lord, and glorify thy name? for thou only art holy: for all nations shall come and worship before thee; for thy judgments are made manifest. Revelation 15:4 (KJV)

6. Lucifer was perfect in all his ways.
   We understand that as human beings it is impossible for us to be perfect without the aid of the Holy Spirit. Yet, we are told in the Scriptures that we should strive to be holy, or perfect.

   as obedient children, not conforming yourselves to the former lusts, as in your ignorance; but as He who called you is holy, you also be holy in all your conduct, because it is written, "Be holy, for I am holy." 1 Peter 1:14–16 (NKJV)

Sinless perfection can only be achieved by the Holy Spirit working within us and us being obedient to Him. Our holiness must come from an inward work of the Holy Spirit motivating us to worship Him, not through outward signs such as hair, dress, and traditions.

O worship the Lord in the beauty of holiness: fear before Him, all the earth. Psalms 96:9 (KJV)

Chapter Seven

"CHAIN OF COMMAND"

THE PRIMARY RESPONSIBILITY OF ALL WORSHIP LEADERS

The responsibility of every worship leader is to bring God's people into God's presence and to bring God's presence to God's people! It is not just to lead music. Music is simply the means to an end. The end goal of worship is God's presence. God dwells in the worship of His people.

> But thou art holy, O thou that inhabitest the praises
> of Israel. Psalm 22:3 (KJV)

To inhabit something is to live there or abide there. God's presence is established in the atmosphere of our worship of God.

THE STRUCTURE OF WORSHIP LEADERSHIP

Before the Lord created mankind, heaven was operational and functioning with what the military calls "chain of command." This system of leadership originated with God and was first seen in the ranks of the angels in heaven.

Once mankind had been created, God revealed this heavenly style of leadership structure to Moses, who implemented it on earth.

And Moses chose able men out of all Israel, and made them heads over the people, rulers of thousands, rulers of hundreds, rulers of fifties, and rulers of tens. Exodus 18:25 (KJV)

Since then, every human organization, business, and country has used this God-originated chain-of-command concept to organize themselves to produce maximum results. It is an established fact that a group of humans will only achieve unity in their goals and purposes when there is leadership.

Because leadership was God's idea, He also requires it in His church. Whenever believers assemble together, God requires that there be leadership who has been appointed by Him. Notice how the writer of Hebrews refers to this chain-of-command-type of leadership three times in the thirteenth and final chapter.

[7] Remember them which have the rule over you, who have spoken unto you the word of God: whose faith follow, considering the end of their conversation. [8] Jesus Christ the same yesterday, today, and forever.

[17] Obey them that have the rule over you, and submit yourselves: for they watch for your souls, as they that must give account, that they may do it with joy, and not with grief: for that is unprofitable for you.

[24] Salute all them that have the rule over you, and all the saints. They of Italy salute you. Hebrews 13:7–8, 17, 24 (KJV)

We know these are spiritual leaders being referred to here, because they are speaking "the word of God" and watching for the "souls" of the people they are leading.

To be a worship leader **in** the body of Christ is to first be a spiritual leader **to** the body of Christ, with the specific job of leading worship.

DAVID'S TABERNACLE

In this chapter, we will look at the best Biblical example of chain of command in a worship setting. It is in the story of how King David organized his worship team. In the Bible, that is referred to as "David's tabernacle," or "David's tent."

We know that David did things right when he organized his worship team, because after he was gone, God continued to point people to the way David had organized his worship team, telling them he wanted to restore what David established.

> *In that day I will restore David's fallen tent. I will repair its broken places, restore its ruins, and build it as it used to be. Amos 9:11(NIV)*

This restoration of David's tabernacle was only possible after Jesus came to earth.

> *After this I will return, and will build again the tabernacle of David, which is fallen down; and I will build again the ruins thereof, and I will set it up: That the residue of men might seek after the Lord, and all the Gentiles, upon whom my name is called, saith the Lord, who doeth all these things. Acts 15:16–17 (KJV)*

Because David's tent is important to God, we need to find out all we can about it. David's tent was not the place where he lived. David's tent was the place he prepared for the Ark of the Covenant, which Moses had built in the wilderness. David lived in houses, but he pitched a tent for the ark.

> *And David made him houses in the city of David, and prepared a place for the ark of God, and pitched for it a tent. 1 Chronicles 15:1 (KJV)*

The ark of God was more than a symbol of God's presence; it was the physical place on earth where God's presence dwelt among men in the Old Testament. Therefore, the ark in David's tent in the Old Testament represents the presence of the Lord in us and in our praises.

Read these Scriptures carefully. They outline for you the New Testament principle of the presence of God.

> *And I heard a great voice out of heaven saying, Behold,*
> *the tabernacle of God is with men, and he will dwell with*
> *them, and they shall be his people, and God himself shall*
> *be with them, and be their God. Revelation 21:3 (KJV)*
> *... the mystery that has been kept hidden for ages and*
> *generations, but is now disclosed to the saints. To them*
> *God has chosen to make known among the Gentiles the*
> *glorious riches of this mystery, which is Christ **in** you, the*
> *hope of glory. Colossians 1:26–27 (NIV), emphasis added*
> *Haven't you yet learned that your body is the home*
> *of the Holy Spirit God gave you, and that he lives within*
> *you? Your own body does not belong to you. For God*
> *has bought you with a great price. So use every part of*
> *your body to give glory back to God because he owns it. 1*
> *Corinthians 6:19–20 (LB)*

THE RE-ESTABLISHING OF DAVID'S TENT

In the old covenant, David's tent was where the ark (the manifestation of God's presence) was placed. In the new covenant "Christ in us," in our bodies, is what makes it possible for the presence and glory of God to be revealed, making our bodies now the tent of God's presence.

But Christ in us is only the beginning of the restoration of David's tabernacle. To discover what else is being restored about David's tent today, we need to look at the record of when David first established his tabernacle for the Ark of the Covenant. That is found in 1 Chronicles 15.

To save the time it would take to read several chapters in the Bible, let me give you a synopsis of what has happened immediately before 1 Chronicles 15.

Years earlier, King Saul took the Ark of the Covenant into battle against the Philistines, thinking it would help him win that battle. Saul had not received directions from God to do that, so consequently, the ark had been captured by the enemy.

After David became King, God put it into David's heart to bring back the ark of God to the kingdom of Israel. Without seeking God as to how that should be done, David ordered that a new cart should be built to carry the ark back home. The new cart was pulled by oxen. On the way back home, the oxen stumbled, and one of David's men, Uza, reached out to steady the ark. When Uza touched the ark with his bare hand, the power of God in and upon the ark was so strong that Uza died.

When this tragedy occurred, David stored the ark in the house of Obededom and went back home to seek God, to find out what he had done wrong. Beginning at 1 Chronicles 15 we learn what God told David about what he did wrong. We also learn God's heart about organizing a worship team to lead the congregation in worship because the ark was being brought back home.

I know we have already been through this chapter looking for the clues it gives us about the qualifications of worship leaders. This time we want to look at how God told David to organize the worship leaders for that event.

THERE MUST BE A PREPARED PLACE

We read this scripture already, but let's read it again.

*And David made him houses in the city of David, and **prepared a place** for the ark of God, and pitched for it a tent. 1 Chronicles 15:1 (KJV), emphasis added*

So we see that the first thing David realized he had done wrong was he had not prepared a proper place for the presence of God. He thought the old place was quite all right. But God had a new order planned, which was not like the old. In the old tabernacle, no one had access to the presence of God except the high priest, and that was only once a year. The ark was kept behind a heavy veil in a place called the "holy of holies."

In the new order, God wanted His presence available to everyone who wanted to draw near to Him. David's tent was pitched on a "prepared place" where all could approach and have access to God's presence. David's new order was the forerunner of what would happen in the New Testament. David's tent was a picture, before its time, of how God intended for His presence to be accessible to all men through Christ.

Just like when God instructed Moses concerning the tabernacle in the wilderness where God told Moses to put the Tabernacle in the center of the camp and have all of the tribes of Israel camp around it,[37] David put the tent for the ark on a knoll or hill so people could stand around it on all sides to worship the presence of God. That was the place David prepared for the ark.

Even now, we cannot experience the presence of God without preparing a proper place for His Spirit as individuals and as a church. We prepare a place for God's presence as individuals by yielding our entire being to Jesus—our spirit, our soul, and our body.

As a church body, we first need to prepare a physical place for the church to gather like David did. David could not build a structure big enough to hold the entire congregation of Israel, so he made his place an open-air worship facility. In today's churches, we build structures that will house the number of worshipers who will worship with us to protect them from the elements. Inside the structure, we provide places to sit and make sure the temperature is comfortable. Extreme temperatures in a place of worship most likely will distract the worshipers from their purpose.

In addition to the physical structure where the worshipers gather, we are providing a spiritual place for God's Spirit to dwell as we worship the Lord. Remember, Gods spirit inhabits the praises of His people.[38]

Also, please remember that the most important and powerful expression of worship God has given to us for our gatherings is music. That is why God has commanded us to prepare a place for His presence with music.

*Serve the LORD with gladness: come before his presence with **singing**. Psalms 100:2 (KJV), emphasis added*

In other words, the presence of God is, and always has been, associated with music. That is why King David used praise and worship expressed by music when he brought the ark of God back home to the place where he had prepared for it.

---

[37] Numbers 2:3–7
[38] Psalm 22:3

DAVID USED THOSE CALLED TO CARRY GOD'S PRESENCE

The second thing David realized he needed to change was that he needed to use those who were called into the specific ministry of carrying the presence of God to do just that.

> *Then David said, None ought to carry the ark of God but the Levites: for them hath the LORD chosen to carry the ark of God, and to minister unto him forever. 1 Chronicles 15:2 (KJV)*

In the church setting, the worship leaders should not be chosen based on their skill level as a musician. Musical skills is not what qualifies someone to be a worship leader! The call of God must be upon a person's life to do that task. We have already spent a great deal of time talking about how to know whether God has called you to be a worship leader.

Also, you may be called to be a worship leader, but you may need to go through a time of preparation before being released into that ministry. For instance, if you do not know how to enter the presence of God on your own, how would you ever hope to lead a congregation into God's presence?

Only those chosen by God to carry the presence of God should be appointed to lead the congregation in worship. In the Old Testament, they were called the Levites. Today we would call them the worship team.

THOSE WHO ARE CALLED MUST PREPARE

The third thing David realized was that those who are called to carry God's presence must make sure they are ready to do so.

> *⁴And David assembled the children of Aaron, and the Levites: ¹²And said unto them, Ye are the chief of the fathers of the Levites: **sanctify** yourselves, both ye and your brethren, that ye may bring up the ark of the LORD*

> *God of Israel unto the place that I have prepared for it. 1*
> *Chronicles 15:4, 12 (KJV), emphasis added*

The word "sanctify" carries with it the connotation of being set apart and prepared both spiritually and naturally for the task God wants you to do. If a leader tries to skip or rush the steps of preparation in those two areas, God will eventually allow that to be seen by the church. That could cause that leader great embarrassment and disqualify the leader from ministry. It is always best to simply submit to the processes God has for us, rather than try to cheat the process.

> *So the priests and the Levites sanctified themselves to*
> *bring up the ark of the LORD God of Israel. 1 Chronicles*
> *15:14 (KJV)*

ORGANIZE THE WORSHIP TEAM INTO RANK AND FILE

The fourth thing David learned from God was how important it is to establish a chain of command in the worship team. That, of course, is the subject of this chapter.

> *And David spake to the chief of the Levites to **appoint***
> *their brethren to be the **singers with instruments** of*
> *musick, psalteries and harps and cymbals, sounding, by*
> *lifting up the voice with joy. 1 Chronicles 15:16 (KJV),*
> *emphasis added*

The following are the pertinent verses describing the establishing of rank and file on David's worship team.

> [16]*David told the leaders of the Levites to appoint their*
> *brothers as singers to sing joyful songs, accompanied by*
> *musical instruments: lyres, harps and cymbals.*
> [17]*So the Levites appointed Heman son of Joel; from*
> *his brothers, Asaph son of Berekiah; and from their*
> *brothers the Merarites, Ethan son of Kushaiah;* [18]*and*

140

with them their brothers next in rank: Zechariah, Jaaziel, Shemiramoth, Jehiel, Unni, Eliab, Benaiah, Maaseiah, Mattithiah, Eliphelehu, Mikneiah, Obed-Edom and Jeiel, the gatekeepers.

[19]The musicians Heman, Asaph and Ethan were to sound the bronze cymbals; [20]Zechariah, Aziel, Shemiramoth, Jehiel, Unni, Eliab, Maaseiah and Benaiah were to play the lyres according to alamoth, [21]and Mattithiah, Eliphelehu, Mikneiah, Obed-Edom, Jeiel and Azaziah were to play the harps, directing according to sheminith. [22]Kenaniah the head Levite was in charge of the singing; that was his responsibility because he was skillful at it.

[23]Berekiah and Elkanah were to be doorkeepers for the ark. [24]Shebaniah, Joshaphat, Nethanel, Amasai, Zechariah, Benaiah and Eliezer the priests were to blow trumpets before the ark of God. Obed-Edom and Jehiah were also to be doorkeepers for the ark.

[25]So David and the elders of Israel and the commanders of units of a thousand went to bring up the ark of the covenant of the LORD from the house of Obed-Edom, with rejoicing. 1Chronicles 15:16–25 (NIV)

I know that passage seems like a lot of hard-to-pronounce names at first, but it is a detailed outline of the chain of command that was established in David's worship team.

The second rank is the only one mentioned in this passage in a clear way.

> *And with them their brethren of the second degree …*
> *1 Chronicles 15:18 (KJV)*

However, because of it, we can understand that the rank before the second degree is the first degree, and the one after the second would be the third. Therefore, we understand the rank and file of this large worship team to have looked like this.

Table 8. David's Worship Team

Chief	Chenaniah (KJV)/Kenaniah (NIV)
First Rank	Heman, Asaph, Ethan
Second Rank	Zechariah, Jaaziel, Shemiramoth, Jehiel, Unni, Eliab, Benaiah, Maaseiah, Mattithiah, Eliphelehu, Mikneiah, Obed-Edom and Jeiel, Berekiah and Elkanah, Shebaniah, Joshaphat, Nethanel, Amasai, Zechariah, Benaiah and Eliezer, Obed-Edom and Jehiah
Third Rank	*verse 15* the Levites [NIV)/the children of the Levites (KJV)]

THE THIRD RANK

Here's what the Bible describes as the third-rank worship team members' responsibilities.

> *And the children of the Levites bare the ark of God upon their shoulders with the staves thereon, as Moses commanded according to the word of the LORD. 1 Chronicles 15:15 (KJV)*

It was not the responsibility of the first- or second-degree worship team members to carry God's presence into the city. It was the lowest-ranking worship team members who had that responsibility. In this passage, the city represents the church. Keep that in mind—it is a worship leader's responsibility to bring God's presence to God's people and to bring God's people into God's presence. We will discuss more about this point under a section called "The Secondary Worship Leader Principal."

We just read that the main responsibility of the children of the Levites was to carry the ark in this grand processional organized to bring the ark back home. That processional was done with singing, accompanied by an orchestra of instrumentalists.

When God gave Moses the design for the tabernacle in the wilderness and all of its contents, He told Moses to put rings on the four corners of the ark. He then had Moses make two long staves out of heavy timber that were inserted through the rings on either side of the ark. That was how the ark was to be transported on the Levites' shoulders.

The ark was made out of heavy materials, so it was not light to carry. There were always four Levites shouldering the weight of the ark, one at each corner. Each Levite could only carry the ark about 10 minutes at a time. Because of that, there was a line of Levites following each of these four who were carrying the ark, ready to take their turn bearing the load.

Here's what the ark would look like looking down from above as the Levites transported it.

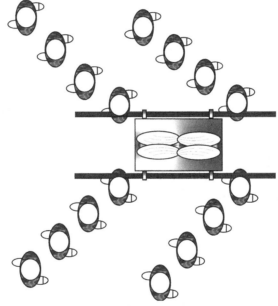

Carrying the Ark

There were probably more than four Levites in each line, but for the sake of space, I have only put four in each line. The number is not as important as the concept.

CHANGING LEVITES

Depending on whether the Levites were at the front or back of the ark, changing the carriers of the ark was either a three- or a four-step process.

At the front of the ark

Step 1: Whenever a Levite could tell he needed to take a break, he maneuvered himself forward on the pole, making room for the next one in line to take his place closer to the ark.

Step 2: When the next Levite in line saw the one carrying the ark move forward on the staff, that was their cue to step up and take the weight on their shoulder.

Step 3: Once the Levite in front felt the weight lift off of them, they were free to go to the back of the line.

Here is a visual step by step of the process I have just described for you.

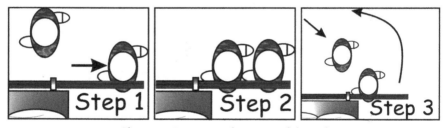

Changing Levites at the Front of the Ark

At the back of the ark

Step 1: Because at the back of the ark the carrier could not move forward when they needed to take a break, they would signal the one following them. Because the music would have been too loud for them to use a verbal signal, most likely the signal was a hand gesture.

Step 2: At the signal of the Levite who was caring the ark, the next Levite in line would come in behind and take the weight from the first one.

Step 3: Once the first Levite felt the weight lift off of him, he was then free to go to the back of the line.

Step 4: When the first Levite vacated his spot, the one who was taking over that position was able to move closer to the ark. The position closest to the ark gave them the advantage to carry its weight further.

Here is another visual showing step by step of what I have just described. Again, these graphics are depicted as though we are looking down at the event taking place.

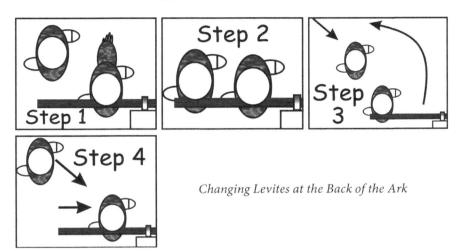

Changing Levites at the Back of the Ark

THE DOORKEEPERS

This crude drawing to the right shows you the simplicity of the design of David's tent for the Ark of the Covenant. I find it very interesting that along with the list of the worship team members, there are four doorkeepers listed as well.

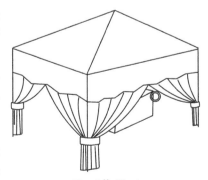

David's Tent

*Berekiah and Elkanah were to be **doorkeepers** for the ark. Shebaniah, Joshaphat, Nethanel, Amasai, Zechariah, Benaiah and Eliezer the priests were to blow trumpets before the ark of God. Obed-Edom and Jehiah were also to be **doorkeepers** for the ark. 1 Chronicles 15:23–24 (NIV), emphasis added*

The four doorkeepers were Berekiah, Elkanah, ObedEdom, and Jehiah. The reason there were four doorkeepers is because there were four sides to the tent. Each was assigned a side to stand at. In today's church, we would call those men security, or ushers.

The doorkeepers' job was to open the tent doors for every person to have visual access to the ark of God's presence and to protect the people from the ark. David did not want what happened to Uza to happen again to a zealous worshiper who wanted to touch the ark.

I believe this is Biblical precedence that the support ministries such as ushers, sound, tech, and projection should be considered as part of the worship team. They may not be playing instruments, but they can sing. And they are still part of the team whose job it is to ensure that the people of the congregation have a wonderful worship experience.

THE CONFIGURATION OF DAVID'S WORSHIP TEAM

We understand that most of the worship by this team was to be expressed by singing. In fact, it would appear that even the instrumentalists who could play their instruments and sing at the same time were encouraged to do so.

> *And David spake to the chief of the Levites to appoint their brethren to be the **singers with instruments** of musick, psalteries and harps and cymbals, **sounding, by lifting up the voice** with joy. 1 Chronicles 15:16 (KJV), emphasis added*

Every Levite who was carrying the ark could also sing, as well as the four doorkeepers of the tent. David's large worship team led the congregation by singing accompanied by an orchestra that also sang, unless their mouth was occupied playing a trumpet. That is why the trumpet players were singled out in the listing of this worship team's orchestra.

> *... Shebaniah, Joshaphat, Nethanel, Amasai, Zechariah, Benaiah and Eliezer the priests were to **blow***

trumpets before the ark of God. ... 1 Chronicles 15:24 (NIV), emphasis added

David's worship team consisted of a large overlapping choir and orchestra. Everyone sang, except for the trumpeters. Because of that, I believe that every instrumentalist on your worship team should also be a singer. Remember, God commanded singing.[39]

We are all commanded to sing. Instrumentalists who refuse to sing are disobeying the Scriptures. Many times, musicians have their self-worth wrapped up in their ability to play their instrument(s). God wants us to find our purpose in worshiping Him, not in the way we express that worship.

Willingness to be used wherever you are needed—singing or playing—will shatter the "star syndrome" attitude with which the devil tempts every worship team member.

On David's worship team, almost everyone was part of the huge choir of singers. The singing was accompanied by this orchestra.

Table 9. 24-Piece Orchestra of David's Worship Team

Bronze Cymbals	Lyres	Harps	Trumpets
Heman	Zechariah	Mattithiah	Shebaniah
Asaph	Aziel	Eliphelehu	Joshaphat
Ethan	Shemiramoth	Mikneiah	Nethanel
	Jehiel	Obed-Edom	Amasai
	Unni	Jeiel	Zechariah
	Eliab	Azaziah	Benaiah
	Maaseiah		Eliezer
	Benaiah		

The orchestra for David's worship team was the first large instrumental ensemble of its kind in the history of the world. Our modern-day orchestras are patterned after David's orchestra. We have many more instruments available to us now than what he had, but we still only have the same three families of musical instruments that David established in his orchestra. The

---

[39] Psalm 100:2

three families of musical instruments are percussion instruments, stringed instruments, and wind instruments. In today's orchestra we divide the wind instruments into two categories: the woodwind instruments and the brass instruments. Trumpets were not made out of brass in David's time but out of ram's horns. Here is how David's instruments fit into the three categories of acoustical musical instruments.

Table 10. David's Instruments in Their Families

Bronze Cymbals	Lyres	Harps	Trumpets
Percussion	Strings		Winds

THE ESTABLISHMENT OF DAVID'S TENT

Bringing back the ark with a parade or processional of worship was just the beginning of what went on at David's tent. In 1 Chronicles 16, we learn what happened once the ark had been returned home.

> *So they brought the ark of God, and set it in the midst of the tent that David had pitched for it: and they offered burnt sacrifices and peace offerings before God. 1 Chronicles 16:1 (KJV)*

Once they got the ark back home, they offered sacrifices to God according to the law of Moses. In fact, they offered so much animal sacrifices that verse three tells us that all the families in the nation were fed from it.

> *And he dealt to every one of Israel, both man and woman, to every one a loaf of bread, and a good piece of flesh, and a flagon of wine. 1 Chronicles 16:3 (KJV)*

I believe that is Biblical precedence to involve food with worship gatherings. We do not need to sacrifice animals to cover our sins anymore, because Jesus was the sacrificed Lamb of God, which takes away our sins.[40]

---

[40] John 1:29

The animal sacrifices offered at David's tent were the same ones that happened at Moses's tabernacle. To learn what was different at David's tabernacle, let's read on.

> ⁴And he (David) **appointed** certain of the **Levites** to minister before the ark of the Lord, and to record, and **to thank and praise the Lord** God of Israel:
> ⁵Asaph the chief, and next to him Zechariah, Jeiel, and Shemiramoth, and Jehiel, and Mattithiah, and Eliab, and Benaiah, and Obededom: and Jeiel with psalteries and with harps; but Asaph **made a sound with cymbals**;
> ⁶Benaiah also and Jahaziel the priests with **trumpets continually** before the ark of the covenant of God. 1 Chronicles 16:4–6 (KJV), emphasis added

Before we read any further in this Scripture passage, I would like to point out a few things we should take note of. The express purpose for the Levites whom David appointed to minister at the tent containing the Ark was to "thank and praise the Lord" using music. The instruments of music mentioned were psalteries, harps, cymbals, and trumpets. That was a full orchestra, and it is the same list of instruments used in the processional when they brought the ark back to Jerusalem. The instruments were to accompany the voices who were giving thanks and praise.

THE CHIEF MUSICIAN

In verse five, we read that Asaph has now been appointed chief. In 1 Chronicles 15, Chenaniah was the chief, but now that they have returned home, Chenaniah has retired or something, and Asaph has been promoted to that position. These are Biblical precedents to raise up music and worship leadership within the local church whenever possible. The two Biblical qualifications for every chief musician is found in this scripture.

> And Chenaniah, chief of the Levites, was for song: **he instructed** about the song, because he was **skilful**. 1 Chronicles 15:22 (KJV), emphasis added

A chief worship leader must know and understand music completely and thoroughly enough to instruct others about music. Second, they must be skillful in playing and singing music. Being skillful implies having professional training on at least one musical instrument, as well as voice training. Of course, if you do not have someone in your local church with that type of training, to start the cycle of raising up your own worship leaders, you will need to send someone out to an institution of higher learning to be trained.

Every worship team member should desire to advance as far as they can on the worship team. Therefore, every worship team member needs to be educated in those two areas for promotion to come. If you wait until you are promoted from third rank to second rank before you begin learning what a chief should know, that will slow down your future promotions.

Every Chief Worship Leader should be holding classes for their worship team in these subjects. I repeat, a chief is one who has been professionally trained in these areas:

1. music theory including music history
2. sight reading for voice
3. music conducting choirs and orchestras
4. song writing/arranging (for instruments and voices)
5. beginner's piano
6. beginner's guitar
7. beginner's voice

When I functioned as a chief worship leader, before I started the worship college, I held these training classes on Tuesday evenings, and our rehearsals were on Thursday evenings. Indeed, it is a commitment to be a member of a worship team. But if God has called you to do that, it is a joy—not a burden—to give yourself to it.

In addition to being able to teach these music classes, every chief worship leader needs to advance their musical skills on an instrument of their choice and their voice. That requires them to take private lessons in voice and their instrument until they have become skilled enough to be able to teach others.

THE SOUND AT DAVID'S TENT

David's worship team was to be playing songs of thanksgiving and praise continually.

> So he (David) left there before the ark of the covenant of the Lord Asaph and his brethren, **to minister** before the ark **continually**, as **every day's work** required: 1 Chronicles 16:37 (KJV), emphasis added

It was this worship team's every day work to lead the congregation of Israel to God's presence with music. This daily activity was their job. Because of it, they had no opportunity to make money or grow food like the rest of the Israelites. This is Biblical precedent that worship ministries should be paid or at least the congregation is to meet their daily needs.

> And with them Heman and Jeduthun, and the rest that were chosen, who were expressed by name, **to give thanks to the Lord**, because his mercy endureth for ever; And with them Heman and Jeduthun with **trumpets and cymbals** for those that should **make a sound, and with musical instruments** of God. And the sons of Jeduthun were porters. 1 Chronicles 16: 41–42 (KJV), emphasis added

So, we see that the establishment of David's tabernacle was a large worship team leading the people into God's presence **continually** with music. Notice also that the design of the musical instruments being played came from God Himself.

Remember, until Jesus came, the presence of God lived in the Ark of the Covenant. Now that Jesus has come, died on the cross, and was raised from the dead, He made it possible for His spirit to reside within us.[41]

---

[41] Revelation 21:3 and Colossians 1:27

Not all of David's psalms are found in the book of Psalms. 1 Chronicles 16 is one of David's psalms that he brought to Asaph to arrange musically to be played and sung by the choir and orchestra at David's tabernacle. This psalm starts in verse eight and goes through verse thirty-six.

Music notation as we know it did not come into being until after 1400 A.D. Therefore, it is impossible for us to know the melody, harmony, and rhythm of this psalm. We can, however, understand a lot about the music used to bring people into the presence of God by reading the lyrics that have been written down. I will not take the space to reprint this psalm for you here, but I recommend that you take a few minutes and read through it in the Bible.[42]

The lyrics of this psalm are all God-centered, not man-centered. Therefore, it is safe to say that the music for it would have also been God-exalting.

I have a friend, Lisa McFarland, who has received revelation from God concerning the sound of heaven. She has done extensive research and studied the Bible on this subject and has concluded that God wants the sound of heaven to invade earth when we worship. I believe that is what took place at David's tent. So, what is the sound of heaven?

There have been only a few people privileged to visit heaven and come back to earth to tell us about it. One of those people was John while he was exiled on the Island of Patmos. Here is the way he described the worship and sound that was going on in heaven when he got to visit.

> Then I looked, and I **heard** the voice of **many angels** around the throne, the living creatures, and the elders; and the number of them was **ten thousand times ten thousand**, and thousands of thousands, saying with a **loud voice**: "Worthy is the Lamb who was slain To receive power and riches and wisdom, And strength and honor and glory and blessing!" Revelation 5:11–12 (NKJV), emphasis added

---

[42] 1 Chronicles 16:8–36

152

Not only were they singing, but they were accompanying the singing with musical instruments.

> And when he had taken the book, the four beasts and four and twenty elders fell down before the Lamb, **having every one of them harps**, and golden vials full of odours, which are the prayers of saints. Revelation 5:8 (KJV) emphasis added

Although John did not report seeing and hearing any other musical instruments in heaven, the fact that he saw and heard harps being played is significant. In heaven, just like at David's tent, the worship leaders of the first and second degree were the ones playing the musical instruments in heaven. The worship team members of the third degree were the singers, like John heard thousands singing in heaven.

Harps are mentioned again in Revelation 15:2. Many people have suggested that because the harps are being played in heaven, angels are playing them. But that Scripture makes it clear that human beings were playing the harps in heaven as they sang. Musical instruments are mentioned in the New Testament in the context worship. Please do not be deceived about this point. God has not done away with musical instruments in worship. If we want the sound of heaven in our worship, we need to use musical instruments!

IT IS MORE THAN THE SOUND

All of these Biblical examples of David's tent style of worship and the sound of worship going on in heaven talk about worship being expressed with a loud noise. If we are not careful, we will misunderstand that the type of worship God wants is not loud because of amplification, but it is loud because of the number of participants.

God wanted a large orchestra and choir in David's tent and in heaven because He wants a maximum number of worshipers to participate. Why is that important to God? To understand the answer to that question, I refer you to *The Importance of Worshiping Together*. It will explain in detail the spiritual power God has placed within our worshiping together.

Our enemy, Lucifer, has been trying to get the church to compromise on this for hundreds of years. Back in the Roman Empire, it was discovered that a pipe organ could fill an entire Coliseum with sound. That permitted one instrumentalist to take the place of an entire orchestra of instrumentalists. Not only did gladiators fight to the death to the sound of the pipe organ, but Christians were fed to the lions and burned at the stake while the organist played loudly.

Not many years later, Satan convinced the church to bring the pipe organ into the church buildings as the primary accompanying musical instrument for worship. One instrumentalist could play just as loud as a full orchestra, eliminating the need for large instrumental ensembles in worship. Lucifer convinced the Church that it was more about volume than the number of worship leaders.

It took Lucifer a lot longer to convince the church to eliminate the choir, or large vocal ensemble of worship leaders. But by the 1990s, church choirs became a thing of the past. That happened in conjunction with electronic musical instruments taking over this sound accompanying our worship.

In the 1940s, secular music developed what is called a big band sound. A big band consists of only the brass instruments from an orchestra, especially trombones and trumpets. The only woodwind instruments in a big band were saxophones and an occasional clarinet. To provide the cohesive rhythm for the big band, a rhythm section was created.

A 1940s rhythm section consisted of someone playing a standup double bass violin by plucking (not bowing), a piano player, a guitar player, and a drummer. That was the first time one person played multiple percussion instruments at the same time and was the invention of what we now know as the drum kit.

By the 1950s we were experimenting with shrinking the size of musical ensembles, so instead of the entire big band, we started using just one of each of the wind instruments in the big band, plus the rhythm section. There were multiple combinations of these smaller ensembles. Some would have all the same instruments of the big band, and others would have only one or two of the wind instruments, as well as a rhythm section. No matter what the combination of instruments, these ensembles were called combos for short.

By the 1960s, the electric guitar and keyboard took over the industry, eliminating the need for an acoustic standup bass and the wind instruments. These sounds were now produced with the electric guitars and keyboards.

Since the 1960s, most live music is created using some variation of this type of instrumental ensemble listed below, which we now call a band but was originally called the rhythm section:

1. electric bass guitar
2. drum kit
3. acoustic guitar
4. electric guitar
5. electronic musical keyboard(s)

Of course, when music is being recorded, a fuller musical sound is always desired and will be created with either a live orchestra or big band or a synthesized orchestra or big band.

Most of today's worship teams have taken on this same configuration of instruments, with varying configurations of vocalists. That results in our worship sounding more like the world's music than heaven's music. Most contemporary Christian worship settings not only sound like the world but also look like the world. They paint the walls black and use the same light shows found at secular rock concerts where the devil or the flesh is being worshiped.

The deviation from God's type of music in our churches has also caused us to deviate from a Godly setting for worship. I ask you this: According to the description of heaven in the Bible, where light is emanating from God's throne,[43] where we are told there is no need for a sun or moon because God is the light of heaven,[44] does a darkened sanctuary look more like heaven or hell?

> And this is the condemnation, that light is come into the world, and men loved darkness rather than light, because their deeds were evil. John 3:19 (KJV)

---

[43] Revelation 4:5
[44] Revelation 21:23

The worship at David's tent always involved large musical ensembles, an orchestra, and a choir. I believe it is not only Biblical but vital to include as many people as possible on a worship team, because there is strength in numbers. The only present-day example of this is the Brooklyn Tabernacle in New York City. Simply do a search on YouTube for the Brooklyn Tabernacle choir and watch any of their live videos to see this in action.

RESTORING DAVID'S TENT'S STYLE OF WORSHIP

David's tent was God's standard of worship throughout history.

And the singers the sons of Asaph were in their place, according to the commandment of David, and Asaph, and Heman, and Jeduthun the king's seer; and the porters waited at every gate; they might not depart from their service; for their brethren the Levites prepared for them. 2 Chronicles 35:15 (KJV)

After the time of David, anytime Israel returned back to God, they also returned back to the type of worship God had instructed David to use, with a large choir and orchestra. When Jehoshaphat was king, several armies joined together against Israel. After seeking God, they received direction from God to put the worshiping singers in front of the Army.

And when he had consulted with the people, he appointed singers unto the LORD, and that should praise the beauty of holiness, as they went out before the army, and to say, Praise the LORD; for his mercy endureth forever. 2 Chronicles 20:21 (KJV)

When King Jehoiada restored the kingdom to follow God, he reestablished the musical choir as David had commanded.

> *Also Jehoiada appointed the offices of the house of the LORD by the hand of the priests the Levites, whom David had distributed in the house of the LORD, to offer the burnt offerings of the LORD, as it is written in the law of Moses, with rejoicing and with singing, as it was ordained by David. 2 Chronicles 23:18 (KJV)*

King Hezekiah also returned Israel to the pattern that David had established with the burnt offerings of Moses and the large orchestra and choir that David had at the tent for the ark.

> *And Hezekiah commanded to offer the burnt offering upon the altar. And when the burnt offering began, the song of the LORD began also with the trumpets, and with the instruments ordained by David king of Israel. And all the congregation worshipped, and the singers sang, and the trumpeters sounded: and all this continued until the burnt offering was finished. 2 Chronicles 29:27–28 (KJV)*

Here are scriptures from the writings of Nehemiah and Ezra that talk about the return to the style of worship that David established.

> *And Maaseiah, and Shemaiah, and Eleazar, and Uzzi, and Jehohanan, and Malchijah, and Elam, and Ezer. And the singers sang loud, with Jezrahiah their overseer. Nehemiah 12:42 (KJV)*

> *Beside their servants and their maids, of whom there were seven thousand three hundred thirty and seven: and there were among them two hundred singing men and singing women. Ezra 2:65 (KJV)*

Ezra listed the number of servants and maids as well as the number of singers. Any way you look at it, a 250-voice choir is a good-sized musical ensemble. The closest I have come to singing in a choir of that size was when my high school choir joined together with several other school choirs for an all-day workshop on a Saturday, with a concert that evening. We had about five choirs, and our number didn't even reach 200 people singing. I still remember the difficulty if was to get that many people to sing together well.

Also, in this scripture it mentions "singing men and singing women." If you know anything about history, you know that for hundreds of years women were not allowed to sing in choirs or perform in theatre. That was Lucifer's attempt to destroy the kind of worship God told David to establish. God created both men and women to sing praise to Him. Anything that says women are not to be used in leading worship is not of God but is of the enemy.

USING CHAIN OF COMMAND IN YOUR WORSHIP TEAM

Do your best to follow David's pattern of rank and file with your worship team. Here is the way your worship team should be structured using David's four levels or ranks.

Table 11. Worship Team Chain of Command

Ranks	Your Worship Team
Chief	➤ minister of music
First Rank	➤ primary worship leaders ➤ assistant music directors ➤ heads of all support ministry departments
Second Rank	➤ choir section leaders ➤ instrumental section leaders ➤ administrative assistant to the chief ➤ shift leads for all support ministries
Third Rank	➤ the choir ➤ the orchestra ➤ the ushers ➤ the A/V department ➤ the projectionists

THE SECONDARY WORSHIP LEADER PRINCIPLE

We have looked at chain of command from the worship team's perspective. Now let's look at the significance of chain of command from the congregation's point of view.

One day I was flipping through the channels on TV and came across a hidden camera show. They set up a gag in a doctor's waiting room. When a beep sounded over the speaker, the person who had been planted there by the show's producers stood up until the sound was heard again. After trying this several times, no one else in the waiting room stood up at the sound of the beep. That prompted the producers to do something different with the gag. They placed another person in the waiting room that was in on the joke and instructed them to follow the lead of the first individual.

With a new room full of waiting patients, they tried the gag again with this new change. To everyone's surprise, this is what happened. When the sound went off, the first guy stood up. Everyone in the room looked up and saw him standing, then went back to reading their phone or a magazine. Soon after the first person stood, the second person stood up as well. Everyone in the room looked at the second person doing what the first person started. Several of them appeared very uncomfortable in that moment.

The sound was heard the second time and the two people sat down, the leader sat a few seconds before the follower sat. A few minutes went by, and the sound was heard again. This time the follower stood up almost immediately after the leader stood up. The people in the room began to look at each other, as if to say, "What is going on?" A few seconds later, one of the people in the waiting room stood up and joined the first two. One by one, all of the remaining people in the room stood up. When the sound was heard again, the leader set down, followed closely by the follower. Then everyone else sat down as well.

This exercise continued a few more times, and everyone in the waiting room was standing and sitting at the audible queue being sounded by an out-of-sight technician.

Then a nurse came and called the name of the initial leader to go back to meet with the doctor, as the show's producers continued having the sound made and watching the people stand in the waiting room until the sound was heard a second time.

Next, they had the initial follower called back, out of the waiting room. That meant that the people left in the waiting room knew nothing about the hidden cameras and the producers' crazy scheme. However, by this time they had been programmed to stand and sit when they heard the sound, so they continued to do so, even without the initial leaders.

They continued the experiment until all of the initial people had been called back for their appointments, except one. Then a new patient walked in to the waiting room. When the sound went off, the person who had been educated by the first two leaders continued the practice to stand and sit after the sound. But the new patient simply looked up from his phone at the man standing, shrugged his shoulders, and went back to reading from his phone.

The producers were bewildered, until they remembered that it wasn't until they planted a follower in the group to follow the leader that everyone began standing at the sound. So, they quickly sent the first follower in to do what he did before. The next time they heard the sound and the patient who had not been in on the initial gag stood up, the follower followed him and stood up as well. The new guy became very uncomfortable, and it wasn't long until he was standing and sitting with the other two.

This entire gag took up most of the one-half-hour show. At the end of the show, the producers talked about their observations of human behavior they had just witnessed. They concluded that human nature does not follow the leader of any given circumstance, but human nature follows the close followers of a leader.

Psychologically people like to wait to follow a leader until they see how well those directly under the authority of a leader follow them. This is called the secondary leadership principle. In other words, the general public will usually watch the subordinates of a leader to see how committed they are in following the leader, before they make a commitment to the leader.

In a worship setting, this means that the primary worship leader of any given worship service is not there to lead the congregation in worship. They are there to lead the secondary worship leaders in worship. It is then the responsibility of the secondary worship leaders to lead the congregation in worship.

Let me say it again this way. The primary worship leader (or chief) leads the worship team in worship, and the worship team (band, choir, and orchestra) leads the congregation in worship. This secondary leadership principle was mentioned by Paul in this scripture.

> Be ye followers of me, even as I also am of Christ. 1 Corinthians 11:1 (KJV)

In this Biblical pattern of leadership, Jesus is the primary leader, and Paul is the secondary leader. The church is being encouraged to follow the secondary leader as he follows the primary leader.

This is also the principal that every worship leader should follow. Even if you are a primary worship leader for a worship service, consider yourself as a secondary worship leader under Christ. Let him be the worship leader, and be present only to support His agenda.

THE BUILT-IN ACCOUNTABILITY OF CHAIN OF COMMAND

Chain of command requires that every person is responsible for their own actions. In other words, only one person can lead at a time. In chain of command, there is no such thing as joint leadership over the same responsibility.

Nowhere in Scripture or in any military type of setting, do we see two people sharing a position of authority. That would not permit accountability for that position. If something went wrong, one could always blame the other. God in His wisdom did not ordain co-leadership in rank and file.

Chapter Eight
"GOD'S PRAISE MUSIC"

BIBLICAL MUSIC

Music is made up of three basic parts: melody, harmony, and rhythm. However, within a melody is the implied harmony and implied rhythm of that piece of music. Therefore, to make melody is to make music. Throughout history, musical melodies have been called tunes.

A song has an additional part—lyrics. If I hum the tune of *Twinkle Little Star*, I am making melody. If I sing the words with the melody, I am singing a song. For music to be a song, it must have lyrics.

The lyrics of a songs contain a specific intelligent message. Therefore, songs are sung by someone for the purpose that someone else might understand its message. Therefore, this is how God defines His different types of songs by who is singing them and whom they are sung to.

In the Bible, God tells us we are to sing four different types of songs. Those four types of songs fit into two categories. The first three types of songs are listed twice in the New Testament and are in the first category, which the Bible calls "praise." Here are the two scriptures where the first song types are listed.

*And be not drunk with wine, wherein is excess; but be filled with the Spirit; Speaking to yourselves in **psalms** and **hymns** and **spiritual songs**, singing and making melody* *in your heart to the Lord; Giving thanks always for all things unto God and the Father in the name of our Lord Jesus Christ; Ephesians 5:18-20 (KJV), emphasis added*

*Let the word of Christ dwell in you richly in all wisdom; teaching and admonishing one another in **psalms** and **hymns** and **spiritual songs**, singing with grace in your hearts to the Lord. And whatsoever ye do in word or deed, do all in the name of the Lord Jesus, giving thanks to God and the Father by him. Colossians 3:16-17 (KJV), emphasis added*

Before we examine what specifically are psalms, hymns, and spiritual songs, let's look at this phrase from the Ephesians Scripture.

... singing and making melody in your heart to the Lord. Ephesians 5:19 (KJV)

Notice the two ways we can make music. We can sing and we can make melody. Again, singing involves words or lyrics. The human voice is the only instrument that can sing a song. We can make melody with our voices or with other musical instruments. Because the Old Testament commands us to worship the Lord with musical instruments, I believe this Scripture in Ephesians is referring to making melody with musical instruments. Here is just one of the places in the Bible where we are commanded to worship God with musical instruments.

Praise him with the sound of the trumpet: praise him with the psaltery and harp. Praise him with the timbrel and dance: praise him with stringed instruments and organs. Praise him upon the loud cymbals: praise him upon the high sounding cymbals. Psalm 150:3-5 (KJV)

The argument comes from some that "we are only supposed to make melody in our heart, not audibly." If that were the case, we should not be singing audibly either, because singing and making melody are mentioned in the same breath. Paul makes it clear that we are to do both—sing with our heart (which is our spirit) and the natural part of us at the same time.

> *What is it then? I will pray with the spirit, and I will pray with the understanding also: I will **sing** with the **spirit, and** I will sing with the **understanding** also. 1 Corinthians 14:15 (KJV), emphasis added*

In *Portrait of a Worshiper*, I explained in detail why the Bible calls the natural part of man the "understanding." The short explanation of this is that everything our body does is controlled by our mind or our understanding. Therefore, this Scripture is clearly telling us we are to sing with our body as well as our spirit. Paul tells us we can do that with just one or the other, but Paul wants us to pray every prayer and sing every song with both parts of our being all the time—our spirit man and our natural man. Therefore, if we are being told here to sing audibly (naturally), we are also to play music Instruments audibly making melody with them.

"But the commandments you read are in the Old Testament," some may argue. So what? Does that mean that because the New Testament does not contain the commandment "Thou shalt not kill" that it is now OK to murder, because we are living in the New Testament era? Of course not! The Old Testament was not done away with when Jesus came; it was just fulfilled.[45]

So, the three types of praise songs we are to sing are psalms, hymns, and spiritual songs. And we are supposed to sing all three of those songs with our spirit at the same time we are singing them with our understanding.

WHAT IS A PSALM?

Remember we said that the types of Biblical songs are defined by who is singing them and to whom they are being sung. In the book of James, we read this, which helps us understand what a psalm is.

---

[45] Matthew 5:17

*Is any among you afflicted? let **him pray**. Is any merry? let **him sing** psalms. Is any sick among you? let him call for the elders of the church; and let **them pray** over him, anointing him with oil in the name of the Lord: James 5:13–14 (KJV), emphasis added*

This scripture is differentiating between when a person should pray for themselves and when they should have a group of elders pray for them. The difference is if you are afflicted, you should pray. If you are sick, you should call the elders to pray. Some people feel that sickness and affliction are the same thing, but they are not. Sickness takes a while to overcome your body, giving you time to involve others in seeking God for healing. Affliction is a sudden thing, like a car accident. If you are afflicted, you can pray yourself immediately, because you may not have time to wait on the elders to pray for you.

Sandwiched between those two reasons to pray for healing is a very interesting statement.

... Is any merry? Let him sing psalms. James 5:13 (KJV)

Many have speculated as to why this statement is stuck in the middle of instructions on prayer. Some have said that when something bad happens you pray and when something "good" happens to make you happy, you sing. That is not the point of this Scripture. God placed this statement where it is to teach us about what a psalm is. This is not a contrast between singing and praying. This is simply showing us that a psalm is a song sung by an individual to God just like an individual can pray when afflicted.

To verify that, I looked into the Psalms that David wrote. I noticed that David wrote most of them to God. Here is a random sampling to show you what I mean.

*Lord, how are they increased that trouble **me**! many are they that rise up against **me**. Psalm 3:1 (KJV), emphasis added*

*Hear **me** when **I** call, O God of **my** righteousness: thou hast enlarged **me** when **I** was in distress; have mercy upon **me**, and hear **my** prayer. Psalm 4:1 (KJV), emphasis added*

*I will praise thee, O Lord, with **my** whole heart; I will shew forth all thy marvellous works. I will be glad and rejoice in thee: I will sing praise to thy name, O thou most High. Psalm 9:1–2 (KJV), emphasis added*

*I will love thee, O Lord, **my** strength. The Lord is **my** rock, and **my** fortress, and **my** deliverer; **my** God, **my** strength, in whom I will trust; **my** buckler, and the horn of **my** salvation, and **my** high tower. I will call upon the Lord, who is worthy to be praised: so shall I be saved from **mine** enemies. Psalm 18:1–3 (KJV), emphasis added*

To select those Scriptures, I simply flipped through the Psalms. I could continue doing that, but I feel like those are enough to prove my point. Therefore, according to the Bible, a psalm is a song sung by an individual to God, as indicated by this graphic.

Some have said that a psalm is any Scripture set to music. Whereas I believe it is a good thing to sing the Scriptures; that is not what defines a psalm.

Psalms

If you sing a psalm with other people in a gathering of the church, it is still a group of individuals singing to the Lord. It is very possible to be in a congregation singing a psalm yet have the experience that your worship of God is an individual thing between just you and God.

WHAT IS A HYMN?

We just discovered that a psalm is a song sung by one person to God. We now must ask: What is the Biblical setting of a hymn? Who sings a hymn and to whom is it sung? Here's what the New Testament has to say about those questions. The setting of this Scripture is at the last supper with Jesus and his disciples.

> And when **they** had sung an hymn, **they** went out into the mount of Olives. Matthew 26:30 (KJV), emphasis added

This scripture answers the question of who sings hymns. The word "they" refers to the group of disciples and Jesus. Therefore, a hymn is sung by a group of people, as opposed to a psalm that is sung by an individual person. This graphic shows what a hymn is.

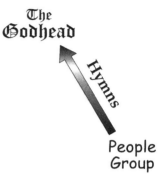

Hymns

Singing a hymn with a group of people is different from singing a psalm with them. This is when the covenant principle we talked about in *The Importance of Worshiping Together*, Chapter three, is experienced. To summarize that principle, God has made a covenant with us so that our worship together becomes exponentially more powerful than our worship as individuals.

There are times when our worship needs to be between us and God only, even in the middle of the church. But there are also times when we need to join our praise with others and experience the dynamic of spiritual power unavailable any other way.

Unfortunately, we do not have any examples of hymns recorded in Scripture. We know Jesus and the disciples sang hymns, because we just read that. However, none of the hymns sung in Jesus' day were written down for us.

According to the Christian History Institute, the two oldest hymns we still sing today are "Shepherd of Eager Youth" written in 200 A.D., and "O Splendor of God's Glory Bright" written in 390 A.D.[46]

---

[46] "2,000 years, 25 hymns," Christian History Institute, accessed April 16, 2021, https://christianhistoryinstitute.org/magazine/article/2000-years-25-hymns.

Let's take a few moments to look at some of the lyrics of these hymns.

"Shepherd of Eager Youth"[47]
Original Greek by Clement of Alexandria (200)
English translation by Henry M. Dexter (1846)

Verse 1
Shepherd of eager youth,
Guiding in love and truth
Through devious ways,
Christ, our triumphant King,
We come Thy name to sing,
Hither our children bring
To shout Thy praise.

The hymn starts off addressing and glorifying God, identifying Jesus as "Christ, our triumphant King." Then the fifth, sixth, and seventh lines show us who is singing and why. The fifth line says, "We come Thy name to sing." Notice the plural pronoun "we" indicating that a group of people are singing to God.

Here are the first two verses of the second hymn listed.

"O Splendor of God's Glory Bright"[48]
Original Latin by St. Ambrose (fourth century)
English translation by Robert Seymour Bridges (early 1900s)

Verse 1
O Splendor of God's glory bright,
O Thou that bringest light from light,
O Light of Light, light's living spring,
O Day, all days illumining:
Alleluia!

---

[47] "471. Shepherd of Eager Youth," Hymnary.org, accessed April 16, 2021, https://hymnary.org/hymn/H1955/471.

[48] "O Splendor of God's Glory Bright, O Thou that Bringest Light from Light," Hymnary.org, accessed April 16, 2021, https://hymnary.org/text/o_splendor_of_gods_glory_bright_o_thou.

Verse 2
Come, very Sun of truth and love;
Pour down Thy radiance from above
And shed the Holy Spirit's ray
On all we think or do or say.
Alleluia!

The reason I shared two verses here is because we have to get into the second verse before we learn who is singing. Obviously from the first verse we know the hymn is praise directed to God. The third and fourth lines of the second verse read, "And shed the Holy Spirit's ray on all we think or do or say." Again, the plural pronoun "we" indicates this hymn is being sung by a group to the Lord.

Let me point out just a few more hymns from church history so you may note that they are all to be sung by a group to praise and glorify God.

"O God Our Help in Ages Past"[49]
CCLI Song # 43152
Lyrics by Isaac Watts (1719)
Music by William Croft, (eighteenth century)

Verse 1
O God **our** help in ages past
Our hope for years to come
Our shelter from the stormy blast
And **our** eternal home

Notice the multiple times the plural pronoun "our" is used and that the group who is singing is addressing God.

---

[49] "O God Our Help In Ages Past," accessed December 31, 2021, https://www.youtube.com/watch?v=z50HteIPWi8

"A Mighty Fortress"[50]
German words and music by Martin Luther (1529)
Translated into English by Frederick H. Hedge in 1853

Verse 1
A mighty fortress is our God,
A bulwark never failing:
Our helper He, amid the flood
Of mortal ills prevailing.
For still our ancient foe
Doth seek to work us woe;
His craft and power are great,
And armed with cruel hate,
On earth is not his equal.

The phrases "our God," "our Helper," and "our ancient foe" indicate the plurality of the group who is singing. However, it is not clear who is being sung to—God or man. For now, we will give this song the benefit of the doubt and call it a hymn. Here is another hymn for us to look at.

"We Praise Thee, O God"[51]
Lyrics by William Paton MacKay (1839-1885)
Music by John Jenkins Husband (1760-1825)

Verse 1
We praise Thee, O God,
For the Son of Thy love,
For our Savior who died and
Is now gone above.

Again, "we" indicates a group singing praise to God. Let me share just one more with you.

---

[50] "A Might Fortress Is Our God," Wikipedia, accessed April 16, 2021, https://en.wikipedia.org/wiki/A_Mighty_Fortress_Is_Our_God.
[51] "We Praise Thee, O God," Hymnal.net, accessed April 16, 2021, https://www.hymnal.net/en/hymn/h/40.

171

"All Hail the Power"[52]
Edward Perronet (1780)

Verse 1
All hail the power of Jesus' name!
Let angels prostrate fall.
Bring forth the royal diadem,
and crown him Lord of all.
Bring forth the royal diadem,
and crown him Lord of all!

This song commands that all—indicating everyone in that group, as well as a multitude of heavenly angels—should praise God. At first glance, this song is being sung to other people, not God. But the issue of who is being sung to is resolved when you know this Scripture.

> *Thou shalt also be a crown of glory in the hand of the Lord, and a royal diadem in the hand of thy God. Isaiah 62:3 (KJV)*

That Scripture tells us that we, God's people, are the diadem that He must be crowned with. That means the singers of this song are asking God to bring forth the Royal diadem of His people and be crowned with that glory. That means that song is being sung to God by a group of people, which makes it a hymn.

So, we see, that a hymn is the type of praise song where a group of people are singing it to the Lord God together.

WHAT IS A SPIRITUAL SONG?

The answer to that question is found in both Ephesians 5:19 and Colossians 3:16. Those are the same scriptures that gave us the three types of praise songs we are to sing. The answer is found in these

---

[52] "All Hail the Power of Jesus' Name," Hymnary.org, accessed April 16, 2021, https://hymnary.org/text/all_hail_the_power_of_jesus_name_let.

two respective phrases, "speaking to yourselves" and "teaching and admonishing one another."

We have already seen that the Bible defines a psalm as a song sung by one person to the Almighty God. It also defines a hymn as a song sung by a group of people to God. That only leaves a spiritual song as the type of song that is about spiritual things but is sung to each other.

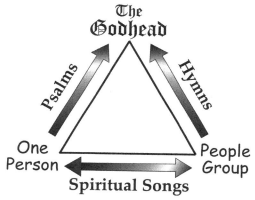

Psalms, Hymns, and Spiritual Songs

A spiritual song is the opposite of a secular song. A secular song talks about everything but holy, spiritual subjects. A spiritual song could cover a variety of Christian subjects including a testimony song, an evangelistic song, a doctrinal or teaching song, an encouragement song, a declaration of faith and intent song, or a scripture set to music. Any Godly song not directed to God in worship but directed to other people is a spiritual song.

Many spiritual songs have been called hymns or psalms out of ignorance. For instance, Bill and Gloria Gaither's wonderful song "Because He Lives"[53] has been placed in several modern hymn books. Because of that, it has been called a twentieth century hymn. However, upon closer examination, that song is not being sung to God but to other people. If it were being sung to God, it would have to read "Because You live, I can face tomorrow." Therefore, this song cannot be a hymn or a psalm but is indeed a spiritual song.

---

[53] William J. Gaither. *Because He Lives*. CCLI Song # 16880, 1971, Hanna Street Music.

Rich Mullins, who was taken from us too young in a car accident, wrote the wonderful spiritual song *"Awesome God."*[54] That song is being sung to other people about "our God." If it were being sung to God, it would have to read, "Oh God, You're an Awesome God."

Back in the 1970s, André Crouch was writing a lot of great spiritual songs. One of his most singable songs is *Soon and Very Soon We Are Going to See the King*[55] That song is being sung to other people, not to God, so it is a spiritual song.

Just because a song is contemporary does not make it a spiritual song automatically. For instance, the lead singer for the band Mercy Me is Bart Millard. In 2001, he wrote the song "I Can Only Imagine," which received the Dove Award's Song of the Year Award that year. At first listen, we might think this is another spiritual song, but on closer examination of the lyrics, we see it is a present-day psalm. It is being sung by one person to the Lord. Here is an example of the lyrics, which shows what I mean.

"I Can Only Imagine"[56]
Words and Music by Bart Millard

Verse 1
I can only imagine
What it will be like
When I walk by **Your** side
I can only imagine
What **my** eyes will see
When **Your** face is before **me**
I can only imagine

---

[54] Rich Mullins. *Awesome God*. CCLI Song # 41099, 1988, Universal Music - Brentwood Benson Publishing.

[55] Andraé Crouch. *Soon and Very Soon*. CCLI Song # 11249, 1971, Bud John Songs, Inc., Crouch Music Corp.

[56] Bart Miller. *I Can Only Imagine*. CCLI Song # 2978857, © 2001, 2002 Simpleville Music.

MAKING A WORSHIP SONG LIST

If you are a primary worship leader, you need to make a list of every song you sing in your church. Make your list in your word processing program on your computer. If you can, set your list up in a table. Here are the columns you should create:

Key. This is the musical key the song is written in or the key that your church does the song in.

Title this is the song's actual published title.

First line or composer(s). This is the song's identifying factor for you, because there are sometimes multiple songs with the same title.

Tempo. Metronome markings are not necessary, unless you think in those terms. I suggest using "F" for fast, "M" for medium, and "S" for slow.

Mode. Simply use a "P" for psalm, "H" for hymn, and "SS" for spiritual song.

Here's what your list should look like. I have used some of the songs that I have listed in this chapter to start this worship song list. Optional additional columns could include the date the song was introduced to your church, the preferred musical feel, and the song's level of music difficulty for your worship team.

Group all the songs in the same key together, and alphabetize the song titles in the key groups. Also, leave extra lines between the key groupings so you can add new songs later.

Table 12. Worship Song List for [church name]

Last Updated [date] by [initials or name]

Key	Title	First Line or Composer(s)	Tempo	Mode
Ab	"Because He Lives"	William Gaither	MS	SS
C	"A Mighty Fortress"	Martin Luther	M	H
D	"I Can Only Imagine"	Bart Millard	MS	P
Em	"Awesome God"	Rich Mullins	MF	SS
F	"All Hail the Power"	All hail the power of Jesus' name!	MS	H
F	"Revive us again"	We Praise Thee, O God	M	H
G	"O God Our Help in Ages Past"	Isaac Watts	MS	H
G	"Soon and Very Soon"	André Crouch	M	SS

Having an up-to-date, customized worship song list is an essential tool for planning all your worship services.

Once you have created your song list, look it over to see how balanced your repertoire is between psalms, hymns, and spiritual songs. Each of those three types of praise songs should make up approximately one-third of your song list. That means that two-thirds of the songs you sing in your church should be directed to God. If you see that you are out of balance in some way, devise a plan to introduce more of the type of songs that you are deficient in.

When you start looking at the lyrics of the songs you sing, you may find songs that the verse(s) are one type of song and the chorus or bridge is a different type of song. If you find that, be sure to note that on the song list. You can do that simply by using this ledger: V = verse, C =

chorus, B = bridge, PC = pre-chorus, etc. Here is an example to show you how to document songs that do not remain in the same song mode throughout the song.

Table 13. Example of Modes

Key	Title	First Line or Composer(s)	Tempo	Mode
?	???	???	?	V1P CH V2SS BP

David even wrote these types of songs. Here is one example. The first two verses of this example are written in a spiritual song mode. David is singing these lines to the congregation. The last verse of this example is in a hymn mode, because it uses the plural pronoun "us" and is directed to God.

Our soul waiteth for the Lord: he is our help and our shield. For our heart shall rejoice in him, because we have trusted in his holy name.

Let thy mercy, O Lord, be upon us, according as we hope in thee. Psalm 33:20–22 (KJV)

Chapter Nine

"GOD'S NEW SONG"

THE TWO CATEGORIES OF SONGS

In the last chapter, I showed you how the Bible defines the praise songs we are to sing according to who is singing them and to whom they are being sung. Those psalms, hymns, and spiritual songs have all been prewritten, rehearsed by the worship team, and sung by the congregation at various times. Those prewritten songs are what the Bible calls "praise."

There is another category of songs that we are also commanded to sing. That category is what the Bible calls a "new song." Here is a Scripture where those two categories are mentioned together.

> *Praise ye the Lord. Sing unto the Lord a **new song**, **and his praise** in the congregation of saints. Psalm 149:1 (KJV), emphasis added*

According to this Scripture, we are commanded to sing praise songs as well as a "new song" to the Lord. I have spent time defining for you the three types of praise songs. Now let me explain to you the two types of new songs.

DEFINING THE NEW SONG

There are two Hebrew words for the English word "new." They are Strong's word numbers 2318[57] and 2319.[58]

Number 2318 is transliterated into "chädash" and is pronounced (khaw-dash'). It means to make new again, restore, renew, repair. The ä is the Merriam-Webster way to indicate this vowel sound, not the IPA method. Here's a Scripture that uses that word.

> *And when Asa heard these words, and the prophecy of Oded the prophet, he took courage, and put away the abominable idols out of all the land of Judah and Benjamin, and out of the cities which he had taken from mount Ephraim, and **renewed** the altar of the Lord, that was before the porch of the Lord. 2 Chronicles 15:8 (KJV), emphasis added*

Strong's Hebrew word number 2319 is transliterated into "chädäsh" and is pronounced (khaw-dawsh'). It means fresh, new thing, never existed, or happened before. That is the word used in the Scripture above (Psalm 149:1) mentioning the "new song." Here is another Scripture that also uses this word. Notice that it likewise contains the two categories of songs we are to sing.

> *Behold, the former things are come to pass, and **new** things do I declare: before they spring forth I tell you of them. Sing unto the Lord a **new song, and his praise** from the end of the earth, ye that go down to the sea, and all that is therein; the isles, and the inhabitants thereof. Isaiah 42:9–10 (KJV), emphasis added*

In verse nine of that Scripture, God is telling us through Isaiah that

---

[57] "2318. Chadash" Bible Hub, accessed April 27, 2021, https://biblehub.com/hebrew/2318.htm.
[58] "2319. Chadash" Bible Hub, accessed April 27, 2021, https://biblehub.com/hebrew/2319.htm.

He is about to do a brand new thing in the earth. It will be something He has never done before, because the word here is chädäsh.

In praying for revival, some Christians take the chädäsh approach to their prayers, praying, "Lord, do it again!" God honored Billy Graham when he prayed that prayer remembering the Welsh revival. Other Christians take the chädäsh approach and ask God to do things He has never done before, to show Himself powerful. William Seymore prayed that way, and God answered him with the Azusa Street revival in the early 1900s. God did things at that revival that He had never done before, fulfilling this Scripture, as well as answering his prayer.

If I came over to your house driving a vehicle that I bought at a used car lot, I would say to you, "How do you like my new car?" That use of "new" is chädash, meaning although the car was a few years old, it is new to me.

If I visited your church and said, "Let me teach you a new song that I wrote last year," that would be a chädash song. The song would have existed for about a year, but it would be new to you.

In Isaiah 42:10, we see the two categories of the songs we are commanded to sing: new song and praise. That is a chädäsh song, not a chädash song. In other words, the new song God has commanded us to sing is one that has never been sung before, by you or anyone else. It is a song that is fresh, brand new in the moment when you sing it.

A song can be chädäsh only once. After it has been sung, it is a song that exists. To sing it again is to re-create or renew the song, making it then a chädash song.

That makes this the important distinction between the two categories of songs we are commanded to sing. First, there are prewritten praise songs we call psalms, hymns, and spiritual songs. Second, there are spontaneous songs we call the new song.

HOW THE NEW SONG WORKS

Remember, God will never command you to do something without making a way for you to do it. This new song concept may frighten you at first, if you think it is all on you to come up with it on your own. That was never God's intention. It is God's responsibility to give you the new song; it is your responsibility to sing it. This Scripture makes it very clear where the new song comes from.

And he hath put a new song in my mouth, even praise unto our God: many shall see it, and fear, and shall trust in the Lord. Psalm 40:3 (KJV)

A new song is not something we are expected to come up with on our own. God gives us the new song to sing. A new song must come from God!

Notice where God places the new song—in our mouth. God does not place a new song in our mind. If He did, we would analyze it before we sang it. God does not want His new song contaminated with our thoughts and ideas. Therefore, He bypasses our mind and puts the new song in our mouth. When I sing a new song, I am hearing it for the first time with my understanding. That is what makes the new song so unique and powerful, it comes from God but is sung by us.

The way that new song works is the exact same way as the gifts of the Holy Spirit that are mentioned in 1 Corinthians 12. If you have operated those spiritual gifts, you will have no problem singing a new song when God gives it to you, because you have already developed the ability to hear God. If the concept of spiritual gifts is new to you, I believe it can be easier to sing a new song than to operate some spiritual gifts, because God will always place the new song in our mouth, not our mind. Some spiritual gifts will actually be placed in our mind when God operates them through us.

The next phrase of this scripture can be interpreted in several ways, *"even praise unto our God."* One interpretation is that every new song will bring praise and glory to the Lord. Another interpretation is that this is another place where the two categories of songs are mentioned—new song and praise. I think that is only part of what God is trying to say to us here. The first phrase of the scripture talks about how the new song is given to us by God. I believe it is possible to insert the word "also" in place of the word "even" to understand a deeper meaning. It then tells us that, just like God should give us the new song, God should also give us the praise songs as we are writing them.

The final phrase of Psalm 40:3 says this, *"many shall see it, and fear, and shall trust in the Lord."* That tells us three very important characteristics of a new song.

First, the new song is intended to be observable by a group of people. There are two types of new songs, defined by who is singing them and whom they are sung to. God wants both of those types of new songs to be observable by "many."

Second, to hear a new song will strike a sense of awe into those who hear it. The word used in the King James Bible is "fear," but it means a sense of wonderment or amazement. Any time you hear a song being sung that has never existed before that moment, it is amazing! I am a songwriter, and I know the hours that it takes to craft a song, even with the Lord's help. But when I hear a song sung spontaneously as though it had been labored over, that is truly an awesome experience. It truly makes me love and respect God more.

Third, the new song will bring other people to God. In that regard, a new song can have the same effect on an unbeliever as prophecy does. Here is what Paul said about the effects that prophesy can have on an unbeliever. This is the same result that a new song can produce, *"and shall trust in the Lord."*

> But if all prophesy, and an unbeliever or an uninformed person comes in, he is convinced by all, he is convicted by all. And thus the secrets of his heart are revealed; and so, falling down on his face, he will worship God and report that God is truly among you. 1 Corinthians 14:24–25 (NKJV)

CONFIRMATION SCRIPTURES

In Chapter 6 of "Portrait of a Worshiper,"[59] I explained that confirmation Scriptures could be found in one of four forms. They are

---

[59] Stone Shamblin, *Portrait of a Worshiper* (Westbow Press, 2018).

commandments, exhortations, examples, and prophecy. I would like to give you some validating scriptures concerning the new song in each of those categories.

Commandment

> *Sing unto him a new song; play skillfully with a loud noise. Psalm 33:3 (KJV)*

Musical instruments should accompany the new song whenever possible.

Exhortation (which means to encourage)

> *O sing unto the Lord a new song: sing unto the Lord, all the earth. Psalm 96:1 (KJV)*

> *O sing unto the Lord a new song; for he hath done marvelous things: his right hand, and his holy arm, hath gotten him the victory. Psalm 98:1 (KJV)*

Example

> *I will sing a new song unto thee, O God: upon a psaltery and an instrument of ten strings will I sing praises unto thee. Psalm 144:9 (KJV)*

Notice the mention of the two categories of songs we are to sing: new songs and praises.

Prophetic

I put these scriptures under the prophetic category because they are found in Revelation, which is a prophetic book of things to come.

> *And they sung a new song, saying, Thou art worthy to take the book, and to open the seals thereof: for thou*

wast slain, and hast redeemed us to God by thy blood out of every kindred, and tongue, and people, and nation; Revelation 5:9 (KJV)

And they sung as it were a new song before the throne, and before the four beasts, and the elders: and no man could learn that song but the hundred and forty and four thousand, which were redeemed from the earth. Revelation 14:3 (KJV)

THE NEW SONG AS PRAISE

God will give us a new song to serve two distinct purposes. The first purpose is to praise Him spontaneously. Here is a Scriptural example of this.

And they sung a new song, saying, Thou art worthy to take the book, and to open the seals thereof: for thou wast slain, and hast redeemed us to God by thy blood out of every kindred, and tongue, and people, and nation. Revelation 5:9 (KJV)

This new song is obviously directed toward God and is being sung by a group of people (not angels) in heaven. We know this is a new song, because it is identified as such right in the scripture. This type of new song is praise to our God. In other words, we can sing prewritten praise songs to God, as well as spontaneous, Spirit-given, new songs of praise to God.

I don't want to take the time to reprint any more of this chapter in Revelation, but you should read Revelation 5:8–14. In it, you will see these groups of beings listed:

1. the four beasts and four and twenty elders
2. many angels, ten thousand times ten thousand
3. every creature which is in heaven,
4. and on the earth,

5. and under the earth,
6. and such as are in the sea, and all that are in them

In the context of this new song, each of these groups were heard singing different words, and probably different melodies, at the same time. This is the biblical precedent for us to sing a new song of praise to God at the same time as the rest of the church. This type of new song of praise can be sung in our private worship times or in the gathering of the church. In that case, everyone in the congregation will receive their own new song from God's Spirit, and we should sing it out loud at the same time along with everyone else. Because everyone is receiving their new song from the Holy Spirit, what you will experience is a harmonious symphony of sound.

THE NEW SONG AS PROPHESY

The second type of new song is a song of prophecy, where one individual sings in the first person as God with a message from God to the church. Prophecy is one of the gifts of the Holy Spirit mentioned in 1 Corinthians 12. I believe that all of the gifts of the Holy Spirit are vital in today's church. However, prophecy is the most important spiritual gift.

> *Pursue love, and desire spiritual gifts, but especially that you may prophesy. 1 Corinthians 14:1 (NKJV)*

Prophesying to music has always been God's preferred method. Let me share with you several scriptures that show you what I mean. In David's tabernacle, David knew the importance of prophesying to music, so he appointed specific people to do that.

> *¹Moreover David and the captains of the host separated to the service of the sons of Asaph, and of Heman, and of Jeduthun, who should **prophesy with** harps, with psalteries, and with cymbals: and the number of the workmen according to their service was:*

*²Of the sons of Asaph; Zaccur, and Joseph, and Nethaniah, and Asarelah, the sons of Asaph under the hands of Asaph, which **prophesied** according to the order of the king.*

*³Of Jeduthun: the sons of Jeduthun; Gedaliah, and Zeri, and Jeshaiah, Hashabiah, and Mattithiah, six, under the hands of their father Jeduthun, who **prophesied with a harp**, to give thanks and to praise the Lord. 1 Chronicles 25:1–3 (KJV), emphasis added*

Defining God's Music

Before David's tent, prophecy had always been associated with music. Centuries before David, the Jewish nation had what was called the school of the profits.[60] Tradition tells us that the curriculum of this school did not only include how to hear from God but also how to play different musical instruments. The reason for that is because it is much easier to prophesy in the atmosphere of worship where the Spirit of God dwells.[61]

When Saul was being anointed as king of Israel, Samuel prophesied a very specific word over him. Here is part of that prophecy. It gives us a glimpse of the day-to-day activities of the school of the profits.

---

[60] 2 Kings 2:5
[61] Psalm 22:3

> *⁵After that thou shalt come to the hill of God, where is the garrison of the Philistines: and it shall come to pass, when thou art come thither to the city, that thou shalt meet a **company of prophets** coming down from the high place with a **psaltery**, and a **tabret**, and a **pipe**, and a **harp**, before them; and they shall **prophesy**:*
> *⁶And the Spirit of the Lord will come upon thee, and thou shalt **prophesy** with them, and shalt be turned into another man. 1 Samuel 10:5–6 (KJV), emphasis added*

The group of profits had just come from a high place, which was a place of worship. It is safe to say that they were continuing to worship God by playing their instruments, on their way home. Being accustomed to singing a new song of prophecy, their worship was mixed with prophetic songs as they traveled. Saul was neither a prophet nor a musician, but in the setting of Spirit-saturated worship, Saul was turned into another man than who he was normally.

A worship leader's responsibility includes releasing the new song of praise and prophecy in the congregation. In the setting of anointed worship, it will be easy for anyone to prophesy, even those who have never done it before, like we see happened to Saul.

Another instance of prophetic song in the Bible is in the story of Elisha in 2 Kings 3. The king of Moab "rebelled" against the king of Israel, so the king of Israel asked the king of Judah and the king of Edom to fight with him against the king of Moab. These three armies set out on a seven-day journey with no water for the troops or their animals. Realizing their mistake, they asked if there was a prophet in the land that they could inquire of the Lord through the profit.

One of king of Israel's servants mentioned that Elisha lived nearby. Elisha had been Elijah's servant and had received his anointing when Elijah was taken up into heaven. Even the great Elisha asked for someone to worship God through music before he began to prophesy.

> *But now bring me a minstrel. And it came to pass, when the minstrel played, that the hand of the Lord came*

upon him. And he said, Thus saith the Lord, Make this valley full of ditches. 2 Kings 3:15–16 (KJV)

OTHER BIBLICAL NAMES FOR THE NEW SONG

There are two other names found in the Bible for the new song. In the Old Testament, the new song is also called the "song of the Lord." In the New Testament, the new song is also called the "song of the Lamb." We read in 2 Chronicles 29 about King Hezekiah coming to reign at 25 years old. God put it on his heart to restore the kingdom back to God. Hezekiah cleaned up the temple of God and restored it to the way it was at the time of King David.

> *And he set the Levites in the house of the Lord with cymbals, with psalteries, and with harps, according to the commandment of David, and of Gad the king's seer, and Nathan the prophet: for so was the commandment of the Lord by his prophets. And the Levites stood with the instruments of David, and the priests with the trumpets. 2 Chronicles 29:25–26 (KJV)*

Since we read that David appointed his worship team to prophesy using their musical instruments,[62] we understand that King Hezekiah also restored David's commandments for that to his worship team, which we just read about. King Hezekiah then ordered the priests and Levites to offer animal sacrifices upon the altar. The song of the Lord began when they first started offering the sacrifices to God, and this spontaneous new song of praise continued until all of the sacrifices were consumed.

> *And Hezekiah commanded to offer the burnt offering upon the altar. And when the burnt offering began, the **song of the Lord** began also with the trumpets, and with the instruments ordained by David king of Israel. And all*

---

[62] 1 Chronicles 25:1–3

the congregation worshipped, and the singers sang, and the trumpeters sounded: and all this continued until the burnt offering was finished. 2 Chronicles 29:27–28 (KJV), emphasis added

We know that this was a spontaneous new song of praise to the Lord, because the Bible tells us that this song started when the sacrifices began, and it continued for as long as the burnt offerings continued to burn. If this "song of the Lord" was a pre-composed song, there would be no way to coordinate that song to last exactly as long as the sacrifices burned. No composer would be able to anticipate the wind on that day and how long it would take for the burnt offering to be consumed. The only option is that the song of the Lord was a spontaneous new song of praise.

In the book of Revelation, we read several places where this type of spontaneous praise to God is called a new song. However, because the Lamb of God takes center stage in Revelation, this new song, this spontaneous worship of Almighty God, is also referred to as the song of the Lamb.

*And I saw as it were a sea of glass mingled with fire: and them that had gotten the victory over the beast, and over his image, and over his mark, and over the number of his name, stand on the sea of glass, having the **harps** of God. And they sing the **song of Moses** the servant of God, and the **song of the Lamb**, saying, Great and marvellous are thy works, Lord God Almighty; just and true are thy ways, thou King of saints. Revelation 15:2–3 (KJV), emphasis added*

John heard two different songs that day in heaven. The first was a prewritten song that he recognized to be the song that Moses wrote thousands of years ago. The song of Moses is found in Exodus 15:1–19. It's a long song by today's standards but was an average length song in its day. Here are just the first two verses of the song of Moses.

Then sang Moses and the children of Israel this song
unto the Lord, and spake, saying,
I will sing unto the Lord,
for he hath triumphed gloriously:
the horse and his rider
hath he thrown into the sea.
The Lord is my strength and song,
and he is become my salvation:
he is my God,
and I will prepare him an habitation;
my father's God,
and I will exalt him.
Exodus 15:1–2 (KJV), poetic structure added

The song of Moses is a prewritten praise song written in the psalm and spiritual song modes. The song of the Lamb is a spontaneous chädäsh praise song that John got to hear everyone in heaven sing. The words of this new song are recorded in Revelation 15:2–4.

MUSICAL KEY CENTERS AND THE NEW SONG

Remember that the three components of music are melody, harmony, and rhythm and that the fourth component of a song is the lyrics. These components make it possible for a group of people to sing and play prewritten songs together. Those components also aid in the releasing of the new song of praise and prophecy.

I gave you Scriptures to show that a new song can be sung by a group of people all at the same time. In that situation, every person is receiving and singing their own melody and lyrics from the Lord. This works best when the instrumentalists provide the key center for the vocalists to sing in. However, in the absence of instrumentalists, simultaneous multiple key centers being sung in by the vocalists can be very beautiful as well.

Most groups, however, will not be able to maintain a new song in multiple key centers for very long. The weaker singers will end up adjusting their key center to the key the stronger singers are singing.

If instruments are being played, all vocalists will gravitate to the key center the instruments are playing in. When you realize this, you will understand how important the instruments are in the releasing of the new song, and you will simply use the instrumentalists to guide the vocalists into the key center you are desiring.

THE ARHYTHMIC NEW SONG

This is a new song that has no specific rhythm or harmony structure. It's easy to release this type of new song at the end of a prewritten song of praise.

Ninety-nine percent of all prewritten songs end on the key center chord of that song. To release this type of new song, simply have the instrumentalists continue to play that final chord in a free rhythmic pattern. This could be arpeggios on the piano or keyboard, random strumming on the guitars and bass, and rolls and swells on the cymbals or drums.

Let God orchestrate this new song by having everyone on the worship team and in the congregation be sensitive to the Holy Spirit's leading. He will tell you when to get loud and when to get quiet. He will also let you know when that new song is over.

THE STRUCTURED NEW SONG

This is a new song that God will lead to take on a specific musical structure. By that I mean a specific rhythm, chord progression, and harmonic rhythm.

Usually, this type of new song will maintain the rhythm and feel of the prewritten song it follows—but not always. If the previous prewritten song has a certain repeating chord progression, the instrumentalists may be led by God to simply carry that chord progression on in the rhythm of the previous song. If the prewritten song has a complex chord progression, it is not recommended that you carry it on into the new song. Simplicity is very important in releasing a new song in your congregation!

As a worship leader, when I sense the Holy Spirit leading the worship team and congregation to do a structured new song in the middle of our preplanned, prewritten song list, it is my responsibility to hear from God and lead that new song. As the primary worship leader, I am responsible for hearing from God as to how every new song's structure should be, which God gives us when I am leading worship. That does not mean that I am the only one who can receive a new song from God! That is not what I am saying at all!

When God releases a new song to a worship team or congregation, he delights in giving parts of that song to people we would least expect God to use in that way. Therefore, my job as a worship leader and chief musician in those moments is to be sensitive to the Holy Spirit as to who He is using at any given time and make a place for them in the corporate setting of worship. That requires me as well as every worship leader to function prophetically.

Once I have heard from God concerning the structure of a new song, I lead the worship team into that structure using two tools. The first tool is the musical beat patterns (music conducting skills), and the second tool is the chord number hand signals.

First of all, I will use the musical beat patterns, which have existed for centuries, to direct my instrumentalists in the rhythm and tempo of the new song. Using musical beat patterns when leading multiple instrumentalists and singers is essential for conveying tempo and the rhythmic structure of a new song to your worship team.

The most important reason for using musical beat patterns is so that everyone knows when the down beat is. Untrained leaders will set the tempo of a new song by simply waving their hand up and down at the speed they desire, but that type of undefined beat pattern does not let anyone know when the first beat of the musical measure is. With the musical beat patterns, the first beat of each measure is always down, and all the other beats are not down.

In addition to directing the rhythmic aspects of a new song, the worship leader is responsible to hear from God concerning the harmonic aspects of the new song as well. By that, I mean the chord progression and how often the chords should change (which is called the harmonic rhythm).

If the new song is a structured new song where everyone is singing at the same time, the worship leader should set the chord progression by the Holy Spirit's leading. If the new song is a solo prophetic song or solo new song of praise, the worship leader must discern the chord progression of the new song by listening to the melody. The melody will give you the indication as to which cords should be played and when they should change. To discern the chord changes of a solo new song requires musical knowledge and the ability to hear from God. Once the worship leader determines the chords of a solo new song, they should indicate the chords to their instrumentalists by the hand signal numbers.

Many worship leaders have skilled instrumentalists who can hear those chord changes more quickly than they can. If that is your case, the primary instrumentalist should verbally (not on a mic) tell the worship leader the chords they are playing, so the worship leader can give the chords to the rest of the worship team instrumentalists. However, to avoid the Babylonian pattern, learn how to hear the chord changes for yourself as quickly as you possibly can.

When leading the worship team in these new songs, use your primary hand (I am right-handed) to do the beat patterns and your secondary hand to show the chords the instrumentalists should play.

CHORD NUMBERS

If you do not understand basic music theory, you have no business being a primary worship leader. Here is a brief summary of the harmonic principles of music you will need to know as a primary worship leader. This summary, however, is in no way meant to take the place of a more complete study of music theory.

Our songs in the western part of the world are based on the eight-tone diatonic scale. These scales will either be major or minor. For every scale or key center, we can play chords starting on every note of the scales.

A basic musical chord is called a triad and is made up of three notes: the root note of the chord, which the chord is named after; a major or minor third above the root note; and a perfect fifth above the root note. The third of the chord defines the chord as either a major chord or a minor chord.

Here are the basic chords of the C major scale. Remember, the C scale has no sharps or flats in its key signature. All major chords are indicated with capital roman numerals, while all minor chords are indicated with lowercase roman numerals. We do not include the xii° chord because it is a diminished chord and is very seldom used in simple western music.

Table 14. Triads of the C Major Scale

Scale → Chords ↓	C	D	E	F	G	A	B	C
I	C		E		G			
ii		D		F		A		
iii			E		G		B	
IV				F		A		C
V		D			G		B	
vi			E			A		C

Triads of the C Major Scale

In all major keys, the I, IV, and V chords are always major chords, and the ii, iii, and vi chords are always minor chords.

Again, to indicate to my instrumentalists the structure of a new song, I set the rhythm with my primary hand, and with my secondary hand I indicate the chord numbers we are to play. To indicate chords one through five, simply hold up the number of fingers representing the chord desired. However, to indicate a six chord, you must use the American Sign Language (ASL) sign for that number. It is done by touching the thumb and pinkie

six

together. Of course, if you are going to do six that way, you must also do three in ASL as well so those two numbers are not confused. Three is formed with the thumb and first two fingers like this.

Concerning the harmonic rhythm, ninety-nine percent of the time, I will set it to change on the down beat of every measure. That keeps the structure simple, which is very important when releasing a new song.

three

195

When giving the signal for a chord change, I show the next chord number slightly before I want it to be played. That is so the instrumentalists have time to prepare for that chord. Then I use the preparatory beat and beat I want the chord played on with the hand I am showing the chord number, so there is no doubt as to when I want that chord played. That requires that a worship leader be able to walk and chew gum at the same time. What I mean by that is you have to do two different things with your hands at the same time.

Different chord progressions will represent different moods of, or messages from, the Holy Spirit. Here are several chord progressions I recommend you have your instrumentalists play through several times while you have your vocalists sing new songs over the top of those progressions. After you have done this for a few minutes and God says it is OK to stop, discuss with your worship team what each chord progression seemed to communicate or represent. It is OK if the same chord progression communicates different things to different people. God knows everyone thinks and communicates differently at different times. You are doing this exercise so that you begin to understand how God communicates through the language of music. Just like words can have different meanings in different settings, so can musical sounds represent more than one thing, depending on the setting of that sound.

SOME SUGGESTED NEW SONG CHORD PROGRESSIONS

INSTRUCTIONS: Consider all these progressions here to be in 4/4 time, unless otherwise indicated. Ask the Holy Spirit what key you should play these exercises in, as well as the tempo they should be in. You may want to try them in several different keys and tempos.

Play each chord for four beats. Once you have played through all of the chords in the pattern, repeat the pattern until the Holy Spirit tells you to stop. Ask your vocalists to sing any melodies and words the Holy Spirit gives them to go with these chord progressions. They can all sing a new song at the same time or take turns singing a solo new song one of a time.

After playing each of these progressions, before going to the next progression, discuss among yourselves what the sound of that chord progression seems to communicate to your spirit. You will find that meanings will change depending on the key and tempo you play them in.

Chord Progressions

a.   I, IV
b.   I, ii, iii, ii, I
c.   IV, V, IV, V, I, I
d.   I, bVII*, IV, V

In C, it would be a major Bb chord made up of Bb D F. In G, it would be an F major chord made up of F A C.

e.   I, vi, IV, V
f.   I, ii, iii, IV
g.   I, ii, iii, IV, V
h.   IV, ii, iii, vi

Combinations of chord progressions are practically limitless, because of the multiple combinations of cords that are available to us. Ask God to give you other chord progressions to worship him and prophesy with. Change the rhythm from four beats per measure to three beats per measure. After you learn about different musical feels, try them out on the chord progressions to see what those sounds communicate to the listeners.

THE PROGRESSIVE NEW SONG

I have been in many worship services where the new song continued for long periods of time without stopping. It may have started with the arhythmic new song, then progressed into a simple chord progression and rhythmic structure, and then evolved over time into multiple different chord progressions and rhythms.

Let me describe one of those experiences to you to help you understand what I am talking about. The new song began as an arhythmic new song on the I chord of a prewritten song we had just sung. After a few minutes of this "free praise," the worship leader began to sense that the Holy Spirit wanted to change that into a structured new song. He then began to beat a 4/4 beat pattern, indicating an I chord for four beats, then an IV chord for four beats. Once the instrumentalists were established in that structure, he stopped giving them direction to simply let them flow in the Holy Spirit. When he made those changes, the difference in the new song that God was giving people throughout the room was audible.

That musical structure continued for several minutes. Then one of the singers stepped to their mic and began to sing a solo prophetic new song from God. The melody of that prophetic song did not follow the harmonic structure we had been singing in, but it took on a completely new pattern of harmony and rhythm. The worship leader quickly detected the new musical patterns and began indicating the chords that went with the new song melody and the rhythm changes by using the beat pattern.

After that prophetic new song was finished, the worship leader led the instruments into an I, IV, V, V7 chord structure to accompany the congregation's new song of praise. That pattern continued for several minutes, until another singer on the worship team stepped up to a microphone and began to sing a solo new song of praise to the Lord. That new song had a completely unique feel and chord progression. The rhythm changed from four beats per measure to three beats per measure and was being sung in a lilting sort of way. Not only that, the melody indicated a chord progression that rocked back and forth from an IV to a V chord several times before it resolved to the I chord.

The worship leader quickly discerned those changes in the music and began indicating them to the instrumentalists. When this new song of praise was finished, the worship leader skillfully took the instrumentalists back into four beats per measure, but adopted the IV, V, IV, V, I, I chord structure based on the previous solo new song's chord progression. That chord progression carried with it a strong anointing, which released the congregation into a five-minute-long structured new song, where high praises ushered in a near-tangible presence of the Holy Spirit.

After at least five minutes of those high praises, I noticed a woman walking down the far aisle toward the front of the church. When she reached the front of the church, I saw her say something to the worship leader, and he indicated to her to step up to one of the microphones. As he did that, he raised his hand, and pointing his palm downward, he slowly lowered his hand. That indicated to his instrumentalists to bring the volume down.

Because the woman was unskilled in music, she began singing a melody of a new song of praise in a completely different musical key center than what we had been in for the last 30 minutes. When the worship leader realized that, he cut all the instruments off and pointed to the piano player. I learned later that the worship leader was asking the piano player to figure out the key center the woman was singing in.

Once the piano player figured out the key she was in, he verbally told the worship leader the key. However, because it would distract from the focus on the woman's new song of praise, the worship leader had to use hand signals to indicate to the rest of the instrumentalist what key to play in. I will go over those hand signals in a later chapter. Once everyone knew the key center to play in, the worship leader was able to return to giving cord numbers to the instrumentalists so they could accompany her new song. As they supported her in her song, you could see her losing her nervousness and gaining boldness and confidence to sing with all her might.

After that solo new song of praise, the worship leader took the instrumentalists back into an I, IV chord progression for the congregation to continue singing their new song of praise. However, because they were in a more difficult musical key, in just a few measures, the worship leader gave the instrumentalists the hand signal to transpose up into an easier musical key.

Shortly after that key change, the trumpeter in the orchestra stood up and began playing a new melody of praise unto God. Because the trumpeter had a background in jazz music, the structure of his new song melody, including both chords and rhythm, took on that feel. The worship leader not only indicated the chords that should be played, he also began directing the instrumentalists to play the chords in a syncopated rhythm.

The trumpeter's new song melody evolved from a jazz feel to a regal feel. The worship leader detected this change by the Spirit of God and directed the orchestra to make that change in real time with the trumpeter. As this new feel took over the new song, everyone felt God's presence once again come into the room stronger than before. Without anyone saying a word, we all knew that the King of kings had entered our place of worship. People began to respond appropriately. Some bowed, some knelt, some stood with their arms raised high, and some laid prostrate before the Lord's presence as they sang a new song.

Out of reverence, many became silent. Others continued singing a new song but were very quiet as they sang. The worship leader once again indicated to the instrumentalists to play quieter. He slowed the tempo way down and establish a bVI, bVII, I chord progression. (In the key of C, that would be an Ab major chord, a Bb major chord, and a C chord.) We could feel that spiritual intensity rise every time we've repeated that chord progression. We also found ourselves being led by the Holy Spirit to raise the volume each time we repeated that chord progression.

This building of sound and spiritual intensity continued for several minutes, until it was beyond loud in that place. At the Holy Spirit's leading, the worship leader indicated to the instrumentalist to hold the I chord, turning the new song back into an arhythmic new song like it had begun, with everyone shouting and clapping as the drummer played a several minute spontaneous drum solo, which was a Spirit-led new song as well. All that lasted more than 45 minutes. None of it was scripted or planned, but it was allowed to take place because the worship leader knew how to hear from God and facilitate what God wanted.

THE GOAL OF ALL WORSHIP

I have gone over this before, but it bears repeating as often as it takes to have it ingrained in our minds and hearts. Worship is not the goal. Worship is the means to an end. The end result of worship is to experience the dynamic, intimate, wonderful, manifest presence of Almighty God. That is the reason we sing our praises and new songs to God, and it is the reason we were commanded to sing!

Serve the Lord with gladness: ***come before his presence with singing****. Psalm 100:2 (KJV), emphasis added*

Praise is the dwelling place of God's presence. Praise is the way we invite God to manifest Himself in our gatherings.

> *But You are holy, Enthroned in the praises of Israel.*
> *Psalm 22:3 (NKJV)*

Our praises are the throne where God's presence sits in any gathering of God's people on the earth. In *The Importance of Worshiping Together* Chapter 1,[63] I showed you how God created music and singing to produce a greater unity among people that is not possible any other way. It is in the unity of God's people where God will manifest His presence. Here is an example of when God manifested Himself on the earth. Notice that this experience came when God's people were in unity.

> *[1]And when the day of Pentecost was fully come, they were all with **one accord in one place**. [2]And suddenly there came a sound from heaven as of a rushing mighty wind, and it filled all the house where they were sitting. [3]And there appeared unto them cloven tongues like as of fire, and it sat upon each of them. [4]And they were all filled with the Holy Ghost, and began to speak with other tongues, as the Spirit gave them utterance. Acts 2:1–4 (KJV), emphasis added*

You have to be in one place to be in unity. Virtual church is not biblical church!

So then, the goal of our worship is to corporately experience God's presence. That means the reason we sing psalms, hymns, spiritual songs, new songs of praise, and prophetic new songs is to experience the manifest presence of God. That is why

> **The first responsibility of a worship leader is to bring the presence of God to the people of God, and to bring the people of God into the presence of God.**

I say a worship leader's first responsibility is to bring God's presence to God's people and to bring God's people into God's presence.

I have experienced many prewritten songs that have brought

---

[63] Stone, Shamblin. *The Importance of Worshiping Together* (LifeRich Publishing, 2020).

a congregation into the manifest presence of God, but I have never experienced the intensity of God's presence during a prewritten song the way I have during a new song. If your congregation is longing for more experiences of epic proportions of God's presence and miracles, you need to be leading them into the new song. A congregation that does not sing a new song will limit their experience of God's presence.

CONCLUSION

Many times throughout Scripture, we are commanded to "sing a new song and His praise." If all you do as a worship leader is lead prewritten songs, you are NOT obeying the Word of God.

Just as two-thirds of the prewritten praise songs you do need to be directed toward God, up to half of your worship time as a congregation should be spent singing a new song to the Lord!

Again, you have to be able to hear from God in the moment to be able to release and direct the new song. That is why I believe that every worship leader MUST flow in the prophetic gifts of the Holy Spirit, without exception! If you cannot hear God's voice, you are not qualified to be a worship leader—I don't care how much musical training you may have had.

Chapter Ten

"MUSIC CONDUCTING SKILLS"

LEARNING THE CONDUCTING SKILLS

This chapter is designed to give you an overview of the fundamentals of conducting music. Keep in mind that you must understand basic music theory if you are going to direct music ensembles of voices or instruments.

The rhythm part of music allows many singers and instrumentalists to make music together. Therefore, a music director's first responsibility is to lead the rhythm of a song. That requires you to understand the rhythm aspect of different note values and the musical time signature.

For this chapter, I will focus on the top number of the time signatures, which tells the number of beats there are in a measure. In this chapter, the beat pattern diagrams I give you will show only the beat patterns for the right hand. You should learn all of these beat patterns with both hands, even though the left hand is not shown. The beat patterns for the left hand should mirror the right hand. In other words, if the right hand moves to the center of the body, the left hand should also move to the center of the body. If the right hand moves away from the body, the left hand should also move away from the body.

Music conducting is a motor skill. Therefore, it must be practiced every day until it becomes automatic. The minimum amount of time you should spend practicing these conducting skills is one-half hour per day. I recommend you do that for at least three months when you are first learning them. That means you are practicing with both hands on all beat patterns, all entrances, and all cutoffs nonstop for one-half hour each day.

THE BEAT PATTERN FRAMES OR BOXES

The musical beat patterns are to be conducted inside a square box. The dimensions of that box will vary depending on the size of the person. The top border of the box is head height. The bottom border is slightly above the waist. The inside border is at the middle of the body. The middle point of the square, both up and down and sideways, is just outside the shoulder. The outside border is an equal distance from the shoulder out as it is from the shoulder into the center of the body.

Music Conducting Boxes

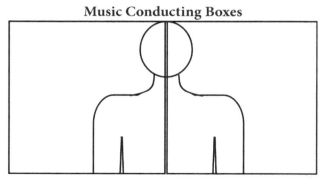

Right-Hand and Left-Hand Music Conducting Boxes

HOW TO HOLD YOUR HANDS

It is important to realize early in your study of music conducting that a conductor's main tool used in communicating with the musical ensemble is their hands. Other communication tools are the conductor's mouth, eyes, and face and sometimes the body language.

Because the hands are so important when conducting, how you hold your hands can indicate a multitude of different things. For all the beat patterns, your hands should be held with the palms facing down.

For most slow to medium tempos, you want to adopt the dragging hand technique. Think of that as the way a pantomime would show resistance as if they were moving their arm through a vat of molasses. As you move your arm down, the wrist bends and the hand points up, showing you have met with resistance, and the hand is trailing the arm through the resistance. Once you reach the bottom and start back up with your arm, the fingers will stay suspended in midair as the wrist begins to bend the other way. To show resistance, the wrist will bend the opposite way, and the fingers will point down as the arm moves up. When moving from side to side, the wrist will bend, always pointing the fingers in the opposite direction from where you are moving your arm.

However, this pantomime style movement does not work on the beat patterns when conducting the faster tempo. For faster tempos, simply keep your wrist rigid.

COMMON TIME

Seventy-five percent of all music is written in common time. Common time means there are four beats in each measure, and the quarter note gets one beat. Because four beats per measure is the most common in music, we will start by learning the four-beat pattern. Don't forget, these diagrams only show the pattern for the right-hand. Make sure you practice the mirrored pattern with the left hand as well. Practice both hands at the same time.

In this diagram, the solid lines represent the motion your hand makes going toward the beats. The dotted lines represent the rebounds after the beats, which put the hand in

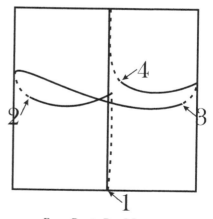

Four Beats Per Measure

the correct position for the following beat. The arrows on the diagram indicate the exact position where each beat takes place. There should always be the same amount of time between each of the four beats, including between beat four and beat one when going from one measure to the next.

Start this beat pattern with both hands at head height above your shoulders. Your elbows should not be straight but slightly bent, placing your hands about two feet in front of your face.

As you practice this beat pattern, you should count out loud the number of the beats. Counting out loud is only done in your personal practice times. Once you learn the beat patterns, your mind will be able to think of other things as you keep the patterns going.

Because you are practicing both hands at the same time, once in a while you should switch from saying the numbers of the beats to saying the actions of each beat. Beat one is always down with both hands. Beat two is always in with both hands. Your hands should almost touch in front of your sternum at the top of the rebound of beat two. Beat three is always out. And beat four is always in and up. Most of the time when practicing this beat pattern, you should say "one, two, three, four" as you beat the pattern. After a few measures, switch to counting the beats "down, in, out, in, and up" for a few measures. The word "in" is spoken on beat four.

WALTZ TIME

The next most common time signature in music is three beats per measure. All waltzes are written in this time signature. Even though there is no beat toward the inside of the body in this beat pattern, you still want the down beat to be in the center of your box from side to side. Resist the temptation to move the downbeat toward the center of your body.

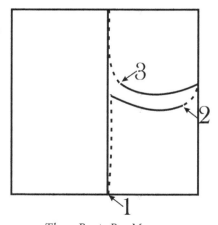

Three Beats Per Measure

Just like the first beat of every measure in all the different beat patterns must go straight down, the last beat of every beat pattern, no matter how many beats are in that measure, must always go in and up. That is why the second beat of a three-beat measure must go out and not in. When practicing this beat pattern, switch from counting the numbers "one, two, three" out loud to saying "down, out, in, and up" like you did on the four-beat pattern.

CUT TIME OR HALF TIME

These are measures with only two beats in them. Again, avoid any temptation to move the downbeat in or out from the center of your box. Because every downbeat must go down and every last beat of a measure must always go in and up, the rebound of the first beat needs to go out so your hand will be in position for the last beat to go in and up. Practice this beat pattern saying the beat numbers out loud, then switch to saying "down, in, and up."

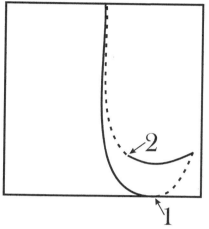

Two Beats Per Measure

PRACTICING YOUR CONDUCTING SKILLS

When you practice these beat patterns, do them nonstop for about twenty to thirty minutes each day. That does not mean you do each beat pattern or skill for thirty minutes, but that all of your practicing time should equal about thirty minutes each day. Depending on what you need to work on, divide that time up accordingly.

Download a metronome app, and choose a different random tempo each day between 40 PBM and 220 BPM, and do all of your conducting skills in that day's chosen tempo. Practice doing each of the three basic beat patterns for five minutes without stopping to change the pattern. Change your beat pattern after three to five minutes, until you have practiced all the beat patterns you are learning. Let one beat pattern flow into the next when it is time to change. In other words, do not stop for about twenty minutes. For the last ten minutes of your practice, work on the entrances and cutoffs for each beat.

THE PREPARATORY BEATS

In addition to directing the tempo and time signature of a song, a musical leader is responsible for directing several other important aspects of a song. Two of the most important are when to sing or play and when not to sing or play. We call those entrances and cutoffs. The reason the music leader directs those actions is so that everyone in the choir and orchestra will do them at the same time.

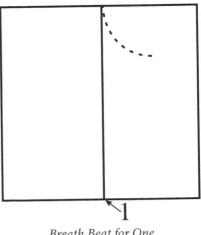

Breath Beat for One

Since songs or musical phrases will start on every possible beat within a measure, a leader needs to know how to bring the singers and instruments in on every beat and off-beat of every different measure of music. The key to that is to always give your ensembles a moment to prepare mentally to sing or play. For the singers and wind Instruments, this preparatory beat is also when they fill up with air. That is why this is sometimes called a "breath beat."

The simple explanation of how to do breath beats is to move your hand in the opposite direction of the beat you are starting on. Practice each of those breath beats and entrances starting on all four of the beats of a common time musical measure. By learning these, you should be able to adapt them to every beat and off-beat you encounter in music.

Notice where your hand starts inside your box for each beat. It is very important that you start with your hand in the right position. Always do the preparatory beat in the same tempo that you want your song to be in. When practicing these entrances, do them followed by completing the measure of four

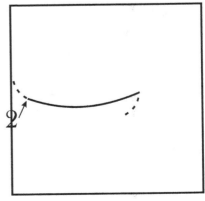

Breath Beat for Two

beats, (e.g., 2, 3, 4), then beat one complete measure of four beats after that. Also, make sure you practice those entrances with both hands at the same time. Don't forget to count the number of the beats out loud. Make sure you do those in the tempo of the day that you have chosen.

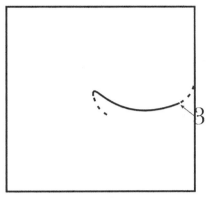

Breath Beat for Three

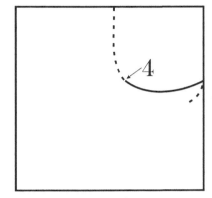

Breath Beat for Four

THE CUTOFFS

Just like you must prepare your musical ensembles to be ready to come in on time, you must also prepare them for when they are to stop singing or playing. That preparation is shown in two ways. The first thing you do is turn your palm up. The second thing you do is make a circle with your hand, as shown here. As you are doing the circle, your palm is turning over so

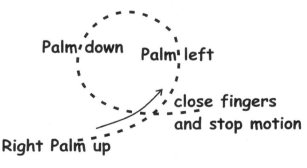

Cut Off With the Right Hand

that when you complete the circle, the palm is once again facing down.

Also, to show the exact moment you want the music to stop, you stop your hand motion at the end of the circle and close the thumb and forefinger together at that moment. It is also permissible to close your entire hand into an ASL hand sign for the letter "S," which represents "stop."

Here are the cutoffs for the right hand for the common time signature. Practice them with both hands at the same time. Beat one full measure of four, then the measure with the cut off. Count the numbers of the beats out loud and say the word "off" as you perform the cutoff motion I

S for Stop

described above. The cutoff will take place in rhythm where the next beat would come. If you are cutting off on three, you would count "1, 2, 3, off." That allows the third beat to have its full time value before you cut it off.

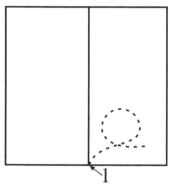

Right Hand Cutoff on One

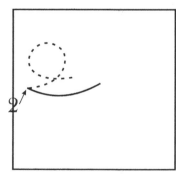

Right Hand Cutoff on Two

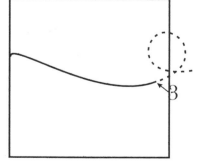

Right Hand Cutoff on Three

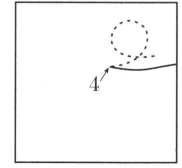

Right Hand Cutoff on Four

DUPLE RHYTHM

There are two ways to divide the beats within a measure of music. The first way is in half, and the second way is in thirds. Dividing the beats into half is what we call a duple rhythm. Dividing beats in thirds is called triple rhythm, or compound rhythm.

If this song you are doing has a duple feel but you want to divide a beat in the song into thirds, you would insert what is called a triplet. If the song is in triple feel and you want to divide a beat in half instead of thirds, you would insert what is called a duplet.

To direct the faster tempos in duple rhythm, simply use the regular beat patterns for measures of two, three, and four. However, count the divided beats by adding an "and" halfway between each number. Toggle back and forth between counting "1, 2, 3, 4" as you direct and "1&, 2&, 3&, 4&" in the same tempo. Make sure the numbers occur on the beats and the "ands" are halfway between the beats. It is also possible to divide each beat one more time. That is counted "1ee&uh, 2ee&uh, 3ee&uh, 4ee&uh." Practice that as well, but make sure you do not vary the tempo of the numbers. Each number must happen exactly on the beat.

To direct a slow or medium tempo song in duple feel, these are the beat patterns you would use. These patterns are not practical if the song tempo is fast. Do not direct more than one division per beat. If you need to divide the beats again, simply count them as you did in the faster tempos, but don't change the beat pattern again. Practice those beat patterns only on the slower and moderate tempos with both hands the way I have described previously.

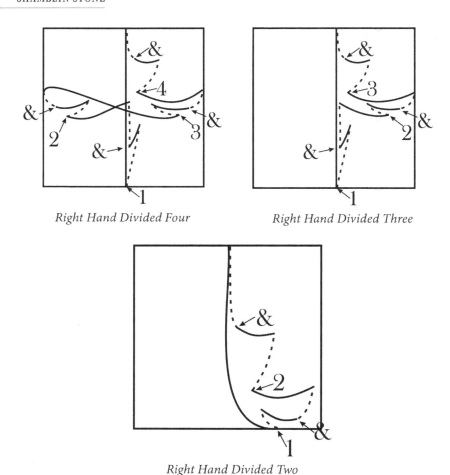

Right Hand Divided Four

Right Hand Divided Three

Right Hand Divided Two

TRIPLE OR COMPOUND RHYTHMS

The compound or triple rhythms in music simply use the three basic beat patterns without directing the beat divisions like we do when directing the slow duple feels. In addition to that, we change the time signatures so that the eight note gets one beat. The number of beats per measure will be multiples of three, six, nine, and twelve.

Because you already know the beat patterns, what you will need to learn by directing these time signatures is how to count the beats with the beat patterns. This is how those compound rhythms are directed and counted.

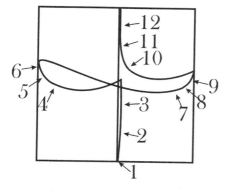

*Right Hand Compound
Twelve Beats*

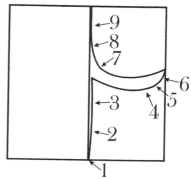

*Right Hand Compound
Nine Beats*

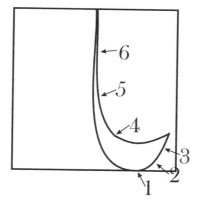

Right Hand Compound Six Beats

The only exception to this rule is when you are conducting a slow to medium 6/8 measure. In that case, this is how you would direct it.

Practice all of those beat patterns the way I have told you to do the others. Make sure you count out loud, conduct with both hands in a mirrored fashion, and keep the beats steady in the tempo of the day.

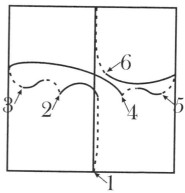

Right Hand Slow Six Beats

ASYMMETRICAL BEAT PATTERNS

Very seldom will you encounter measures like these in music. However, they do exist, so I would like for you to be familiar with how to direct them when you encounter them. Practice them some, but definitely do not give them as much attention as the other beat patterns.

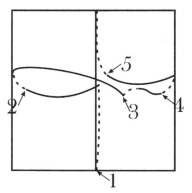

Right Hand Five Beats   Right Hand Seven Beats

ADVANCED MUSIC CONDUCTING SKILLS

What I've covered so far in this chapter is just the introduction to music conducting. I do not intend to get into the advanced studies of conducting in this chapter. I will say, however, that the primary hand is responsible for maintaining the beat pattern, and the secondary hand is responsible for all the entrances, cutoffs, and expressions. Also, before you are going to give someone direction, you should look at them first to let them know something is coming.

Chapter Eleven
"NONVERBAL COMMUNICATION"

WORSHIP LEADING HAND SIGNALS

In addition to the music conducting skills, a worship leader has several other things they must communicate to their worship team. Because verbal cues and directions in the middle of a worship experience would be very distracting, I recommend that all worship leaders adopt hand signals.

I will give you the hand signals I use, many of which have their origin in American Sign Language. I picked up these from my wife, who taught sign language at the college level for many years. I wish I could tell you that worship leader hand signals are universal, like the music conducting techniques, but unfortunately they are not. Some of these signals are widely used, and others may simply be unique to me. If you have other hand signals that you already use, feel free to continue using them. If you do not have hand signals for all of these situations, I recommend adopting mine.

Give hand signals in such a way that all of the singers, instrumentalists, projectionists, A/V personnel, and movement ministries are in sync. The congregation will begin to pick up on these hand signals as well, but they are not the reason you give them. Remember, the worship leader leads the secondary worship leaders, who then lead the congregation.

STOP

I introduced this to you in the last chapter. The sign language "S" is widely used among musicians for "stop." Use this signal a few bars before you want to stop, so everyone can prepare. Then use the cutoffs I showed you to cut everyone off at the same time.

S for Stop

MUSICAL DYNAMICS DIRECTION

To indicate you want more volume from the vocalists or instruments, turn your palm up and move your hand upward as aggressively as you desire the volume to change. To indicate you want less volume, turn your palm down and move your hand downward, showing the amount of the volume adjustment needed by the intensity of your movement.

EQUIPMENT VOLUME ADJUSTMENTS

If the volume of a microphone needs to be turned up, look toward or catch eye contact with the sound person, point to the mic needing adjustment, then give a thumbs-up while moving your hand up a couple of inches. If the volume needs to go up quite a bit, do that gesture twice or even three times if necessary. Please understand, when you are asking the sound person for volume changes, you are only asking the individual to change the volume in the monitors. The sound person has final say over the sound mix in the main speakers.

Likewise, if you want the overall volume in the monitors to go up, point to a monitor speaker or an in-ear monitor and make the thumbs-up gesture I just described. You can avoid having to use those hand signals if you provide a monitor system with individual volume controls. If you want decreased volume on a particular microphone or the

Less Volume

216

overall monitor mix, DO NOT indicate that with a thumbs-down hand signal. Historically, kings did that hand gesture to indicate a death sentence. To indicate less volume for a mic or overall monitor mix, catch eye contact with the sound person, point at the mic or monitor, hold your thumb and forefinger wide apart vertically with the finger above the thumb, and close the gap between them by lowering the forefinger. That indicates to the sound person to "pull the slider down" for that mic or the monitors.

SONG SECTIONS

Songs will follow multiple different forms. A song form is identified by its line groupings. The most typical song form has verses, a chorus, and a bridge. Often it becomes necessary to let the worship team know which line grouping you are going to sing next. Here's the way you would indicate to your worship team where you want to go next.

C for Chorus

To show your team you want to do the chorus of a song, do a sign language "C" with either hand. Always do the signs a few bars early so your worship team can anticipate where you are going. If there is only one verse in the song you are doing, to show your worship team you want to do the verse, simply use the sign language "V." If there is more than one verse in the song, show the "V" followed by the verse number you want to sing. Here are the numbers one through six in sign language. I doubt that you will need any higher numbers than six, but if you do, you can find sign language numbers on the internet. Although the number two and the letter "V" are the same sign, if you use that sign twice in a row,

V for Verse

your worship team should know that what follows the "V" will always be a number, not a letter.

ASL Numbers 1 - 6

B for Bridge

To indicate that you want to go to the bridge of a song, use a sign language "B." It resembles the number four, but the fingers are together, not spread apart.

These days, worship songs can take on any number of different forms. Some songs have multiple choruses and bridges as well as verses. If that is the case, simply use the numbers to identify which chorus or which bridge you want to go to.

Some songs have adopted the use of a pre-chorus. To show that you want to go to the pre-chorus, first hold your hand vertical with the outside edge of your hand facing away from your body and your thumb beside your fingers closest to your body. Then do the sign language "C" right after that. If there are multiple pre-choruses, follow these signs with the number of the pre-chorus you want to go to.

If the song is an AABA form, here is the sign language sign for the letter "A."

If you want to repeat the entire song, there is a universal signal to indicate that and is not based in

A for A Section

sign language. I am not sure of the signal's origin, but I believe it dates back to early radio days when all music was performed by a live band or

From the Top

orchestra. This signal is drawing a circle in the air with your index finger. It stands for "from the top," which means go back to the beginning. Back then, musicians played from sheet music, and the top meant the top of the first page of the music.

To repeat the last line or phrase of a song, turn the wide sign language "G" up like this. This sign represents "do only this much." If you have not had the chance to rehearse this repeat, the worship team will have to anticipate where you are going back to or wait on the vocal cue to know how much of the last line(s) is to be repeated. If you have had the chance to

Repeat Last Line

define the repeat in rehearsal, the worship team will know exactly where to go back to when you give the team this sign. On the rare occasions that you would like to repeat just the last phrase or words of the song, shorten the distance between your thumb and forefinger to show you want to do a smaller amount of words.

CHANGING KEYS

First, in the up-tempo section of your worship service, avoid modulating down from the key you are in, unless you cannot avoid that. Modulating down reduces the energy level. Of course, you may want to use this technique when moving into the slower section of your worship service to reduce the energy on purpose.

Second, you and your worship team need to know the musical key signatures. That is basic music theory knowledge. A key signature is found at the beginning of each line of music on the staff. For the key of "C," there are no sharps or flats. For every other musical key, there will be a specific number of sharps or flats in the key signature. Here is a quick ledger of the major and minor key signatures.

Table 15. Key Signatures

KEY SIGNATURE	MAJOR KEY	RELATIVE MINOR KEY
NO sharps or flats	C	Am
1 sharp	G	Em
1 flat	F	Dm
2 sharps	D	Bm
2 flats	Bb	Gm
3 sharps	A	F#m
3 flats	Eb	Cm
4 sharps	E	C#m
4 flats	Ab	Fm
5 sharps	B	G#m
5 flats	Db	Bbm
6 sharps	F#	D#m
6 flats	Gb	Ebm
7 sharps	C#	A#m
7 flats	Cb	Abm

I do not recommend that you expect your instrumentalists to be able to play in every one of those key signatures. Professional musicians may be expected to know how to play in all of those keys, but volunteer musicians should not have to do that. The most I expect from my worship team is for members to be able to play in four sharps and four flats. Once I was able to do music in five flats with my team, but that is the exception, not the rule. I recommend that you try to stay in the keys with three or fewer sharps or flats, and the fewer accidentals the better.

You need to establish with your worship team in rehearsal

which keys you will play music in and expect the instrumentalists to memorize those keys. These are the major key centers a well-rounded worship team should work toward being able to play in: C, D, Eb, E, F, G, Ab, A, Bb. Your team may need to strike some of those keys if they do not possess the skill level to play in all of them. For instance, if you have mostly guitars on your team, you may need to drop some keys with flat key signatures. If you mainly have piano or keyboard instruments, you may need to drop some of the sharp keys.

For the minor key centers a well-rounded worship team would not be expected to play in as many keys as it does in the major key centers. These are the minor keys you should attempt to the master: Cm, Dm, Em, Gm, Am.

Once your worship team has established the specific keys it will be playing in, to modulate up to the next key, the worship leader should simply give a thumbs-up sign in plenty of time for the instrumentalists to prepare for the modulation. If you are playing a song in the key of Eb and give a thumbs-up on the last line of the chorus followed by a sign language "C," that means you would repeat the chorus but modulate up to the E key. The thumbs-up means go to the next key established that you play in. In this instance, the thumbs-up means go up one half step. However, if you are playing in the F key and indicate to modulate up on the next chorus, you would modulate up to G, which is a full step up. That is because

Key of Eb

you established in rehearsal that you would not be playing in the keys of F# or Gb.

To recap, a simple thumbs-up can either mean to transpose up one half step or one full step, depending on which keys you have established in rehearsal that you will play music in.

To modulate up to any other key, you will need to show the key signature by giving the number of sharps or flats after you give the thumbs-up. To show the sharps, the numbers should be normal and face upward. To show the flats, the numbers should face down after the thumbs-up, as pictured here.

SONG SELECTION

If you want to go back to the previous song, hold your hand flat with the palm down, then turn the palm up to simulate turning back one page. If you want to go back two songs, simply make this gesture twice.

Previous Song

When it is time go to the next song on your list, use the sign language "H." The reason we do not reverse the "back one song" sign to make it mean "ahead one song" is because those signs would look too much alike and could cause confusion in the middle of worship. We use the sign language "H" because there will be no misconception with it as to where you want to go. This sign simply means "go to the next song." Some people say the "H" stands for "head" as in the word "ahead." Others say it means "hop to the next song." Whatever you want to think when you give the sign is OK. Just keep in mind it means to go to the next song. If you want to

Next Song

skip a song, make this sign then hop your entire hand foreword the distance of the length of your hand. If you want to skip two songs, hop this sign twice away from your body one hand length at a time.

NEW SONG

To indicate to your worship team that it should play a new song, hold your hand out with your palm facing down and your fingers spread apart. As you move your hand side to side, wiggle your fingers up and down, with each finger moving randomly, not in sync with the others. When you give this sign, the worship team should move into an arhythmic new song on the tonic chord of the prewritten song it just finished. Also, give this sign to your worship team before you are about to launch a structured new song so that the team will watch you for the tempo, rhythm, and chord changes. Also give this sign to the instrumentalist or vocalist you want to prophesy on their instrument or voice within the structured new song you are in at the moment. Practice this in a rehearsal setting before you implement it in a worship service. Only appoint those to prophesy in a service when God leads you to do so and only after you have given that person multiple chances to do so in a rehearsal setting! NEVER expect someone to sing or play a new song in the worship service if they have not freely done so within several rehearsal settings.

SUMMARY

Always remember to show all your hand signals in plenty of time so your worship team knows where you want to go. Also remember you are giving these signals to every member of your worship team, including the sound people and projectionists.

Chapter Twelve

"MUSIC FEELS"

MUSIC IS FELT AND HEARD

This written text is no substitute for hands-on musical training. Music is an audible medium; therefore, you must hear it to learn. However, there is something else we have discovered about music. The rhythm of music can be felt in our body.

In *The Importance of Worshiping Together* Chapter 1, I explained how music can be done with our spirit as well as our understanding. That means music effects all three parts of our being—spirit, soul, and body. The way the rhythm of music effects our body is the way music feels to us. That then explains how dancing to music came into being.

For centuries, the feeling of music was limited to the basic time signatures. However, over time, we began to develop different rhythms, which also gave music various feels.

This chapter is an overview of the different rhythmic feels available to be used in our worship music today. Keep in mind that you will not experience these different feels by just reading about them. You must hear music to feel it.

To convey these rhythms to you in this chapter, I will be using the traditional note values. If you are not familiar with music note values, you will need to learn them. I suggest you clap each of these examples so you can hear these rhythms.

MUSIC FEELS VERSES MUSIC STYLES

It is easy to mix up these two things. The way you tell them apart is think of music feels as having to do with the rhythm of music and music styles as having other factors in the music and presentation of the music that defines them.

For instance, a barbershop style of music, as well as most jazz music, is defined by the harmonies. Hip-hop or rap music does have a distinguished rhythm, but it is defined by being spoken throughout most of the song, not just the rhythms used. There can be multiple rhythms in hip-hop music. Country music is defined by its arrangement, the selection of musical instruments used, the vocal stylings, and the subject matter. You will find the same rhythms in country music that you find in all other styles of music. The musical feels can be applied across many musical styles or genres.

FOUR CATEGORIES OF MUSIC FEELS

There are four categories of music feels. These categories are 1) the straight or even feels, 2) the dotted feels, 3) the triple feels, and 4) the off-beat feels (also called the syncopated feels). Let's go over each of those categories. Keep in mind that you can do the different rhythmic feels at any tempo you choose.

THE STRAIGHT DUPLE FEELS

I introduced this concept in the last chapter. Duple rhythm is the musical term. Straight or even is the language used in recording studios. Here's what the straight four and straight eight rhythms look like when written in musical notes. Music in common time (4/4) has four beats per measure, and the quarter note gets one beat. That means there are four quarter notes in each measure. It takes two eight notes to equal one quarter note, so you can have exactly twice as many eighth notes in one measure.

Within the same song, you could have different instruments and voices doing the straight four and the straight eight at the same time. As a matter of fact, it is preferred to do it that way when arranging a song. You can also trade off throughout the song. Maintain variety throughout any musical arrangement.

It is also possible to divide the notes again and again. To divide eighth notes would give you sixteenth notes, which are very busy musically and should only be used once in a while.

To divide sixteenth notes would give you thirty-second notes, but they are not practical in most songs.

THE DOTTED FEELS

There are two different rhythms that fit into this category. The first is called the Shuffle, and the second is called the Swing. Those two music feels use dots beside notes to form their rhythm. A dot beside a note or rest receives half the value of the note or rest it is beside. Another way of saying it is that a dotted note or rest gets one and a half times its value.

The Shuffle is named for a lazy way to walk. If every time you take a step you slide your foot along the ground briefly and then put it down, that is a shuffle. There are two ways to notate and do a shuffle. The first way uses the dotted rhythm I was telling you about. Here is that rhythm.

The Dotted Shuffle

When this rhythm gets going, it resembles the human heart beat. The short note (sixteenth) leads the longer note, which happens on the beat. This is the traditional way to do a shuffle and can be laid over the straight rhythms for variety. However, the other way to do a shuffle is to use the triplet feel instead of the duple feel. I personally like this way to do the shuffle much better. It just feels more right to me. Here is the way it is notated.

The Triplet Shuffle

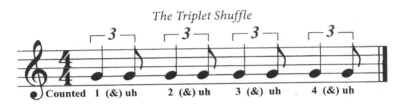

This way of doing the shuffle is not as driving or clinical. It has a more laid-back, natural feel to it, in my opinion. Using this version of the shuffle makes it very easy to overlay it on top of any of the triple family of time signatures.

The second dotted musical feel is called the Swing. It is a variation of the shuffle feel but with a distinguishable difference. Here is the way the swing is notated.

The Swing

In music, in common time, the first and third beats are the strongest. The downbeat is always the strongest beat of every measure, but the third beat is still much stronger than beats two and four. Because of that, the quarter notes in this pattern always seem stronger, and the dotted eighth and sixteenth notes are the lead in notes for beats one and three.

THE TRIPLE FEELS

I introduced these to you in the last chapter. Now let me show you how they are notated. The primary triple feel has three beats per measure, and the quarter note gets one beat. This time signature is also named for the way it feels when listening to it. It has been called a waltz for centuries. Again, the downbeat is the strong beat, and beats two and three are equally weak beats.

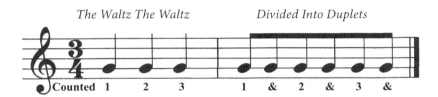

To divide a triple rhythm into duplets as indicated above will suppress the waltz feel. It is OK to divide random beats for the sake of notating lyrics, but it is not a good idea to design an entire song around this musical feel. It will produce an anxiousness in the listeners, because it is not easy to listen to for a prolonged time.

The basic rhythms of 2/2 or 2/4, 3/4, and 4/4 are divided into the triple feel by making the eight note get one beat, then changing the time signatures to 6/8, 9/8, and 12/8. Here is the way these are notated.

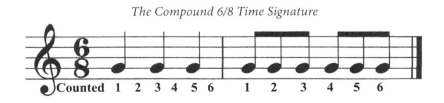

The first measure above with the three quarter notes feels like a measure of 3/4, because the downbeat is always the strongest beat in a measure. It is recommended that you do not write a complete song with quarter notes in a 6/8 time signature, because that destroys the waltz feel. Simply keep the time signature in 3/4 to maintain the waltz feel.

The second measure above is a true 6/8 triple feel or compound rhythm. In the 6/8 time signature, the first beat and the fourth beat of a measure are the strongest beats. Of course, the downbeat is always the strongest, but the second strongest in this measure is beat 4. Beats 2, 3, 5, and 6 are equally the weakest beats in the measure. This combination of strong and weak beats gives this its waltz feel. This triplet feel is maintained in measures of 9/8 and 12/8, the other compound rhythms.

The Compound 9/8 Time Signature

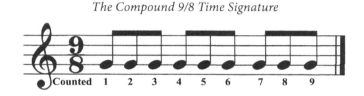

The Compound 12/8 Time Signature

THE SYNCOPATED FEELS

For centuries, these patterns of strong and weak beats have dominated our music. Then song writers and composers began to play around with changing these patterns. With their melodies and accents they begin to see if they could create music by violating those traditional strong and weak beats.

It was discovered that it is almost impossible to give importance to the weaker beats in all of these time signatures. That's when composers began experimenting with accenting the off beats. They found that it was easier to do that by accenting weak beats.

Once it was discovered that people can provide infinite variety in music by stressing different off beats, syncopation was born. The combinations of syncopated rhythm is so extensive that I will only introduce you to it in this chapter. In other words, I will only give you two or three examples of how syncopation can be used in music.

If you were to syncopate every beat in common time, it would look like this.

The Syncopated Beat

Reggae music pretty much follows this pattern. There are a multitude of Latin and African rhythms that adopt syncopation to one degree or another. Here are just a couple of examples. Notice how they flirt with the beats enough to maintain their integrity yet deviate enough from them to show the listener that these rhythms are different from the traditional ones.

A Basic Latin Beat

The Cha Cha Cha Beat

Chapter Thirteen
"THE WORSHIP FORMULA"

GOD SELDOM WORKS WITH FORMULAS

Human nature desires formulas—neat little packages of prethoughtout steps to follow to obtain a predictable result. For that reason, God has given us very few formulas in the Bible to use in our relationship with Him. God prefers that we have an ongoing total dependency upon Him in which we seek Him for everything in our lives. We seek His face for fellowship. We seek His hand for His unscheduled intervention in our lives. We seek His mind for wisdom and knowledge. And we seek His heart for love and holiness.

Formulas would not promote a relationship with God. Formulas would teach us to "use" God but not seek God. Formulas would show us God's power without requiring us to know His heart.

However, just because God has not given us many formulas does not mean He hasn't given us any formulas at all. There are two situations where God wants us to know that if we do certain things, it will have the same promised and predictable results every time.

Healing is not one of those formulas. It is not God's will to always heal. I have been healed many times but not every time. Prosperity is not one of those formulas. True riches are not measured by the earth's standards but by heaven's treasures. Happiness is not one of those formulas. There are only two things that I am aware of in the Bible that God has given us formulas for: His presence and defeating the enemy.

THE DELIVERANCE FORMULA

In the model prayer where Jesus was teaching His disciples how to pray, He taught them to pray this:

> *And lead us not into temptation, but **deliver** us from evil: For thine is the kingdom, and the power, and the glory, for ever. Amen. Matthew 6:13 (KJV), emphasis added*

Even before the disciples knew anything about the struggles they would have against demonic forces, Jesus taught them that they would need to be delivered out of these attacks. If you as a Christian have not yet been attacked by the enemy, don't worry, you will be. None of us will escape demonic attacks.

Because that is the case, God wanted to give us a way that we could experience deliverance from these attacks, so He gave us "The Deliverance Formula." Remember, a formula has a guaranteed result. If you follow a formula, it works every time. In the times when we are experiencing demonic attacks, God wants us to know there are some steps we can take that will insure our deliverance from any devil. Here is that formula in Scripture:

> *Submit yourselves therefore to God. Resist the devil, and he will flee from you. Draw nigh to God, and he will draw nigh to you ... James 4:7–8a (KJV)*

Anyone who has walked out this formula has experienced deliverance from their satanic attacks. I have never seen it fail! The reason it will not fail is because God put promises within this formula, what some may call guarantees. Those guarantees are attached to steps two and three of the formula.

234

Table 16. The Promises of the Deliverance Formula

Step #	Instruction	Promise
1	*Submit ... to God*	
2	*Resist the devil*	*he will flee from you*
3	*Draw nigh to God*	*He will draw nigh to you*

This three-step formula is progressive. That means you must do step one before you can do step two. If you do not do step one, the guarantee attached to step two is null and void. That also means it will be impossible to do step three and receive that promise as well.

Because the entire formula depends on step one, we have to seek out in Scripture what it means to submit to God. Keep in mind, the mysteries of God must always be searched out according to this Scripture.

> *It is the glory of God to conceal a thing: but the honor of kings is to search out a matter. Proverbs 25:2 (KJV)*

Even the only two formulas God gave us are given in such a way that they are not complete without us searching out their meanings. Also, the only way we know we have discovered their truth is by the Holy Spirit's confirmation.

> *(Jesus said) I have yet many things to say unto you, but ye cannot bear them now. Howbeit when he, the Spirit of truth, is come, **he will guide you into all truth**: for he shall not speak of himself; but whatsoever he shall hear, that shall he speak: and he will shew you things to come. John 16:12–13 (KJV), emphasis added*

So, what does it mean to submit to God? What is the secret to making this entire formula work? Let me briefly answer these questions for you so you are not left guessing.

According to 2 Corinthians 10, the effectiveness of demonic attacks against us is when we accept lies from our enemy as if they are truth. Then in 2 Timothy 2 we are told what to do if we have believed a lie.

> *In meekness instructing those that oppose themselves;
> if God peradventure will give them repentance to the
> acknowledging of the truth; And that they may recover
> themselves out of the snare of the devil, who are taken
> captive by him at his will.* 2 Timothy 2:25–26 (KJV)

There is a lot to unpack in those two Scriptures, however we will only focus on the two things necessary to complete the deliverance formula. The first thing we must do is repent for believing the specific lie the enemy told us. The second thing we must do is acknowledge the truth concerning that lie. That is how we recover ourselves. That is what gives us the legal right to resist the devil and know that he must flee from us every time.

THE WORSHIP FORMULA

Just like God wants us to know there is a way to defeat the devil whenever needed, God also wants us to know there is a guaranteed way to experience His presence. Remember I told you that worship is not the goal. The intimate presence of God is the goal, and worship is the way we experience God's presence, because God's presence inhabits our worship.[64]

There is, however, a bit more to this formula than to simply say we worship God to experience his presence. That is the equivalent of telling you to submit to God without telling you how to do so. Hidden in Scriptures are the details of this formula. I will start at Psalm 100. Verse two tells us that this Psalm is all about experiencing God's presence. Then in verse four we start to learn about the steps of the worship formula.

> *Enter into his gates with thanksgiving, and into his
> courts with praise: be thankful unto him, and bless his
> name.* Psalm 100:4 (KJV)

In this Psalm, David is explaining to us how to approach God's presence. He is likening it to going to God's house. Step one of that process

---

[64] Psalms 22:3

is going through the gate. Step two is spending time in His courtyard. Just like we had to search out one of the steps of the deliverance formula in other scriptures, we will find the third and final step of the worship formula in these Scriptures.

> *Exalt ye the Lord our God, and worship at his footstool; for he is holy. Psalm 99:5 (KJV)*

> *We will go into his tabernacles: we will worship at his footstool. Psalm 132:7 (KJV)*

The three-step worship formula is this: 1) Enter His gate, 2) enter His court, 3) then enter His tabernacle to sit at His footstool. As a westerner, we think of a courtyard as being surrounded by the house, as

A Typical Eastern Style House

modeled by so many of the European castles. But David was not familiar with that model of courtyard. He was thinking of an eastern style house where the courtyard is what westerners call their front yard, like this drawing to the right. During my stay in Danang, Vietnam, in 1971, I saw hundreds of this style of home, both elaborate ones and modest ones.

In *Biblical Worship*,[65] I talked about this Scripture when explaining Hebrew parallelism. I told you that once you enter through the gate of an eastern house, you are immediately in the courtyard. That is where most people entertained their guests. It was a place for food, fellowship, and celebration. Only the most special guests were invited inside the tabernacle or dwelling place.

Please understand this: Jesus considers us all His very special guests and always wants us to end our time with Him at His footstool, expressing intimate worship to Him.

---

[65] Stone, Shamblin. *Biblical Worship* (Westbow Press, 2012).

Just like the deliverance formula, this formula is also progressive. You cannot skip steps one and two and go directly into His tabernacle. You must first go through the gate. Next you need to spend time in His courtyard with Him and His other guests. He deserves to be celebrated, and the courtyard is the place for celebration. These two steps are very necessary before you enter the tabernacle.

HOW IT WORKS

Now that we have the correct mental picture of what it means to enter into God's presence, let's look and see exactly how we are supposed to do this.

Table 17. The Worship Formula

Step #	Instruction	How
1	*Enter into his gates*	*with thanksgiving*
2	*(enter) into his courts*	*with praise*
3	*go into his tabernacles:*	*we will worship*

What we learn here is that the act of giving thanks to God is the same thing as walking through God's gate when approaching His presence. Giving God praise is the equivalent to spending time with Him in His courtyard. And worshiping God is the same thing as an intimate time at his footstool.

Therefore, the way we enter into God's presence is with thanksgiving, praise, and worship—in that order. In the beginning of our study about worship in *Biblical Worship*, I told you to consider these three words as synonyms. While that is a great way to think of them in the broad sense, thanksgiving, praise, and worship also have distinct meanings when we examine them more closely in light of this worship formula.

THANKSGIVING

To be thankful is a mental/emotional attitude. To give thanks is an action. It is impossible to give thanks to God if you do not have a thankful attitude. It is also impossible to offer praise and worship to God if you are unthankful. Therefore, every worship experience MUST begin with a thankful attitude! Expressing our thanks gets us inside the gate.

As a worship leader, when you are planning your worship service, make sure the first song or two reminds people of what they should be thankful for. Once they have expressed thanksgiving to God, they have passed through the gate and are ready to offer praise and worship to God.

PRAISE

Praise is associated with high energy. In Psalm 149, the phrase "high praises" is used. This is talking about extremely animated and exuberant praise to the Almighty God. In other words, out of your thankful heart will gush the magnificent adoration of God our father, His son Jesus, and the Holy Spirit.

True praise puts God in his rightful place in our minds as king over all the universe. It exalts Him! It magnifies Him! It causes our vision of Him to transcend our earthly realm. It produces a sense of awe within the worshipers.

WORSHIP

Worship is a time of intimacy with God. Intimacy is earmarked by tenderness, not exuberance. Intimacy is where lovers get to know each other in ways they did not know were possible. Intimacy is a time of vulnerability not experienced any other way. It is a time of deep joy, not ecstatic joy. It is a time when love is expressed the way the Bridegroom initiates it. It is the culmination of the expression of our love for God and His love for us.

THE WORSHIP FORMULA IN THE CONTEXT OF MUSIC

Keep in mind this worship formula was given to us to work in the setting of music. Remember it tells us that in Psalm 100:2, ... *come before his presence with **singing**.* Therefore, the distinctions between the three steps of the worship formula will also have something to do with music, not just the song lyrics. Of the three components of music—melody, harmony, and rhythm—rhythm can have the most variation. Therefore, we understand that the rhythm of those three steps of the worship formula will also provide an important distinction, especially in the tempos. Those rhythm distinctions are vital to the worship formula.

GOING THROUGH THE GATE

When we first begin a worship experience, we are excited and full of anticipation. Therefore, slower tempos would not represent this step in the formula properly. However, there is a problem when several people try to go through a gate too quickly. Most doorways or gates are only wide enough for one person to go through at a time. If a group of people try to run through a gate, they will experience what we call a bottleneck, forcing them all to slow down and walk through the gate.

For that reason, songs that take us through the gate need to be a brisk walking tempo. Whenever possible, I use songs with a shuffle feel as well to get as many people of the congregation as possible through the gates.

Be aware as a worship leader that very seldom will you be able to get everyone in the congregation to go through the gate in a reasonable amount of time. There are thousands of variables that keep people from having a thankful heart and readily expressing thanksgiving at the beginning of a time of worship. As a worship leader, you must stay sensitive to the entire congregation you are leading.

If you move into praise too quickly, you could leave some people outside the gate. Those people will then not participate in the worship experience that day but will stand around the wall looking over it into the courtyard, watching everyone else worship. It's easy to spot those who never made it through the gate that day before you went on into praise. They will be the ones not participating in the praise and worship.

On the other hand, you will have people show up at church who have already been in prayer and personal worship. Their thanksgiving meter will already be in the red zone, pegged out. If you wait too long to move into praise, those people will start doing their own thing in worship, which will destroy the unity God wants for that worship time. Once you lose control of a worship setting, it is impossible to gain it back. Therefore, you must be led by the Spirit as to when to move into praise so that you will bring the maximum number of people with you.

By the way, this is impossible to do when you are not flexible with your worship song list. A worship list or service plan should be considered as ONLY a guideline for the worship leader. You MUST listen to God throughout the service to know how to lead every minute of that service.

INSIDE THE COURTYARD

In *Biblical Worship* Chapter 4,[66] I gave you the definitions of the Hebrew word "halal," which is translated into the English word "praise." Let me remind you of those definitions.

1. to shine / to give light
   When Moses returned from being in God's presence, his face shone brightly.[67] When people have spent all their energy praising God, they will visibly glow.

2. to be clear (of sound or color)
   Sound and light (color) are part of the electromagnetic spectrum, which are vibrations. To praise God with all our might will tune our being's vibrations to His.

3. to sing
   Singing and shouting are the ways God has given us to make vibrations to glorify Him.

4. to celebrate
   Praise is a high energy party celebrating the King of kings and the Lord of lords.

5. to make a show
   When we praise God, we are not supposed to hide our light under a bushel but let it be seen by all.

---

[66] Stone, Shamblin. *Biblical Worship* (Westbow Press, 2012).
[67] Exodus 34:35

6. to boast

Here is a Biblical example of this.

> ***Great is the Lord, and greatly to be praised*** *in the city of our God, in the mountain of his holiness.* ***Beautiful*** *for situation,* ***the joy of the whole earth****, is mount Zion, on the sides of the north, the city of the great King. Psalm 48:1–2 (KJV), emphasis added*

7. to commend

Here is the chorus of a song sung by Chris Tomlin commending God.

> "You made it all, said let there be
> And there was all that we see
> The sound of Your voice
> The works of Your hands
> You do all things well
> You do all things well
> You do all things well"[68]

8. to rave

Here is a Biblical example of this.

> *For unto us a child is born, unto us a son is given: and the government shall be upon his shoulder: and his name shall be called* ***Wonderful, Counsellor, The mighty God, The everlasting Father, The Prince of Peace.*** *Isaiah 9:6 (KJV), emphasis added*

---

[68] Tomlin, Chris, Jesse Reeves, and Michael John Clement. *You Do All Things Well.* sixsteps Music, Vamos Publishing, and worshiptogether.com songs, admin. by Capitol CMG Publishing], CCLI Song # 4403605, 2004.

9. to rage

Here's where things start to get a little over the top. Most of the time when we hear the word "rage," it is used in a negative way. But here we are being told that our praise of God should rage to the point of appearing out of control.

10. to act madly

Our praise of God can be so demonstrative and expressive that we appear to be crazy to the unbelieving onlookers.

11. to be clamorously foolish (while giving glory)

When I hear this phrase, I immediately think of someone who is intoxicated. When we praise God, we should be so full of His Spirit that we resemble someone who is drunk. After all, that's what they thought about the disciples of Jesus on the day of Pentecost.[69]

All those definitions are what it means to spend time in God's court with praise. Does your praise and the praise in your church resemble those definitions of praise? If not, it should!

The musical tempos and feels that represent the court of God are the up-tempo ones. Celebration is done with high energy and a driving, straight beat. That is where unity is very important. This is where the church executes the judgments written against Lucifer, with high praises of the Almighty God.[70]

INSIDE THE TABERNACLE AT HIS FOOTSTOOL

Also, in *Biblical Worship* Chapter 4,[71] I gave you the definitions of the Greek word "proskuneo," which is translated into the English word "worship." Let me remind you of the origin of that word.

This word is formed from two Greek words. The first word is "pros," meaning "toward." The second word is "kuneo," which means "to kiss."

---

[69] Acts 2:15
[70] Psalm 149
[71] Stone, Shamblin. *Biblical Worship* (Westbow Press, 2012).

A kiss is the most intimate publicly accepted expression of love we have been given by God. Therefore, to worship God is to express intimate love to Him.

It is totally inappropriate and unholy to be intimate in the courtyard. Public intimacy is called an orgy, which is satanic in its origin. Lovers go into their chambers to express intimacy. When it comes time, the Bridegroom will invite the bride into His chamber for intimate expressions of love. This is the goal of every time we praise God, but it may not happen every time. However, if we have not spent ourselves in celebration of the Bridegroom, we are not ready for intimacy with Him.

> *Yet you have not called on me, Jacob, you have not* **wearied yourselves** *for me, Israel. Isaiah 43:22, (NIV) emphasis added*

It has been my observation that we will experience the comparable depth of intimacy with the Bridegroom in His tabernacle to the same degree that we gave ourselves to celebrating Him in the courtyard.

Inside the tabernacle things slow way down. Volumes also adjust to accommodate the closer proximity the bride is to the Bridegroom. These are the two most distinguishable musical traits of worship. Shouting in someone's face "I love you" is not an appropriate way to be intimate.

It is in this setting that the holiness of Jesus becomes magnified in our eyes, and we often feel inadequate to be considered a candidate to be inside His tabernacle. Yet, the longer we stay there in the secret place with him, the more we never want to leave. We then realize that this is what we were created to do. We get addicted to God's presence and cannot live without it. Because of that, we will find ourselves hurrying through the gate and court next time we approach God's presence, because we want desperately to experience the close intimacy we felt the last time with God. We then find ourselves dreaming of that secret place with God throughout our day, and we are never satisfied without experiencing God's intimate presence at least once every day.

THE WORSHIP LEADER'S RESPONSIBILITY

As a worship leader, I recommend that you plan your prewritten songs for every worship service following this formula. Again, let me remind you, a worship song list/plan should only be considered as a guideline. You do not have to do every song on your list. Follow the Holy Spirit's leading as to when to lead the congregation into the next phase of this formula. If God tells you to spend more time going through the gate or celebrating Him in the court, you can always redo songs on your list or facilitate an appropriate new song.

In planning a service, I will usually plan the prewritten songs for the gate, court, and tabernacle phases to have an equal amount of time, each having about one-third of the time allotted for worship. However, once the service is underway, I never pay attention to how much time we spend in each phase. I only pay attention to the way the Holy Spirit is leading me so I can obey Him. A day or two later I will analyze the way God led me in that service to see how much time we spent in each of the three phases. Some services I will have spent more time in one of those phases than the other two combined. That is alright, because God knows the people who are present at each meeting and what their needs are. He also is the one who knows His own heart's desire for every meeting.

I do, however, keep track of the overall time we are spending in group worship. Don't be mistaken by thinking the amount of time you spend worshiping together determines the quality of your corporate worship. Your congregation will need to grow into being able to spend lengthy periods of time in group worship. The Holy Spirit will know how long your worship sessions should be. It is vital that you follow His leadership in this area. You and a select few others may be able to worship for an hour at a time, but the majority of your congregation may not be there yet.

It is not about how long you spend in worship that determines the quality of a worship service. It is only if you and most in your congregation have experienced the three steps of the worship formula culminating in the intimate presence of God that matters.

Several times throughout my lifetime I have been asked to lead worship but was told I only had ten or fifteen minutes because of the packed agenda of the rest of the meeting. I even remember once being told to keep worship under five minutes. Because I knew this worship formula, even with five minutes I was able to bring the congregation into a moment of intimacy with God. Just a moment with God can be extremely satisfying and rewarding.

> For a day in Your courts is better than a thousand.
> I would rather be a doorkeeper in the house of my God
> Than dwell in the tents of wickedness. Psalm 84:10
> (NKJV)

In this scripture, David is saying that, even if he never makes it into the tabernacle of God, just being in His courtyard is a thousand times more satisfying than anything else. Likewise, one minute in the tabernacle of God is a thousand times better than not experiencing God's presence at all.

Guard your relationship with your pastor! Do not allow Satan to accuse them in any way, especially concerning worship. Too many times I have heard worship leaders complain that their pastor did not understand how important worship is or otherwise they would give the worship leader more than twenty or thirty minutes to lead worship. NEVER accuse your pastor of not understanding the importance of worship! Be willing to work with the time allotment you have been given for worship, knowing that is all the time necessary to bring the people into God's presence, because you know the formula for doing so.

THE ENERGY LEVELS

The "gate, court, and tabernacle" formula will result in a predictable pattern of energy levels throughout the progression of this pattern of worship service. Here is a graph of the energy levels you can expect from this formula.

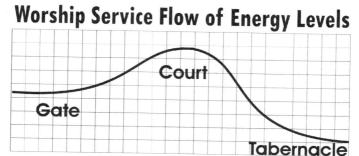

Flow of Energy Levels

A QUICK DEMONSTRATION

When I teach this to a group of people, at this point in the teaching I will grab a guitar and demonstrate this worship formula. I usually use the chorus of a song written in 1989 called "The Name of the Lord" for this demonstration. Here is the chorus of that song.

The Name of the Lord[72] by Clinton Utterbach

Chorus 1
Blessed be the name of the Lord
Blessed be the name of the Lord
Blessed be the name of the Lord most high
Blessed be the name of the Lord
Blessed be the name of the Lord
Blessed be the name of the Lord most high

I use this song for several reasons. First, it's lyrics are very simplistic, so they do not get in the way of this demonstration. Second, most people have at least heard the song, and if they have not, it is so simple they can learn it in one hearing.

In this demonstration, I lead everyone through this chorus only three times. The first time I will do it in a shuffle about 75 beats per

---

[72] Utterbach, Clinton. *The Name of the Lord.* Universal – Polygram International Publishing, Inc., Utterbach Music Publishing Company, admin. by Universal Music Publishing Group, CCLI Song # 265239, 1989.

minute (BPM). The second time I will do it in a straight eight feel at about 120 BPM. And the last time I continue with the straight feel but slow it down to about 55 BPM. If everyone participates in this exercise, by the middle of the third time through this chorus, the presence of God is extremely detectable, even by those who have never spent much time in God's presence before.

This worship formula works every time because of the promise or guarantee found in Psalm 22:3. As a worship leader, plan all of your services around this formula.

ONCE YOU ARE IN THE TABERNACLE, STAY THERE

Because the goal of worship is to get into God's intimate presence, once you get there, NEVER go back to the court in that worship service. Once you have slowed your tempo down in worship, never speed it up again!

AT YOUR FOOTSTOOL

Knowing how effective and important this worship formula is, I wrote a song about it. I also recorded this song live twice and put them both on YouTube. To find them, go to YouTube, search for "Shamblin Stone At Your Footstool." The first version is simply called "At Your Footstool"; the second one is called "At Your Footstool Version Two."

Here is the chord chart for this song. Keep in mind it is a tabernacle song, so it is slower in tempo and very slow by the time you get to the bridge.

At Your Footstool[73]
Shamblin Stone May 30, 2015

Verse

D
We have entered through Your gates today
 G
with a thankful heart
     D   G
We have spent time in Your courts with our praise
     D
Now we enter through the only door,
 G
Into Your tabernacle
     D   G
Where we long to worship You all of our days

Chorus

       G   A7   D   Bm
At Your footstool, we have peace, there are no fears
       G   A7   D   Bm
At Your footstool, we are safe, no need for tears
        G   A7   D   Bm
We've not come to ask anything from You
      Em   G6   A7   D
At Your footstool, all we need is You

Bridge
 G   D   A   *Women*
We love You,   *there's no God quite like our God*
 G   D   A   *Women*
We love You,   *there's no Lord above our Lord*
 G   D   A   F#m A7 D   G2   (D)
We love You, we love you Lord!

---

[73] Stone, Shamblin. *At Your Footstool.* Shamblin Stone Music, 2015.

Chapter Fourteen
"IN THE BEAUTY OF HOLINESS"

RIGHTEOUSNESS AND PRAISE

In *Biblical Worship*, Chapter 1 is entitled "What Is God Doing in the World Today?" I based my answer to that question on this scripture.

> *For as the earth brings forth its bud, As the garden causes the things that are sown in it to spring forth, So the Lord God will cause **righteousness** and **praise** to spring forth before all the nations. Isaiah 61:11 (NKJV), emphasis added*

In other words, although God has told us of many things that will take place in the last days, for His followers, this is the most important thing, which will take place in the last days: God will establish righteousness and praise in the earth, "*before all the nations.*" I dedicated that chapter to exegeting that scripture.

The first thing I did was establish that the last few chapters of Isaiah were written to the last days Saints. Then I showed you how this promise applies to our lives today. If you have not yet read that book, I recommend that you do so, as well as all the books in this series on worship.

The most important concept I established from this scripture is that praise is not complete without righteousness, and righteousness is not complete without praise. They must go hand in hand!

Another way of saying those two words (righteousness and praise) is "holiness" and "worship." David exhorted us to worship the Lord while being holy at the same time.

> O worship the Lord in the beauty of holiness: fear
> before Him, all the earth. Psalm 96:9 (KJV)

Why do holiness and worship go hand in hand? Because the object of our worship is holy! We cannot worship who God is without worshiping His holiness because He is Holy. It is an impossibility to separate God from His Holiness, just like it is impossible to separate God from His love. God is love![74] God is holy![75] He is the definition of love and holiness. Because of that, it is impossible to have love or holiness without God.

Whenever we approach God's presence by expressing our love to Him with our worship, we also will encounter His holiness every time. To come face to face with God's holiness will quickly reveal our unholiness. That explains why some people are so uncomfortable with the last stage of the worship formula. To experience intimacy with God, we have to address His holiness and our unholiness without Him.

Sinful man cannot stay in the same place with a holy God. Man either must repent and be cleansed from sin or he will have to leave God's presence. That is why some people do not mind going through the gates and spending time in the courts in praise but fear the intimacy of the tabernacle of God.

HOW ISAIAH WAS CHANGED IN GOD'S PRESENCE

Like many young preachers, Isaiah was what we would call a "hellfire and brimstone" preacher in his younger years. If you are not familiar with that term, it means someone who tries to bring the conviction of sin on their congregation by preaching hard against the various sins that can enslave mankind.

---

[74] 1 John 4:16
[75] 1 Peter 1:16

We see Isaiah preaching this type of sermon in Isaiah 5. Here is an excerpt from his sermon. As you read this Scripture, picture in your mind an impassioned young preacher yelling these words from a pulpit.

> *8* **Woe** *to those who join house to house; They add field to field, Till* there is *no place Where they may dwell alone in the midst of the land!*
>
> *11* **Woe** *to those who rise early in the morning, That they may follow intoxicating drink; Who continue until night* till *wine inflames them!*
>
> *12 ...And wine ... in their feasts; But they do not regard the work of the Lord, ...*
>
> *14 Therefore Sheol (**hell**) has enlarged itself And opened its mouth beyond measure; ...*
>
> *18* **Woe** *to those who draw iniquity with cords of vanity, And sin as if with a cart rope;*
>
> *19 That say, "Let Him make speed ...*
>
> *20* **Woe** *to those who call evil good, and good evil; Who put darkness for light, and light for darkness; Who put bitter for sweet, and sweet for bitter!*
>
> *21* **Woe** *to* those who are *wise in their own eyes, And prudent in their own sight!*
>
> *22* **Woe** *to men mighty at drinking wine,* **Woe** *to men valiant for mixing intoxicating drink,*
>
> *23 Who justify the wicked for a bribe, And take away justice from the righteous man!*
>
> *24 Therefore, as the **fire** devours the stubble, And the **flame** consumes the chaff, ...*
>
> *25 Therefore the **anger of the Lord** is aroused against His people; ... Isaiah 5:8–25 (NKJV), emphasis added*

In my younger years, I was like this young preacher Isaiah. I grew up in a denomination that glamorized the evangelistic screaming of a sermon. The overall tone of condemnation was expected in every sermon. The best preachers were judged to be the ones who could bring the most visible conviction of sin upon a congregation. Young Isaiah would have been their poster child preacher.

But something happened to Isaiah at the beginning of Chapter 6, which changed him completely. It was the presence of the Almighty God. It was the holiness of his Creator that was revealed in God's presence. Here's how Isaiah shared this life-changing experience.

> *1 In the year that King Uzziah died, I saw the Lord sitting on a throne, high and lifted up, and the train of His robe filled the temple. 2 Above it stood seraphim; each one had six wings: with two he covered his face, with two he covered his feet, and with two he flew. 3 And one cried to another and said: "**Holy, holy, holy** is the Lord of hosts; The whole earth is full of His glory!" 4 And the posts of the door were shaken by the voice of him who cried out, and the house was filled with smoke.*
>
> *5 So I said: "**Woe** is **me**, for I am undone! Because I am a man of unclean lips, And I dwell in the midst of a people of unclean lips; For my eyes have seen the King, The Lord of hosts."*
>
> *6 Then one of the seraphim flew to me, having in his hand a live coal which he had taken with the tongs from the altar. 7 And he touched my mouth with it, and said: "Behold, this has touched your lips; Your iniquity is taken away, And your sin purged." Isaiah 6:1–7 (NKJV), emphasis added*

In his sermon in Chapter 5, Isaiah declared "Woe" seven times on those to whom he was preaching. The word "woe" represents God's judgment against sin. Then, in the time that it took the angels to sing one chorus of their song praising God's holiness, Isaiah saw himself as the sinner he really was. Seeing God's holiness by being in God's presence took Isaiah's focus off of others' sins and showed him how unholy he was compared to the holy God.

That's when Isaiah cried out, "Woe is me, for I am undone!"

Every time we enter into God's tabernacle, He will reveal more of

Himself to His worshipers. That means he will reveal more of his love and holiness to us. Seeing God in the beauty of holiness will always reveal to us every little sin we have. Sin cannot remain in the presence of holiness. Therefore, every time we truly enter into God's presence, we will be forced to deal with our unconfessed sin. We will either confess our sins and be cleansed from our sins as Isaiah was, or we will remove ourselves from God's presence.

Never run from God's presence! Always run into God's presence! By that I mean be quick to repent and confess your sins when God's holiness reveals them to you.

WHAT HAPPENS WHEN WE CONFESS OUR SINS?

Let me answer that question from the New Testament. John concisely explains this answer in one verse of scripture.

> *If we confess our sins, he is faithful and just to forgive us our sins, and to cleanse us from all unrighteousness.*
> 1 John 1:9 (KJV)

First of all, nothing will happen until we confess our sins. The feeling of conviction does not qualify as a confession. Even confessing the feeling of conviction is not enough. We must confess, "Lord, I am guilty of …" Then we name the specific sin that God's holiness has revealed to us. We must be specific. A general confession of sin does not qualify as acknowledging our sin.

There are two directions we can confess our sins. The most important way is to confess our sins to God, as Isaiah did. However, the New Testament gives us a second way to confess our sins, in addition to confessing to God.

> *Confess your trespasses to one another, and pray for one another, that you may be healed. The effective, fervent prayer of a **righteous** man avails much. James 5:16 (NKJV), emphasis added*

What qualifies us to be righteous? It is when we are quick to confess our sins when they are revealed to us in the presence of God's righteousness. Unrighteousness is established when we do not confess our sin when it is revealed to us by God's holiness.

Once we have confessed our sin, our part in this process is over. What happens next is God's responsibility. We are told in 1 John 1:9 that God will then do two things. Before we discuss those two things, we need to understand the way He will do these things.

... he is faithful and just to ... 1 John 1:9 (KJV)

This is another place in the Bible that explains step one of the deliverance formula. When it says God will be faithful to do something, that is our guarantee that He will do it! In other words, if we do our part, which is to repent[76] by confessing our sins, we are guaranteed that He will faithfully do His part.

Not only will He be faithful, He will also be just. An unjust judge will be lenient to some and harsh to others. God's holiness does not permit Him to be unjust.

After we confess our sins, the two things God will do faithfully are:

... forgive us ... and to cleanse us ... 1 John 1:9 (KJV)

It is the cleansing part that is painful. If you don't believe me, just ask Isaiah. God sent an angel to burn his lips with a hot coal. The cleansing part of that process always involves pain as a deterrent to keep us from doing what we did again. Without the cleansing by pain, there cannot be lasting forgiveness! The consequences of pain for our actions is the way God has always intended for mankind to grow. That's why this Scripture is in the Bible.

He who spares his rod hates his son, But he who loves
him disciplines him promptly. Proverbs 13:24 (NKJV)

---

[76] 2 Timothy 2:25

Because God is our father and He loves us, He will not withhold the pain of our cleansing from sin. Human behavior is **ONLY** changed by pain as a deterrent. Timeouts do not cause enough pain to change human behavior! Being grounded does not cause enough pain to change human behavior! Being sent to your room does not cause enough pain to change human behavior! Losing privileges do not cause enough pain to change human behavior!

You may be thinking, "Why doesn't he shut up about parenting and go back to teaching about worship?"

Because true biblical worship is "in the beauty of holiness." You cannot have worship without the painful cleansing process that God designed to bring about holiness in us.

Again, that is the reason some people resist the intimacy that comes from biblical worship. In their mind, getting into God's presence is simply too painful for them. They need to be taught that the benefits of being in God's presence far outweigh the moment of cleansing we must endure to experience it!

IN GOD'S PRESENCE, OUR CALLING IS REVEALED

After Isaiah went through the cleansing process, he could stay in God's presence for as long as he and God desired. In God's presence, Isaiah received his call into the next phase of his ministry.

> *Also I heard the voice of the Lord, saying: "Whom shall I send, And who will go for Us?"*
> *Then I said, "Here am I! Send me." Isaiah 6:8 (NKJV)*

I believe that it is safe to say that, if Isaiah had not submitted to God's cleansing process for him, he would not have heard God speak at that moment. Isaiah would have missed out on the call of God, which changed the complete direction of his entire life. We will never know what we miss out on if we stop ourselves from entering into God's intimate presence, because it is much easier to hear God's voice when you are in His presence than any other time.

SANCTIFY YOURSELVES

Remember that David told the Levites to sanctify themselves before they carried the Ark of God's presence. A worship leader must be ready to enter God's tabernacle before they try to lead others into His intimacy. Make sure you as a worship leader have gone through the cleansing process before you try to lead others into God's holy presence. If you are having to repent and confess your sins as you are leading others, that will not permit you to help the congregation through this process the way you should.

As a worship leader, you need to sanctify yourself every time you are to lead worship, without exception. Do not get lazy with this! Do not try to skip this. If you do, you will either immediately or eventually regret it.

Chapter Fifteen
"LEADING THE CONGREGATION IN WORSHIP"

WORSHIP IS A PARTICIPATORY EVENT

Ideally, the only one who should be observing in a time of worship is the One being worshiped—that is the Lord. This, of course, is the goal of our worship gatherings, but in reality, the inexperienced worshipers will need to observe the experienced worshipers to grow as worshipers. We want to see everyone participate in worship with all their heart, soul, and strength as God commanded; however, we want to help people get to that point, not condemn them because they are not there yet.

The first step to reaching this goal is accomplished when everyone realizes they are supposed to participate and not observe. The world has trained us that in musical settings those on the stage are the performers and everyone else is an observer or audience member. The only audience participation acceptable at a concert or show is the expression of appreciation toward the performers. In the worship setting, however; the audience now becomes the performers, the Lord becomes the audience, and those on the stage are only there as facilitators to serve the audience in their performance for the Lord.

There is no place for stars on the worship team, only servants. If you want to be a worship leader to show off your musical ability, then you are not called to be a worship leader! A worship leader should care more about helping people experience God's presence than performing as a musician. Music is only the means to experience God's presence.[77]

THE MOTIVE FOR BEING MUSICALLY SKILLFUL

Please do not misunderstand what I am saying. It is vital for every worship leader to become skillful at playing and singing music! The motivation for obtaining this skill, however, cannot be the applause or appreciation of people. It must be to invisibly facilitate the congregation's worship of the Almighty God.

If you are an excellent musician, no one should notice that. They should leave the worship experience raving about God's presence, not your musical abilities! If the congregation notices you, you are not doing your job well as a worship leader. You should be hidden in Jesus. They should see Him, not you!

If you are a poor musician, you will distract the congregation from the presence of God with your poor musical skill level. Wrong notes and poor musicianship will bring attention on the worship leaders, which takes the attention away from the presence of God. We should desire to excel as instrumentalists and singers so as to not bring negative attention upon ourselves, thereby keeping the congregation from experiencing the presence of God.

ENCOURAGE, DON'T SCOLD

The most effective way to lead people into God's presence is to show them how to do it rather than tell them. We call that leading by example. However, even when leading by example, the Spirit of God will lead you to give the congregation brief words of encouragement from time to time. Here are a few rules to follow when you feel God is leading you to say something during the worship time.

---

[77] Psalm 100:2

Be Led by the Spirit

If you are going to interrupt the flow of a group worship time to say something, make sure the Holy Spirit is leading you before you do so! One word spoken from the flesh can halt the progress you have made toward God's presence. However, one word spoken by the Holy Spirit's leading can ignite the congregation's passion for God's presence.

Keep It Brief

Every second you are talking is time the congregation is not worshiping. Worship time is for worshiping, not sharing. Never say more than a couple of sentences in the middle of a worship time.

Using Scripture

If God reminds you of a scripture that applies to the moment, quickly share it. Resist the urge to give a long explanation of that Scripture. Let the word of God speak for itself. Of course, say what God wants you to say—just don't get longwinded.

Encourage, Never Scold

The saying goes, you catch more flies with honey than vinegar. If you as a worship leader are disappointed in the way the congregation is worshiping, NEVER tell them that! The two biblical reasons we worship God is because of who He is and what He does. If the congregation is worshiping half-heartedly, simply remind them of something God has done or something about His character to provide them with the needed motivation to worship wholeheartedly.

FACILITATE THE SPIRIT'S LEADING

Remember I taught you that worship ushers in God's presence. When God shows up, let Him be in charge of the agenda for that meeting. Be willing to stop your preplanned ideas and let Him direct what happens in the gathering from that point on.

God will lead you to facilitate one of three things when His presence shows up in a meeting. The first thing He may do is ask you to lead a prewritten song that is not on your song list plan. Your ability to obey Him in that moment depends on how well you and your team know the song He is asking you to do or your ability to play by ear. Sometimes only a few of your instrumentals will be able to play songs by ear. Don't let that deter you from obeying God's leading. If you do this very often, the other instrumentalists will start to pick up on how to do so. If you never ask them to play a song that they do not have music or chord charts for, then they will never learn how to play by ear.

Of course, springing a song on the worship team will also have the projectionist scrambling. That's OK. They will get there eventually. Never apologize for obeying the Holy Spirit's leading.

The second thing the Lord may ask you to facilitate is a new song. I have already told you how to facilitate that, if God leads you in that way.

The third thing God will want facilitated is the gifts of the Holy Spirit. Remember, music/worship has always been used to release the prophetic gifts. Therefore, be aware that as you lead people in worship, God will release those gifts in the body of Christ.

DO NOT quench those gifts when God releases them in your gathering! Also, do not fear those gifts. Because we are human, we will make mistakes, which is how we learn. But that is no reason to stop trying to get it right. We are even told in the Bible that every time we try to operate in a prophetic gift of the Holy Spirit, it will always be only partially right.

For we know in part and we prophesy in part. 1 Corinthians 13:9 (NKJV)

Because of that, God has given us specific instructions as to how the prophetic gifts should operate within the church gathering. Those instructions are found in 1 Corinthians 14. Part of the chapter compares speaking in tongues with prophecy, encouraging us to exercise the prophetic in our gatherings. Here are the specific verses that address how prophecy should be handled in the church gatherings.

> *Let two or three prophets speak, and let the others judge. But if anything is revealed to another who sits by, let the first keep silent. For you can all prophesy one by one, that all may learn and all may be encouraged. 1 Corinthians 14:29–31 (NKJV)*

The first thing Paul tells us here is that any more than two or three prophetic words in a meeting can be excessive. One of the reasons for that is human attention span. If more than three people share prophetically in a meeting, most of us will forget what the first one or two people shared. When God speaks to us prophetically, He intends for us to remember and execute what He has told us. Human nature learns line upon line.[78] Each person can reach a place of information overload, meaning they are incapable of taking in any more information until they process the information they have received.

The second thing we learn in this Scripture is that all prophecies must be judged by seasoned prophetic ministries. Because of that, a worship leader should never be the only one judging the prophetic in a gathering. I recommend that you encourage anyone who believes God wants them to share a prophetic word in the gathering of believers to first run it by one of the pastors or church elders.

Of course, this screening process is only done for the novices in the congregation. The worship leader can release proven prophetic ministries as soon as they indicate they have a word from God to share. All others should find one of the recognized church leaders and quietly share the prophetic word they believe they have received from God, and that church leader should decide one of the following.

1. The individual indeed received a word from God and should share it in the service. (If that is the case, the elder or pastor should get the worship leader's attention to let them know to facilitate that person's prophetic gift within the service.)

---

[78] Isaiah 28:10

2. The prophetic word may be from God, but it does not fit into the flow of the service at that time. (If that is the case, the elder or pastor should gently tell the person to wait to see whether God will indicate the proper time for them to share it. When the elder or pastor feels the time is right in the gathering for that word to be shared, they should get the worship leader's attention at that time. If God never releases that prophetic word in that gathering, the elder or pastor MUST encourage that person to not give up but to keep listening for God's voice.)

3. This is not a word from God, but the individual should not be discouraged and should keep listening for God's voice.

WAYS THE PROPHETIC CAN BE SHARED

Seasoned prophetic ministries will usually speak in the first person for God. However, that is not the only way we can share a word from God. This scripture found in the same chapter in 1 Corinthians gives us leeway to share a prophetic message from God with the congregation in other ways as well.

> *Well, my brothers and sisters, let's summarize. When you meet together, one will **sing**, another will **teach**, another will tell some special **revelation** God has given, one will speak in **tongues**, and another will **interpret** what is said. But everything that is done must strengthen all of you. 1 Corinthians 14:26 (NLT), emphasis added*

In Chapter 9, I have already talked about singing a prophetic new song. Those who teach usually share a scripture, then briefly exegete it. That too can be considered a prophetic word from God. A revelation from God is usually not based on a Scripture but is something God revealed to a person in their day-to-day life. Tongues as a prophetic utterance requires a lot of faith by the speaker, because they will not know what they are speaking or if someone in the gathering will be able to interpret what they are saying. However, it is biblical to speak in tongues, then interpret by the Spirit what you just said in tongues.

> *Wherefore let him that speaketh in an unknown tongue pray that he may interpret. 1 Corinthians 14:13 (KJV)*

Chapter Sixteen
"THE WORSHIP TEAM CONFIGURATION"

MULTIPLE TEAMS VERSUS ONE TEAM

It is not biblical to have multiple worship teams in your church. Everyone involved in the worship ministry of a church should be considered a member of that church's worship team. That presupposes that you are following David's tabernacle pattern of having a large orchestra and a large choir. If you have adopted the world's model of using a few singers with an instrumental rhythm section, you have already strayed from the biblical model. That makes it easy to take things one step further and create multiple teams when trying to involve more people in worship leading.

If your church uses multiple worship teams, inevitably the congregation will compare the teams and choose their favorite. That leads to the congregation choosing to show up late for church when their favorite team is not leading. That promotes disunity, not unity, within the church. In addition to the congregation comparing the worship teams, the people on the worship teams will also compare themselves among themselves, which is not wise!

*For we dare not make ourselves of the number, or compare ourselves with some that commend themselves: but they measuring themselves by themselves, and comparing themselves among themselves, are **not wise**. 2 Corinthians 10:12 (KJV), emphasis added*

When you have multiple worship teams, it will always result in comparisons being made. Human nature will never do anything different. That, in turn, will promote a spirit of competition, which is deadly in a spiritual setting.

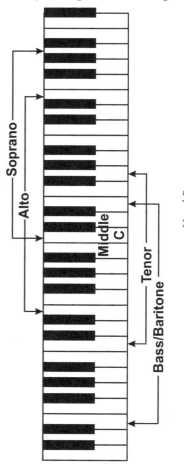

Even if your church has multiple services, do not promote the idea that each service has its own worship team. Instead, promote the idea that every person involved in the church's worship ministry is on **THE** church's worship team. Not everyone can participate in all of the services because of personal obligations. However, there will be some who can and will participate in all of the services, if you give them that opportunity.

CONFIGURING YOUR CHOIR

The average untrained singer has a vocal range of 1.5 to two octaves. With training, a person can expand their vocal range, but most of the singers you will have in your volunteer choir will not be trained.

Here is the average vocal ranges for the typical four-part harmony choir (SATB). These are general guidelines. Each individual will have their own vocal range. They may not be able to sing every note within the range they fall into.

Others may have an extended range on one end. Those people can sometimes fit into either of two voice ranges. In that case, you can use them in this section of your choir where you need them the most. Those people are rare. Most people fit into only one voice range.

When testing people's voice ranges, make sure they are filling up with air to sing. Also, make sure they always sing with their throat open and relaxed. If they do these two things, it is easy to figure out when they have reached their limitations on both ends of their vocal range. When they get too high, their voices will crack or tighten up. When they get too low, their voices will growl from trying to close up. Every one of us has our limitations in all parts of life. Singing is no different.

Test the vocal ranges of every person in your worship ministry, even the instrumentalists. Once you have determined everyone's vocal range, assign each a place to stand or sit in the choir configuration. There are many ways to configure a choir. Here are just two ways you can try.

When you do a vocal a cappella song, have your instrumentalists leave their instruments and take

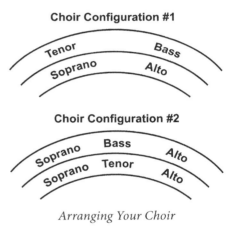

Arranging Your Choir

their place in the choir configuration. Using the Bible as the precedent, every worship team member, including the instrumentalists, should also sing.

THE APPOINTED SINGERS

These are singers on microphones. I recommend that they stand together on one side of the worship leader. Because of their close proximity, they could share a music stand, but they should all have their own microphone.

Here is the configuration of appointed singers that I recommend. Each position is to be filled by only one singer.

Melody Double

If the worship leader is male, the melody double should be a female and vice versa. The melody double needs to have a strong voice. They cannot be easily distracted from their vocal part, no matter what others are singing around them. Inexperienced congregational worshipers listen to a voice of their own gender to follow. For most inexperienced singers, their mind is unable to follow a voice of a different gender.

Alto and Tenor

These are two people out of their respective sections of the choir who lead their section from their microphone. They should be able to harmonize by ear! Their responsibility is not to sing the melody of songs but to harmonize their part (alto or tenor) in such a way that their section can follow them. In other words, they need to keep their part simple enough to follow.

From time to time, you will have a soprano who is capable of harmonizing by ear on the tenor part. I do not recommend this for the same reason we use a melody double of the opposite gender. It can be very difficult, even for your choir men in the tenor section, to follow a soprano.

Sometimes an alto has a low-enough voice to sing the tenor part by ear in the proper range. That is definitely preferred over a soprano singing the tenor part up an octave above the tenors.

Bass/Baritone

This is an optional appointed singer position. If you do not have someone to lead the bass section of the choir who can hear the bass part by ear, simply have the men who can sing with the tenors do so. If that part gets too high, have them revert to the melody.

CONFIGURING YOUR INSTRUMENTS

How you configure your instruments will depend on your church facility mostly. Keep in mind that the instruments are there to accompany the singers. Therefore, the instruments should never take center stage. The choir should always be center stage! That leaves three places where the instruments can be: to either side of the choir or in front of the choir.

Instrumentalists who are in front of the choir should always be sitting and possibly be on the floor in front of the stage. If they are in front of the choir on the stage, make sure there is enough room in front of them for the appointed singers and worship leader. If they are on the floor in front of the stage, their chairs should face the center and the stage somewhat, so they can see and follow the worship leader.

Group the instruments into sections of the same or similar instruments. I recommend that you look up the layout of an orchestra or band online to get some ideas as to how to configure the instrumentalists that you have.

Always keep the rhythm section instruments together. I recommend that you put them to one side or the other, so as to keep the drums away from center stage. It is important for the bass guitar and the drummer to be close together so they can coordinate the bass sounds. The kick drum of the drum kit provides the percussion part of the bass sound, and the bass guitar provides the pitch of the bass sound. Those two instrumentalists should work at coordinating their sounds.

Don't put your drums behind Plexiglas, and don't build a cage for them. Don't mic your drums. All of those things steal the musicianship from your percussionists. Put your drums with all the other instruments, and tell the drummers to blend their sound with the overall musical ensemble. That is the only way they will learn musicianship on their instrument.

On the following page is an example configuration for a worship team that has a large choir, appointed singers, a full rhythm section, and orchestral/band instruments.

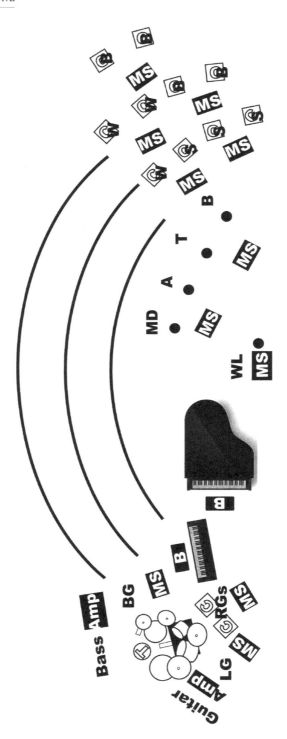

A Worship Team Configuration

LEGEND FOR THE ABOVE GRAPHIC (L TO R)

BG = Bass Guitar Player
T = Drummer's Throne
RGs = Rhythm Guitar Players
B = Piano/Keyboard Bench
· = Mic Stand
A = Alto Appointed Singer
B = Bass Appointed Singer
W = Woodwind Instrument

LG = Lead Guitar Player
C = Chair
MS = Music Stand
WL = Worship Leader
MD = Melody Double Singer
T = Tenor Appointed Singer
S = String Instrument
B = Brass Instrument

WORSHIP TEAM CHAIN OF COMMAND

Once you have made a list of everyone in your worship team and the vocal part they sing, make a list like I have outlined below. It includes everyone who can lead worship as a primary worship leader, those who play each of the rhythm section and orchestral instruments, and those who can sing by ear on the various vocal parts. That list could look something like the list below.

I started filling in the blanks with names so you get the idea of the list. When you make your list, in the Skill column write a "B" for beginner, "I" for intermediate level, and "A" for advanced level. In the Read column, write a "Y" for yes or an "N" for no to indicate whether the person can read music in this capacity. I have only put one blank line under each section; however, you may have four or five or more people listed in each section.

Once you have populated the names of people from your church in the list, as the chief musician appoint the most skilled and most spiritually mature person in each group as the section leader over that group, carrying on the chain-of-command concept. Depending on how many orchestral instruments you have, you could appoint one section leader over them all or divide them into sections of strings, woodwinds, and brass Instruments, each having their own section leader.

Table 18. 1st & 2nd Rank Worship Team Members

Name	Phone	Email	Skill	Read
Primary Worship Leaders				
Shamblin Stone – CM[79]	000-000-0000	ss@xxxxx.com	A	Y
Men Melody Double				
John Smith – SL[80]	000-000-0000	js@xxxxx.net	I	N
Women Melody Double				
Alto Appointed Singers				
Tenor Appointed Singers				
Bass Appointed Singers				
Drum Kit				
Percussion Traps				
Bass Guitar				
Lead Guitar				
Rhythm Electric Guitar				
Rhythm Acoustic Guitar				
Piano or Primary Keyboard				
Secondary Keyboard or Organ				
Orchestral Instruments				
Name	Instrument	Phone	Email	Skill	Read

The chief musician should hold regular meetings with all the section leaders together. Depending on your church, those meetings may be quarterly, every other month, or once a month. Section leaders should pass down to the section members information communicated in those meetings.

Section leaders' responsibilities include the following.

SECTION LEADER JOB DESCRIPTION

Spiritual Responsibilities
1. Check on the spiritual well-being of your section members weekly.
2. Encourage your section members as often as is necessary.
3. Report any lingering spiritual issues to the chief musician/music pastor, who should follow-up and get the person the appropriate help.

Musical Responsibilities
1. Correct musical mistakes within the section.
2. Train the section members musically.
3. Recruit new members for your section.

Administrative Responsibilities
1. Build a participation schedule:
   a. that is fair to all section members
   b. that uses the more skilled people in the prominent gatherings of the church
   c. that gives those developing opportunities to grow
2. Submit this quarterly schedule to the chief musician for approval.
3. All scheduling issues should go through the section leaders.
   a. Section members are to report to the section leaders when they cannot fulfill their obligations as scheduled.
   b. Section leaders are responsible to find a replacement in those cases.

---

[79] CM = chief musician or music pastor
[80] SL = section leader

c. Section leaders are to report any of these changes to the chief musician before the event being changed.

SPECIAL NOTE

Most of these sections listed in Table 18 "1st and 2nd Rank Worship Team List" can use only one of the team members in each service. The other individuals in that section are expected to sing in the choir at the services when they are not playing their instrument or functioning as an appointed singer. Second-rank worship team members who only show up when they are scheduled should be removed from that section until they learn a servant's heart.

THE MASTER LIST

The chief musician is responsible for compiling the master list of who is scheduled to minister at every meeting or service based on the schedules the section leaders provide. On the next page is a template you can use for that. I also include information on the service plans I put together for each service. Use the top part of the following template for a master list of who is scheduled when. When you add the bottom part to the template, it becomes a service outline form or worksheet.

If your church has multiple services, identify each service by its time and date on the master list and service plan.

Table 19. [Church Name] Worship Service Plan

Date:	Time:
Special Day/Event:	
Special Music:	
Worship Leader:	
Piano:	2nd Keyboard:
Melody:	Alto:
Tenor:	Bass:
Drums:	Percussion:
Bass Guitar:	Lead Guitar:
Rhythm Guitar:	Acoustic Guitar:
Audio Technician:	Projectionist:
Orchestral Section Leader of the Day:	

Preservice Plan

Key	Song/Item	Note

Service Plan

Key	Song/Item	Note

Ending Song(s)

Key	Song/Item	Note

Chapter Seventeen
"PLANNING YOUR WORSHIP SERVICE"

THE IMPORTANCE OF PLANNING

I have discovered two extremely different schools of thought concerning the planning of worship services. I have known those who do not plan anything but just get up and follow the Holy Spirit's leading. Then I have known others who plan their services down to the minute and refuse to deviate from that plan.

I confess that after having led worship for over 50 years, I have done it both ways. I don't think we should choose either method exclusively but both. We should seek God in the planning of a service and follow God in the execution of the service.

Planning is important to everything we do. Even Jesus taught us that.

> *For which of you, intending to build a tower, does not sit down first and count the cost, whether he has enough to finish it Luke 14:28 (NKJV)*

However, if you are not flexible in the executing of your plan, you can miss God when He calls an audible. For those of you who are not familiar with that term, it is taken from the game of football. The offensive coordinator of a team may have a game plan, but many times the defense of the other team figures out what the offense is planning. In that case, the quarterback—when he sees by the way the other team's defense is lined up that it has figured out the plan—can call an audible, thereby changing the play at the last second on the line of scrimmage.

The worship time is the battleground where we fight for the souls of everyone in attendance at that worship service. If the Holy Spirit (our quarterback) sees that our enemy has figured out the game plan for the worship service, He will call an audible in the middle of the worship service. As worship leaders, we must hear and obey when He does that. The key is to allow the Holy Spirit to lead us as we plan a service and also lead us as we execute that plan.

PREPARING TO PLAN

There is no substitute for prayer before you begin to plan a worship service. Let me remind you, prayer is the most powerful expression of individual worship God has given to us. Prayer reminds us that He is in charge. Therefore, the most important prayer we can pray before we start to plan a worship service is that God will give us His plan for the service.

That prayer is not accomplished just a few minutes before you sit down to plan. It must be an ongoing prayer from the moment you find out it will be your responsibility to lead worship, until you sit down to make the plan for that service. Please do not skip or shorten this prayer time.

KNOW YOUR PARAMETERS

Each church or denomination will have adopted a template for the structure of its gatherings. You need to understand the template you are expected to function within. Some templates do not permit the biblical gate, court, tabernacle pattern to flow from start to finish. Those are gathering templates that break up the worship with well-meaning items such as Scripture reading, offering, special music, responsive readings, testimonies, coffee time, announcements, fellowship, liturgy, communion, and on and on the list can go.

If your church has adopted a worship service template that does not permit uninterrupted worship so you can take them through the gate, court, tabernacle pattern, work on getting that changed as soon as possible. Many times, it can be a simple change or rearranging of the service components to allow time for the worship flow to happen.

KNOW YOUR CO-LABORERS

One of the reasons I always list the people who will be ministering with me at any given service is because of how they will affect the worship in multiple ways. I strive to know the following about every person on the worship team.

1. Their musical skill level

This is one of the most important things to know about your fellow team members. First of all, everyone who participates in a volunteer worship team will be at different skill levels. That is simply a fact of life you cannot avoid. As a worship leader, you need to know your worship team members' current and potential skill levels.

One reason to know that is so you do not expect more from them than they are currently capable of doing. Some prewritten songs require a particular musical arrangement to sound right. However, if your instrumentalists are incapable of doing that arrangement, stop expecting them to do it. Be happy with a simplified version of the song or avoid doing the song altogether.

On the other hand, if you have some very accomplished musicians on your team, you should search out prewritten songs that will utilize their musical skills. Understand that they will become disheartened if all you do is simplified music.

2. Their leadership style and skill

I have seen worship leaders scold a congregation when they did not think the congregation was worshiping correctly. Biblical leadership styles need to be from a spirit of meekness, not authoritativeness. I have also known worship leaders who lead with the attitude of "do as I say, not as I do." A shepherd models biblical leadership. A shepherd leads the sheep and does not drive the sheep. Cattle are driven; sheep are led.

3. Their spiritual maturity

If someone does not spend personal time worshiping and reading the Bible, it will become obvious. A worship team member is in a highly visible position in the church. For that reason, they should demonstrate a willingness to seek God and grow spiritually in their personal lives. I am not saying that every worship team member needs to be a mature Christian. All I am saying is that every worship team member needs to be a maturing Christian.

4. Their teamwork ability

Are they a team player? Do they think in terms of "team" instead of individuality? I said it before and will say it again: There is no place on a worship team for a star—only servants.

5. Their knowledge of the repertoire

Every church will have its own repertoire of prewritten worship songs. You need to know how well your team members can play or sing those songs or whether anyone needs individual rehearsal before the team rehearsal and worship service. If I am aware that someone on the team needs to work on a particular song privately, I make sure to encourage the individual to do so early in the week in a personal conversation.

6. Their ability to accompany or do a new song

There are two things concerning the new song you need to be aware of about every worship team member. First, can they hear, based on the cues in a spontaneous new song melody, what chords they should play to accompany that melody? Second, can they sing or play a new song on demand? The worship team must be proficient in a new song before the congregation can be released in it.

PLANNING YOUR SERVICE TO FLOW

I have explained to you how worship is the journey and God's presence is the destination. If you are going somewhere in your car, the worst way to reach your destination is to plan to stop every five minutes. In other words, on a short journey, you usually do not stop once it begins until you reach your destination.

You will want to convey this concept to your congregation in the way you plan your worship service. The most effective way to demonstrate that is to group your prewritten songs into medleys so there is no break whatsoever between most of the songs.

A medley is two or more songs grouped together that flow easily from one song to the next. For songs to flow together, they must have at least one or more aspects in common. Here are the song aspects you should coordinate when planning a worship service, starting with the most important to the least important.

KEY CENTERS

Do your best to choose songs in the same key when building your medleys and worship service. If I can plan an entire service in the same musical key, I consider that a great plan. The fewer key changes throughout a worship service, the better the flow can be.

One of the main reasons for that is because volunteer instrumentalists can get confused as to which key they are in when you change keys a lot. Every time you change musical keys, the inexperienced musicians will have to momentarily think through the new key center. This brief mental exercise takes their focus away from hearing God's voice, making it difficult for them to maintain a prophetic edge to their music.

Worshipers (that is, the congregation) subconsciously interpret random key changes as having a lack of purpose or direction. Your worship plan may be based on a lyrical theme, but if you have to change keys for every song, that theme will be overshadowed by the lack of continuity displayed by the multiple key centers.

Don't get me wrong—most worship services will have to change keys at least two or three times. There is nothing wrong with using two or three key centers within one worship service. However, you will need to remember these things when planning your key changes.

1. Changing to a higher key will increase the energy or intensity level in your worship service, while modulating to a lower key reduces the energy level in an awkward and unpredictable way. Modulating up is always the best way to go! You cannot predict the effect a downward modulation will have on your group of worshipers. The drop of energy and direction caused by modulating downward is completely uncontrollable; therefore, avoid it at all costs.

2. The strongest modulations are always up by either one-half step or one full step. I gave you a list of the key centers that your worship team should aspire to be able to play in. That list will show you when to modulate up one-half step or one whole step. Either way, that is called a modulation by step.

   The strongest place to modulate up by step is within a song. This modulation then becomes part of that song's arrangement, helping to build the song's energy. Of course, you can still modulate between songs if that is needed.

3. Modulations by skip are ones going higher than one full step. In reality, you can modulate to any key center you desire from any key, but the way you modulate will either promote "flow" or cause an awkward break in the flow. Keep in mind when modulating by skip, you need to play at least one measure of the new key center to acclimate everybody to it before you start singing the next song.

   One of the best ways to promote flow when modulating by skip is to make use of secondary dominants. The word "dominant" refers to the chord built on the fifth note of any scale. A dominant seventh chord is audibly the strongest leading chord of any key center and <u>must</u> be resolved to the root chord. To modulate by skip using a secondary dominant in 4/4 time, simply play the dominant seven chord of the key you want to modulate to on the fourth beat, then resolve it to the new root chord on the next beat (the down beat). It is still recommended that you play the new root chord for one measure (minus musical pickups) before beginning the next song.

TEMPOS

There is a direct correlation between songs' tempos and their energy level. In Chapter 13, I gave you a diagram of the energy levels (tempos) you should try to follow as you are planning your worship service. If you do your best to follow the flow of that pattern, you will be following the biblical gate, court, tabernacle formula.

Don't be married to a certain tempo for every song. Be open to adjusting the tempos depending on where you are at in the gate, court, tabernacle process. In other words, a song used to enter the gate may work in the tabernacle as well, if you slow it way down. The important question when placing a song into your worship service plan is, "How fast does the Lord want us to play that song?" It is not, "How fast do we usually play this song?"

TIME SIGNATURES

It is extremely difficult to successfully execute a medley using songs with different time signatures. Don't mix the triple feel time signatures with the duple time signatures. Even if your volunteer worship team is able to pull it off, I guarantee you the congregation will not be able to. Simply group the duple rhythms together and the triple rhythms together.

MUSICAL FEELS

Some songs dictate their musical feel by their melodic rhythm. For example, in 1983, Graham Kendrick wrote and published the song

Rejoice.[81] The very melody of that song is written in a shuffle. Doing it any other way would change the song into a different song.

Other songs are more flexible and can fit into multiple different music feels and time signatures. For example, I like doing the hymn *Amazing Grace* in a triplet-based shuffle. The song is written originally in a 3/4 time signature. I change four to 9/8 in the instrumentalists. When you overlay the melody in 3/4 on top of the 9/8 in the instruments, it gives it the shuffle feel based on triplets. However, if I choose to do Chris Tomlin's chorus[82] to these verses, I have to do the verses in a straight 4/4, elongating certain notes to make the 3/4 melody fit, because Tomlin wrote his chorus in 4/4.

Sometimes you can find songs that use the same musical feel in the same key and in the same tempo which fit well together in a medley. Other times, you will have to change the musical feel in the middle of the medley. When changing feels in the middle of a medley, make sure you practice that transition in the rehearsal time right before the worship service, so all of your instrumentalists make the change together.

LYRICAL THEMES

Sometimes the Spirit of the Lord will lead you to put together a worship service with a particular lyrical theme. First of all, it is very rare to find enough songs to carry a theme throughout the entire worship service. I'm not saying it can't be done; I'm just saying it is difficult. Most of the time you can be successful at planning one or two medleys around themes, but don't think you have to follow that theme through for the entire worship service.

Some themes I have been successful in using in the past for worship services include:

1. The name of the Lord
2. Blessing
3. Celebration
4. Holidays like Christmas and Easter

[81] Kendrick, Graham. *Rejoice*. Make Way Music, CCLI song #1338, 1983.
[82] Tomlin, Chris, John Newton, and Louie Giglio. *My Chains Are Gone*. sixsteps Music, Vamos Publishing, worshiptogether.com songs, CCLI song #4768151, 2006.

5. Repentance and forgiveness
6. Joy
7. Peace and comfort

PLAN TO INTRODUCE NEW PREWRITTEN SONGS

In Chapter 8, I told you to construct a song list of all the prewritten songs your church knows. That is not supposed to be a stagnant list but one that is growing all the time. I suggest you make a separate list of the potential prewritten songs you would like to introduce to your church. Every week or so, review that list and prioritize the songs that God wants you to introduce first.

I also recommend you add a column to your song list showing the date you introduced each song to your church. For the older songs, you won't be able to put a date, but you can put a date on the songs you introduce from this day forward. Here's the columns you should set up for your list.

Table 20. Repertoire of Prewritten Songs

Worship Song List for [church name]

Last Updated [date] by [initials or name]

Key	Title	1st line or Composer(s)	Intro'd	Tempo	Mode
			MM/YY		

Never let the criteria for selecting new prewritten songs for your congregation be because they are the latest and greatest releases by the music publishers. The most important criteria for choosing new prewritten songs is "What is God saying to your church in this season?" Your church's praise song repertoire needs to reflect the history of everything God has taught your church throughout the years.

Fortunately, God will reveal certain truths to the body of Christ all over the world at the same time. That means we can use some songs written on the other side of the world in our church. However, sometimes the Lord has specific things to teach a local church that He is not teaching the rest of the body of Christ at that time. As a worship leader, you must be sensitive to what God is saying to your local church and support those truths with the songs you select to do in that season.

Many times, God will give original songs within a congregation to punctuate the current truths He is revealing to a local church. That has happened everywhere I have been throughout my ministry, because I encourage it to happen. If God births a song in someone who doesn't understand music, I help them figure out the words, chords, and melody to their song, because I, as a chief musician, must understand music. I believe God wants to release songs in every congregation. That is one of the motivating factors for the song writing course I have put together: to help average people release the songs God is giving them.

I remember in the late 1980s when I was the music pastor of a large church in Canada, the senior pastor, Tim Osiowy, was preaching a three-sermon series on God's Grace. On the Sunday afternoon that he preached the second sermon in that series, one of the congregation members, Lock Cameron, knocked on my door in the middle of nap time. He was absolutely overwhelmed by God's presence as he told me that God had given him a song about grace.

Lock plays the guitar and had brought his with him. I was speechless by the anointing of God as he sang his song for me. I taught the chorus of that song to our worship team at the Thursday evening rehearsal, and we did that song before Pastor Tim's third sermon on grace the next Sunday, as well as several weeks following. I still do the chorus of that song to this very day. I wish I had learned the verses. The profound chorus, which simplified the truths we were learning, goes like this:

> By Your grace You are able to save me
> By Your grace You are able to change me
> By Your grace You are able to sustain me
> Till I come to the image of Your Son

This is just one of the many times God has birthed songs within a local church to support the truths He was establishing. Please be open to Him doing that in your local church as well.

On some occasions we have taken the recording of a spontaneous new song that was released in a previous service and learned it as part of our prewritten song repertoire. You may be surprised to learn how many published praise songs were actually birthed that way.

Never introduce more than one new prewritten song in the same worship service. More than one will be overwhelming to your congregation. I recommend that you plan to introduce one new prewritten song about every month. That gives you the opportunity to do it every week for a month, which will establish the song in the congregation's minds as a familiar song. Make sure your worship team knows a song well before you introduce it to the congregation.

MAKING YOUR SERVICE PLAN

Now it is time to use these tools to construct a worship plan for your service. In the last chapter, I gave you a worksheet to use when you plan your services. If you are familiar with Microsoft Word or an equivalent software, you should be able to set up the tables for these worksheets on your computer. If not, feel free to photocopy this form for your use.

For an average-length worship service, I usually plan about six prewritten songs to do. If God's presence shows up and releases a new song or the gifts of the Spirit, I simply drop one or two of the planned songs to give place to the spiritual spontaneity God is desiring.

Once I have put together the service plan, I email it to the entire worship team, along with chord charts for all of the prewritten songs, and YouTube links (if available). If I want someone on the worship team to practice one or more of those songs on their own, I will give them a call to personally request that.

PLANNING A TIME FOR THE NEW SONG

You should plan at least one place in your service to release a new song. You can indicate this on your worship plan. I even tell my instrumentalists the chord progression we are going to start with, expecting that God will change it as He leads us.

WHAT ABOUT MULTIPLE SERVICES?

Some churches have multiple services on a Sunday morning. Other churches will have a Saturday evening service, as well as a Sunday morning service. Your worship plan should be the same for all services each week, unless you have a Sunday evening service. In that case, you should plan two different services for that weekend.

Some churches change their worship plan for services, according to the demographic they are targeting for each service. It is a Satanic idea to separate the generations to their own worship service and choose music that will appeal to each generation. Worship music should never be chosen based on musical style! Every worship service should contain songs that remind us of past revelations as well as present truths.

Chapter Eighteen
"PRACTICALITIES"

THE IMPORTANCE OF PUNCTUALITY AND COURTESY

The larger your worship team is, the more important it is to manage rehearsal times well. One minute wasted is not simply one minute. If you have 30 people on your worship team and you waste one minute in rehearsal, you have just wasted 30 minutes. One of the biggest reasons for a high dropout rate from worship teams can be traced back to quality musicians' frustration levels over wasted time in rehearsals.

For that reason, a chief musician or primary worship leader must plan rehearsals down to the minute and do their best to maintain the integrity of that plan. Make sure you start your rehearsals exactly on time and end on time—or better yet, start a couple minutes early. Respecting people's time is an outward demonstration of respect for them.

Teach your worship team to respect all of their teammates by showing up early for all rehearsals and ministry times so they can be in their place when it is time to start. Instrumentalists who must tune or set up their instrument(s) need to show up even earlier so they will be ready to rehearse or minister on time. The audio/visual department personnel must also arrive early to make sure their equipment is ready.

By the way, in the rehearsal setting, the chief musician will need to work with just one section of the worship team from time to time. Keep those times brief to maintain the attention of the entire team throughout the rehearsal. Teach your worship team that this is not a waste of time for the sections not being worked with. They can still learn by listening. Also, rehearsal is not the time for people to talk to each other. Talking while another section is working on something is the height of disrespect!

Another action of disrespect to the entire team, as well as the chief musician, is when people leave in the middle of the rehearsal to go to the bathroom. Teach your team to take care of restroom needs before the rehearsal and time of ministry. No one should have to leave in the middle of a rehearsal or service, unless it is a dire emergency! Also, no one should leave without first getting the chief musician's attention to seek permission.

A rehearsal is not the time to voice your personal opinions about anything, even music. A worship team is not a democracy. The chief musician is responsible before God to make all final musical decisions. That does not mean the chief musician is always right but simply responsible to make the decisions, which makes their decisions the right ones. Once in a while, it can be good for a chief musician to ask team members for their musical opinion. However, if a leader chooses to not accept those suggestions, team members must graciously accept that decision. The chief musician should also try to do their best to explain why they did not use the idea to the team member's satisfaction.

BEFORE THE REHEARSALS

The worship leader of any service should plan the service(s) at least two weeks in advance. That gives the leader time to arrange the music and transpose any music needed for the service. On the Monday before the Sunday service(s), I send out an email to the entire worship team. Attached to that email is a Word document containing the service plan(s) for that coming Sunday.

If the songs we are doing are available on YouTube, I include links to them in the song list(s). That way, if anyone is not sure of any of the songs, they can click on the links and familiarize themselves with the songs before the midweek rehearsal.

Along with the service plan, in the same Word file, I put the chord charts for all of the songs in their concert keys. I expect the worship team members to print that file for themselves. If they require the printed music for the songs, I allow them access to the church's CCLI (Christian Copyright Licensing International) account online so they can go on "Song Select" and print the music out for themselves. Of course, if we are doing a locally written song, I am responsible for writing it out musically for those who require it.

For the instrumentalists and appointed singers, I expect them to purchase their own three-hole punch and a black three-ring binder to hold the printed chord charts or music. The church should provide Manhasset style music stands to hold those binders. For the choir, they should pair up inside their own section so they can share two to a binder. Those pairs can work out between themselves the purchase of a black binder and the song printing each week.

Everyone is responsible for bringing their binder to rehearsals and ministry times, along with a pencil and eraser. I require everyone to write down everything that applies to them on the chord charts or music in their binders. No one will be able to remember everything required to execute a worship service without writing things down! Be sure to use a pencil, not a pen.

WEEKLY WORSHIP TEAM REHEARSALS

Regardless of the size of your church or worship team, rehearsals are critical to the success of your worship. I recommend two rehearsals per week. The primary rehearsal should be a weekly weeknight, all-worship-team rehearsal not to exceed two hours. Everyone involved in the church's worship ministry should be required to attend. That includes the audio/visual department. When the entire worship team rehearses together on a regular basis, every instrumentalist and singer is learning the same songs at the same time the same way.

The second weekly rehearsal should take place 45 minutes prior to the worship services and should involve only the team members scheduled to minister in that service. If your church has multiple services on Sunday, you may have to shorten the rehearsal(s) between the services.

TIMING FOR THE WEEKNIGHT REHEARSAL

I suggest either beginning at 6:30 p.m. and ending at 8:30 p.m., or beginning at 7 p.m. and ending at 9 p.m. The time you choose must fit the community in which you live. Some communities tend to go to bed earlier than others.

If I want to meet with a smaller ensemble or soloist to practice special music, I will have the entire worship team come at 6:30 p.m., then hold that ensemble or soloist over for not more than a 30-minute rehearsal. The only time I will exceed 2.5 hours on this rehearsal night is when we are preparing for a special presentation, such as a Christmas or Easter concert. In that case, three hours is the absolute maximum time to expect people to be at a rehearsal. Also, any time you keep people for more than two hours, you must give them a restroom break. Make sure everyone knows the time frame of their commitment before they commit, and honor the time frame you asked for.

If you think you need to hold rehearsal over five or ten minutes, do one of two things. The first action is the preferred one, which is simply stop the rehearsal before starting the last thing you want to practice.

The second option is to ask the team's permission to go five or ten minutes overtime. If you do not receive a consensus from the group, stop the rehearsal! Never seek permission to go overtime more than two or three times per year. Any more than that will be construed as an abuse of time.

OUTLINE FOR A WEEKNIGHT REHEARSAL

The following is a suggested template for your week night rehearsals. Feel free to adapt it to fit your situation.

Table 21. Week Night Rehearsal Template

Time	What	Who
7:00 p.m.	Opening Prayer	TBA
7:02 p.m.	Instrumental Warm-ups	Instruments
7:07 p.m.	Vocal Warmups	Everyone
7:12 p.m.	Fix Musical Issues	Everyone
7:15 p.m.	Sunday Morning Service Rehearsal	Everyone
7:45 p.m.	Sunday Evening Service Rehearsal	Everyone
8:15 p.m.	Scripture based Devotional	Chief Musician
8:24 p.m.	Announcements	Chief Musician
8:30 p.m.	"New" song / new songs rehearsal	Everyone
8:55 p.m.	Closing prayer (including requests)	TBA
9:00 p.m.	Dismiss	Chief Musician

INSTRUMENTAL WARM-UPS

In Chapter 11, I told you to have your instrumentalists learn to play in these key centers: C, D, Eb, E, F, G, Ab, A, Bb, Cm, Dm, Em, Gm, Am. The best way to warm up your instrumentalists is to have them play together through one octave, ascending and descending, of those keys.

Obviously, there are too many keys to play through all of them every time you warm up, because we have only allotted five minutes for instrumental warm-ups at the weeknight rehearsal. Conceivably you will have even less time to warm up in the rehearsals before each service. I recommend that you always do the keys of C, D, F, and G and add one other major key and one minor key every time you warm up. Make sure you remember which keys you have done in the past so you are rotating the keys equally.

On the next page, you will see the C major scale written in quarter notes, then in eighth notes. Do all of the scales following that pattern. If you must write out these scales for your instrumentalists, be aware that some of the instruments require you to transpose their music.

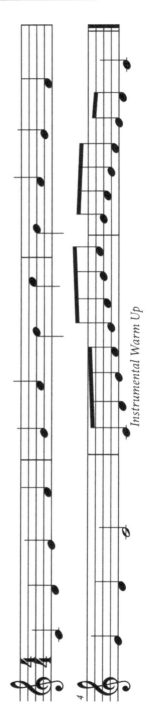

Instrumental Warm Up

You will notice this exercise is entitled "Concert C Warm-Up." A piano or keyboard is tuned to concert pitch. So are a guitar and bass guitar. However, some of the orchestral instruments are not tuned to concert pitch. As a chief musician or primary worship leader, you must know which instruments must be transposed to play in concert with everyone else.

Fortunately, the string family of instruments—violin, viola, cello, and double bass—all play in concert pitch. Look out for the wind instruments. For instance, a trumpet and a clarinet are both B flat instruments. That means, whenever they are playing a C, they are playing a concert Bb. For them to play in the key of concert C, they have to be playing in the key of D. Alto saxophones are Eb instruments. That means they must play in the key of A to play in concert C.

After you have done those scales several times, your instrumentalists will have them memorized and will be able to play them all from memory. The rhythm section instruments should also play those scales with the orchestral instruments. The pianist and keyboardist should strive to play the scales with both hands. The lead guitarist and bass guitarist should play the scales as well. The rhythm guitarist is the only one exempt from this exercise. Instead of the scales, that individual should play these chords on these notes of every scale.

Table 22. Warm-Up Chords for the Rhythm Guitar

Ascending

Note #	1	2	3	4	5	6	7	8
Chords	I		I		I		V	I

Descending

Note #	8	7	6	5	4	3	2	1
Chords	I		I		IV		V	I

The drummer and percussionists should provide rhythm for this exercise at the tempo the chief musician sets.

VOCAL WARM-UPS

Just as it is important to stretch before you work out, it is also important to warm up your voice before placing strong demands on it. On the following page, I provide a great exercise for all the singers to warm up with. The vocalists will need instrumental support on this exercise from the piano and drums only. All other instrumentalists should sing these warm-ups with the choir.

This warm-up is an arpeggiated triad in every major key indicated by the key signatures on the exercise. The pianist should play the motif as the singers sing it on either "zing ee eh ah oo" or "moh ee moh ee moh." I recommend alternating these syllables. At one rehearsal, do the first; then at the next rehearsal, do the second.

The benefits of the "zing ee eh ah oo" syllables are these:

1. This allows everyone to practice rapidly singing multiple vowels, which requires changing the vocal cords and mouth quickly.
2. It also allows everyone to practice placing the sound high in the nasal cavity as you sing the word "zing." Every singer should feel a buzz in their eyes and forehead when they sing that word.
3. The benefits of the "moh ee moh ee moh" syllables is practicing rapidly changing the shape of the mouth between two extremely different mouth shapes.

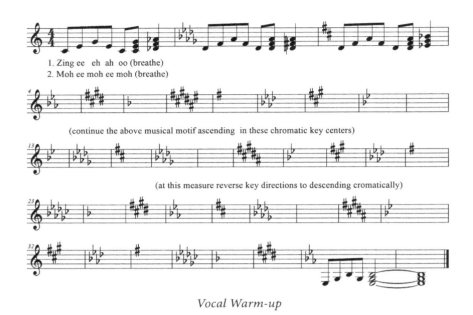

1. Zing ee eh ah oo (breathe)
2. Moh ee moh ee moh (breathe)

(continue the above musical motif ascending in these chromatic key centers)

(at this measure reverse key directions to descending cromatically)

Vocal Warm-up

The singers should not sing while the pianist is playing the chords of the key they just sang in and that they will be singing in. These piano chords provide two very important things. First, they give the singers the new key center for the next arpeggios so they can be mentally ready for it. Second, they give the singers the opportunity to fill up with air.

No one will be able to sing this exercise in every key indicated. That means each singer must pay attention to their personal vocal range. When the keys start to get too high for the altos and basses, they should drop out and count the number of key centers the exercise continues ascending. Then count the same number of descending keys before rejoining the exercise. When it gets too low for the tenors and sopranos, they can simply drop out and wait for the altos and basses to finish the exercise.

A second vocal warm-up that helps the choir to blend its sound is this one:

Choral Blending Exercise

Again, the humming sound provides the opportunity for the singers to feel the buzz in their eyes and forehead. You should not do this exercise in a strict rhythm but with total ad-lib. Only move to the next measure when your choir has achieved a unified, blended sound where no individual voices can be detected.

FIX MUSICAL ISSUES

In the middle of a worship service is never the time to fix musical issues. If the worship team makes a mistake, just keep going. Then, if a musical issue showed up during the Sunday service, at the beginning of the weeknight rehearsal, take three minutes to fix that issue. It is better to fix small problems shortly after they have happened than to wait several months to address them. However, don't spend a lot of time on those issues. If it will take more than two or three minutes to fix a musical problem, schedule time to do that after the announcements.

REHEARSAL FOR SUNDAY SERVICES

The appointed singers, rhythm section instrumentalists, and audio/visual technicians who are scheduled for the service you are rehearsing for should play, sing, and operate the equipment for that rehearsal. The rest of the people in those sections who were not scheduled should take their place in the choir.

If your church does not have a Sunday evening service, that frees up some time in rehearsal to allow you to spend a little more time on the Sunday morning service and on learning new songs. If you have both Sunday morning and Sunday evening services, you need to be very expedient with your time in rehearsal.

This rehearsal time is not the time for spontaneity or learning new songs. It is the time to make sure everyone can play and sing the prewritten songs you have chosen for the services. If a musical problem arises with a song, you must quickly decide:

- whether you have enough time to fix that problem in this rehearsal time.
- whether you should substitute that song with a more familiar one.
- whether you should drop the song for that service until the worship team knows it better.

All of the songs on your worship service plan should be familiar to everyone, because you have taken the time to learn the songs when they were new to you. You do not have a lot of time to waste in this rehearsal on songs you should already know. Never plan to do a song in a service before you know it well and are ready to teach it to the congregation.

Because the worship team should know all of the songs you are planning to do for the services, you may not need to do every verse of the multiple verse hymns or songs in the rehearsal. You may choose to do only the less-familiar verses. Of course, you may choose to not do all of the verses in the actual service either.

More than the songs themselves, these rehearsals are about practicing the flow of the service. That means practicing the transitions between songs is the priority. If you have to waste time learning a song in this rehearsal, you are not ready to do the song in a service. This rehearsal is more about practicing the flow than learning songs.

SHORT DEVOTIONAL

A chief musician or principal worship leader should spend time every day reading the Bible. When doing that, ask God to direct you where to read in the Bible. As you read the passage that God leads you to, ask Him to teach you.

A the chief musician or principal worship leader, you should also spend time every week praying by name for every member of your worship team.

Then, a day or two before the rehearsal, ask God what truth you should share at the rehearsal. Your devotional should be only one truth that God has shown you in your times with Him, supported by one or two Scriptures. Keep it brief—don't ramble! End your devotional with a short prayer asking God to seal that truth to the heart and mind of everyone.

ANNOUNCEMENTS

There are always things you must communicate that affect the entire worship team. Some worship leaders use this time to announce birthdays or anniversaries or social events. You may also have instructions concerning a special time of ministry coming up. The church may be planning a series of special meetings for which you will need to give the team instructions.

This is not a time for group discussions or to air out personal feelings!

LEARNING NEW SONGS

For this part of the rehearsal, the section leaders of the rhythm section instruments and the appointed singer vocal parts should either be the one to play or sing or appoint someone in their section. I recommend that each section leader give their section members equal opportunities to participate during this time of the rehearsal. Some section leaders may choose to switch out every one in their section in one rehearsal. If you have a lot of people in one section, everyone will only get a few minutes playing or singing. In that case, you may prefer to have the same person for each rehearsal and rotate a different person every week.

Practicing the Chädäsh Song

I recommend that at least once per month at this rehearsal you take the time left after announcements to practice singing and playing the new song. Because the Bible tells us that David appointed certain people to prophesy in song,[83] once you have established an initial chord progression for the new song in rehearsal, randomly appoint different instrumentalists and singers to play or sing a new song. Don't just select the appointed singers and instrumental section leaders for this. Try to give every person in the choir and orchestra chances to practice the new song.

I realize this puts them on the spot, but the Bible gives you the right as their chief musician to appoint them to play or sing a new song. A new song is released in the exact same way the gifts of the Spirit are, especially prophecy. In Paul's instructions to the Corinthians concerning the operation of prophetic spiritual gifts, Paul reveals a very important truth.

> And the spirits of the prophets are subject to the prophets. 1 Corinthians 14:32 (NKJV)

That means that, when operating spiritual gifts and a new song, God will work with a person **IF** they choose to yield themselves to the Lord. He does not override anyone's free will.

Practicing a new song in rehearsal prepares the worship team to do it in a church service. Then, the more the congregation members experience a new song, the more chance they will allow God to give them a new song as well.

Practicing the Chädash Songs

At the other three rehearsals of the month, you should be learning new prewritten songs. I suggest you have three prewritten songs you are working on at all times. Those songs should be in various stages of preparation. One of the three songs should be very new to the worship team. Make sure your best vocal harmonizers, which should be your section leaders, are on the microphones when you first introduce a song to your team to establish the correct vocal harmonies for that song.

---

[83] 1 Chronicles 25:1

Another song you are working on should be one you are more familiar with but still need rehearsal on it before you can teach it to the congregation. Because the vocal harmonies will have already been established, you can rotate the appointed singers for these other two songs. The third song is the one you are very familiar with and are about ready to teach to the church.

When it is time to teach the congregation a new prewritten song, I suggest that the first time you do so in a service, do it as a special number by the choir and orchestra. These specials work well if your church still passes the plate for offering time or has people get out of their seat to walk their offering to an offering station.

After you have introduced this prewritten new song to the congregation as a special, for the next two weeks include that song in the song list or worship plan. By that time, the song should be established in the congregation's repertoire of worship songs.

THE PRESERVICE REHEARSALS

Have your worship team be ready to rehearse 45 minutes before each service. That means the instrumentalists who must tune or set up must get there earlier so they are ready on time. At these preservice rehearsals, talk through the service plan and practice the transitions between songs. Here is a preservice rehearsal template that I recommend.

Table 23. Preservice Rehearsal Template

Minute	What	Who
45	Opening Prayer	TBA
43	Instrumental Warm-ups	Instruments
40	Vocal Warmups	Everyone
36	Talk through the service plan	Worship Leader
27	Practice the difficult transitions	Everyone
20	Prayer for service	TBA
15	Restroom break	Everyone
10	Preservice music	Insts./audio
5	"Places"	Everyone

TALK THROUGH THE SERVICE PLAN

At the weeknight rehearsal, the worship team rehearsed everything concerning the service. Now that it is time to execute what was rehearsed, remind the worship team of what they practiced.

To demonstrate what I would do to talk through a service plan, let me share with you an actual service I put together and led on June 20, 2021. Keep in mind as you read through it that my church has a worshiping congregation. Therefore, I plan for the worship time in our services to last anywhere from 45 minutes to an hour. Depending on how long God leads the new song to go or if the gifts of the spirit are released, I would shorten this list as the service progresses. If I was planning a worship time for only twenty to thirty minutes, I would have planned only three or four prewritten songs.

Table 24. City Church of Wichita Worship Service Plan

Date: June 20, 2021	Time: 10:30 am
Special Day/Event: Father's Day	
Special Music: N/A	
Worship Leader: Shamblin Stone	
For the sake of privacy the second-rank names have been removed.	

Preservice Plan

Key	Song/Item	Note
N/A	**Prerecorded music** (Audio Technician's Choice)	Moderate Tempo

Service Plan

D	*Great Is Thy faithfulness* © 1923	Hymn
E	*Thrive* Casting Crowns © 2014 https://www.youtube.com/watch?v=qQ71RWJhS_M	CCLI # 7006228
E	*My Redeemer Lives* Hillsong © 1998 https://www.youtube.com/watch?v=bj_BvlYFyEg	CCLI # 2397964
E	*We Believe* Newsboys © 2013 https://www.youtube.com/watch?v=E00j5xGeDm8	CCLI # 6367165
E	*Be Glorified* Billy Funk © 1991 https://www.youtube.com/watch?v=b2FwHBPIi9k	CCLI # 429226
Em	*Take Me In* © 1987 https://www.youtube.com/watch?v=zxWRe-dHFg0	CCLI # 19272
Em	**"New"** song (C 2 bts, D 2 bts, Em 4 bts)	
E	*Awesome in This Place* © 1992 https://youtu.be/faiLQCuoskM	CCLI # 847554

Ending Song

	TBA	

The keys of E and Em are very difficult to play in for the transposing instruments. Before I plan a worship service in those keys, I have to know that my wind instrumentalists can play in them. If not, I will transpose all the songs to Eb and Ebm and tell the guitarists to put a capo behind the first fret and play in the key of D and Dm. Of course, I will have to transpose their chord charts to those keys. With my present worship team, I do not need to go to all that trouble, so I left the songs in the concert pitches of two sharps, four sharps, and one sharp.

I want to take you through what I would say to the worship team in the preservice rehearsal. I have given you the lyrics of all the songs so you can refer to them as you read my comments. Keep in mind that, if this were the rehearsal, you would be hearing my words as you are looking at the songs. That way you will be reading my words and will have to glance back at the lyrics to keep up with what I am saying. In other words, this will take longer to read through and make sense of than it would for me to talk through it as you follow along with the songs.

At every rehearsal I expect every worship team member to have a pencil with which they write on the song sheets everything that is pertinent to them. I suggest that, as you read through what I would say at the rehearsal, that you pretend you are there and write it down on the lyrics sheets here in pencil the things that would apply to you.

Everyone develops their own shorthand for taking these notes. For instance, instead of writing out the words appointed singer, I will simply use *AS*. For soprano, alto, tenor, or bass, I will use the letters *S, A, T, B*. Clarinet is *Cl*, trumpet is *Tr*, drums is *D*, lead guitar is *LG*, piano is *P*, etc. Also, unison is *U*, harmony parts is *pts*, and if we are going to repeat a section, I use the musical repeat signs around the section we are to repeat. The musical repeat symbols are two vertical lines and a colon. The colon is to the right of the two lines at the beginning of the section and to the left of the two lines at the end of the section, like this: ||: ... :||. Here are the lyrics to the songs on our list.

Great Is Thy faithfulness[84]
Thomas Obediah Chisholm and William Marion Runyan

Verse 1:
Great is thy faithfulness, O God my Father, There is no shadow of turning with Thee;
Thou changest not, Thy compassions they fail not As Thou has been Thou forever wilt be.

Chorus:
Great is Thy faithfulness! Great is Thy faithfulness! Morning by morning new mercies I see.
All I have needed Thy hand hath provided Great is Thy faithfulness, Lord unto me.

Verse 2:
Summer and winter, and springtime and harvest, sun, moon, and stars in their courses above
Join with all nature in manifold witness to Thy great faithfulness, mercy and love.

Verse 3:
Pardon for sin and a peace that endureth, Thy own dear presence to cheer and to guide.
Strength for today and bright hope for tomorrow Blessings all mine, with ten thousand beside.

++

Thrive[85]
Mark Hall | Matthew West

Beginning
Oh oh Oh oh

Verse 1
Here in this worn and weary land Where many a dream has died
Like a tree planted by the water We will never run dry

Pre-Chorus
So living water flowing through God we thirst for more of You

---

[84] Chisholm, Thomas Obediah and William Marion Runyan. *Great Is Thy Faithfulness.* CCLI Song # 18723, 1923.
[85] Hall, Mark and Matthew West. *Thrive.* Be Essential Songs, My Refuge Music, Highly Combustible Music, House of Story Music Publishing, One77 Songs, CCLI Song # 7006228, 2014.

Fill our hearts and flood our souls With one desire

Chorus
Just to know You and to make You known We lift Your name on high
Shine like the sun make darkness run and hide
We know we were made for so much more Than ordinary lives
It's time for us to more than just survive We were made to thrive

Verse 2
Into Your Word we're digging deep To know our Father's heart
Into the world we're reaching out To show them who You are

(Bridge)
Joy unspeakable, Faith unsinkable, Love unstoppable, Anything is possible

ending
Oh oh Oh oh We were made to thrive

+++

My Redeemer Lives[86]
Reuben Morgan

Verse
I know He rescued my soul, His blood has covered my sin, I believe I believe
My shame He's taken away, My pain is healed in His name, I believe I believe

Pre-Chorus
I'll raise a banner 'Cause my Lord has conquered the grave

Chorus
My Redeemer lives! My Redeemer lives! My Redeemer lives! My Redeemer lives!

Bridge
You lift my burdens! I'll rise with You!
I'm dancing on this mountaintop to see Your kingdom come

+++

---

[86] Morgan, Reuben. *My Redeemer Lives*. Australia: Hillsong Music Publishing, CCLI Song # 2397964, 1998.

We Believe[87]
Matthew Hooper, Richie Fike, and Travis Ryan

Verse 1
In this time of desperation When all some know is doubt and fear
There is only one foundation we believe we believe
In this broken generation When all is dark You help us see
There is only one salvation we believe we believe

Chorus
We believe in God the Father we believe in Jesus Christ
We believe in the Holy Spirit and He's given us new life
We believe in the crucifixion We believe that He conquered death

1st ending
We believe in the resurrection And He's coming back again. We believe!

2nd ending
We believe in the resurrection and He's coming back again

3rd ending to ending
We believe in the resurrection and He's coming back

Verse 2
So let our faith be more than anthems Greater than the songs we sing
In our weakness and temptations, we believe we believe

Bridge
Let the lost be found and the dead be raised In the here and now let love invade
Let the church live loud our God will save We believe we believe
And the gates of hell will not prevail For the pow'r of God has torn the veil
Now we know Your love will never fail We believe we believe

Ending
He's coming back again, He's coming back again, We believe we believe

+++

---

[87] Hooper, Matthew, Richie Fike, and Travis Ryan. *We Believe*. Integrity Worship Music, Integrity's Praise! Music, Life Worship, and Travis Ryan Music, CCLI Song # 6367165.

Be Glorified[88]
Billy Funk

Verse 1
Be glorified, be glorified, Be glorified, be glorified

Chorus 1
Be glorified in the heavens Be glorified in the earth Be glorified in this temple
Jesus Jesus Be Thou glorified, Jesus Jesus Be Thou glorified

Verse 2
Worship the Lord, worship the Lord, Worship the Lord, worship the Lord

Chorus 2
Worship the Lord in the heavens Worship the Lord in the earth Worship the Lord in
this temple
Jesus Jesus Be Thou glorified, Jesus Jesus Be Thou glorified

+++

Take Me In[89]
Dave Browning

Verse
Take me past the outer courts Into the Holy place
Past the brazen altar Lord I want to see Your face
Pass me by the crowds of people The priests who sing Your praise
I hunger and thirst for Your righteousness And it's only found one place

Chorus
Take me in to the Holy of Holies Take me in by the blood of the Lamb
Take me in to the Holy of Holies Take the coal, cleanse my lips, here I am

+++

---

[88] Funk, Billy. *Be Glorified*. Integrity's Praise! Music, CCLI Song # 429226, 1991.
[89] Browning, Dave. *Take Me In*. Curb Dayspring Music, CCLI Song # 19272, 1987.

Awesome in This Place[90]
Dave Billington

Verse
As I come into your presence Past the gates of praise,
Into Your sanctuary, 'Till we're standing face to face.
I look upon your countenance, See the fullness of your grace.
I can only bow down and say ...

Chorus
You are awesome in this place, Mighty God! You are awesome in this place, Abba Father!
You are worthy of all praise, To You our lives we raise.
You are awesome in this place, Mighty God!

Now here is what I would say in the preservice rehearsal.

Great Is Thy Faithfulness

"Remember this first song is in three, and we want to do it about 90 beats per minute." NOTE to reader: If your instrumentalists are not familiar with metronome markings, simply use the three-beat pattern to beat out a couple of measures in the tempo desired. Also, I use this faster tempo when using this song as a gate song. If I use this song in the tabernacle, I do it about 75 bpm.

"We will do an instrumental introduction in tempo using the last half of the last line of the chorus beginning at 'Great is Thy ...'." NOTE to reader: To do an instrumental introduction requires that someone plays the melody. I prefer it when the orchestral instruments do that; however, it is still OK to have the pianist or lead guitarist play the melody.

"We will do all three verses; however, there will be no chorus after the second verse. For the third verse, the soprano melody double and alto appointed singers will sing the melody and alto part while the rest of us sing 'oos.'" NOTE to reader: You will have had to teach all the "oo" parts to the choir in the midweek rehearsal. Don't let them "oo" what

---

[90] Billington, Dave. *Awesome in This Place*. Integrity's Hosanna! Music, CCLI Song # 847554, 1992.

the appointed singers are singing. When a choir "oos," it should only change notes once per measure at the most. The less changes the better. The tenor and bass appointed singers can still lead their sections in the "oos," but you will need to make sure there are internal leaders in the soprano and alto sections.

"After the third verse, everyone come in very strongly on the chorus. Trumpets, play up an octave for this last chorus. Also, we will slow the tempo down to 80 BPM. I want this last chorus to sound very regal. On the last line of this chorus, we will repeat the words 'Great is Thy faithfulness,' singing them three times in total, progressively retarding on each time. Do a very slow and regal retard as you finish that line, 'Lord unto me.'"

Thrive

"On the downbeat of the word 'me,' change the time signature to four/four and change the tempo to 120 BPM. Play one measure of the D chord and one measure of the E chord. Then begin this next song on the A chord, singing the 'ohs.'

"We will only do the 'ohs' at the beginning and at the end of this song, not in the middle the way Casting Crowns does it. The ohs are always done in unison.

"Here's the format we will do this song in: Ohs, verse one, pre-chorus, chorus, verse two, pre-chorus, chorus, the bridge three times, chorus, and end on the Ohs. Maintain the tempo throughout the song, including the final ohs.

"Now let's discuss the details of this song. I will sing the first line of the first verse solo. On the second line the tenor appointed singer will join me with a tenor harmony.

"All the appointed singers join me in unison on the pre-chorus. Instrumentalists, please keep your parts simple but driving.

"Everyone please come in on the chorus in full vocal harmony, until the last line of the chorus, which everyone—including the instrumentalists—will do in unison.

"The alto appointed singer sings the melody of the first line of the second verse solo. She is joined by the soprano appointed singer on the last line of verse two singing a tenor harmony.

"Everyone comes in on the pre-chorus in unison. At the chorus, we go into full vocal harmony, including the last line. Notice this is different from the first time.

"The bridge is done in harmony but with contrasting dynamics. Start the three times through the bridge at piano, gradually increasing the volume to a double forte. Then vocally harmony parts on the entire last time through the chorus, but go back to unison on the ending ohs."

My Redeemer Lives

"Don't slow down at all from the 120 BPM, and everyone go immediately into the chorus of *My Redeemer Lives* in vocal parts.

"On the verse, the tenor appointed singer sings solo the first line, harmonized by the clarinet on an alto part. At the end of that line, everyone sings and plays in parts on the words 'I believe, I believe.' The tenor and clarinet also do the next line of the verse like they did the first line, and again everyone joins them on the 'I believe I believe' in parts like before.

"On the pre-chorus, the tenor sax joins the tenor singer and clarinet with a tenor harmony part, while the choir 'oos.' Then the voices are tutti again on the chorus.

"On the bridge, the tenor sings the melody solo with no harmonies from the clarinet and tenor sax. The choir 'oos' for the first line and 'ahs' for the last line of the bridge. At the beginning of the bridge, bring the dynamics down to mezzo piano and gradually crescendo to a mezzo forte by the end of the bridge.

"On the chorus after the bridge, everyone stops playing except for the drums and percussion, and everyone claps on beats two and four and sings a cappella in parts. After the a cappella chorus, repeat the chorus with everyone playing and singing in parts. After that chorus, the choir goes back to 'oos' as the tenor, and clarinet does the first line of the verse progressively slowing to about 90 BPM."

We Believe

"On the very next measure, everyone sings and plays the chorus of the song *We Believe* in full harmony parts. The tempo will be about 90 BPM. Take the first ending going to verse two. We will not be doing verse one of this song in this service.

"The soprano appointed singer sings the first half of the first line of verse two. The alto appointed singer sings an alto part with the soprano on the second half of that line. The tenor appointed singer joins with them with a tenor harmony part on the first part of line two of verse two. The bass appointed singer joins the other appointed singers with a bass part on the words 'we believe we believe.' We are tutti again on the chorus, taking the second ending and repeat the chorus. We will not be singing the bridge in this service.

"On the last time through the chorus, all voices sing the melody in unison on the first line. On the second line of the chorus, break into four-part harmony for the rest of the song. Take the third ending of the chorus going to the ending of the song. Retard the last line of the ending, 'we believe we believe.'

"Move into an arhythmic new song on the E chord. Be sensitive to the Holy Spirit here in case He wants to use you at this time to sing a structured new song, or flow into the gifts of the Spirit."

Be Glorified

"I will start this song out of the new song when I feel the Spirit telling me to go on with the service plan. I anticipate doing it about 65 BPM. When you hear me start the song, let the keyboards carry the accompaniment for the first time through the verse. The choir and appointed singers will 'oo' on the notes you have been taught as I sing through the verse one time.

"We will repeat the first verse after I sing it with everyone in parts. On the chorus, I need everyone singing with me in parts. Instrumentalists should play very simplistically and worshipfully. Sing in parts every time we do the chorus of this song, except the first time when I sing it solo.

"On the verse, everyone sings in parts, then go into unison when we sing 'Jesus, Jesus,' then back to parts on 'be Thou glorified.' We will do this song as many times as the Lord leads. On the last time we sing 'be Thou glorified,' slow the tempo to 60 BPM."

Take Me In

"On the syllable '-fied,' play one measure of the E chord, then play one measure on the Em chord. Start the song on the pick-up to the next measure.

"On the first time through the verse, the alto appointed singer will sing the entire verse solo while the rest of us 'oo.' Everyone comes in on parts on the chorus. When we go back to the verse after the first chorus, everyone sings in unison. We then go back to parts on the chorus. Repeat the chorus singing 'oos' while the alto appointed singer sings the chorus solo.

"We repeat the line, 'take the coal, cleanse my lips, here I am' with every one singing parts several times. Use this chord progression to break into a structured new song for as long as the Holy Spirit leads."

Awesome in This Place

"When the spirit leads us to draw the structured new song to a close, we will end it with a Picardy third." NOTE to reader: This is a musical term meaning to end a minor key song on the major I chord.

"The soprano appointed singer, accompanied only by the piano, will sing the verse in a total ad-lib tempo." NOTE to reader: Ad-lib is the absence of any rhythmic structure.

"At the chorus, the tenor and alto appointment singers join her in three-part harmony at about 45 BPM. We then will repeat the verse and chorus in tempo with everyone singing parts and playing simplistically.

"We will repeat the verse and chorus as many times as we are led to by the Holy Spirit. When it comes time to end the song, we will sing the last line of the chorus three times, retarding each time. Between the repeats, we will go to a C#m chord. After that, we will once again move into an arhythmic new song on the I chord.

"Anytime we move into a new song, be praying and asking God if He wants to use you to sing a prophetic new song or to flow in a gift of the Holy Spirit. If I feel God wants to give you a solo new song, I will point to you like I did in practice and expect you to sing or play the new song."

PRACTICE THE DIFFICULT TRANSITIONS

You will not have time in this preservice rehearsal to go through any of the songs completely. What you should use this time for is to practice as many of the transitions as you can. That helps to set the tempos in everyone's minds as well.

PRAYER FOR THE EVENT

Now that you have done your part to prepare for worship, it is time to ask God to make up for your inadequacies and to inhabit your offering of praise.[91] It is important to do this corporately, not just as individuals, because unity in worship is extremely important.

RESTROOM BREAK

Insist that everyone on the worship team visit the restroom before ministering. Nothing distracts a person more from worship than the call of nature. Also, I'm sorry to have to say this, but every woman should check herself in the mirror before leaving that room, and every guy should check his fly at the door. Our responsibility is to lead the congregation in worship, not to distract them from it.

PRESERVICE MUSIC

I know it is easiest to play prerecorded music before your service starts, as people are coming in to find their seat. There is nothing wrong with that. However, it is important that you realize how preservice music can set the expectations for a service and how you can select the right music for this.

---

[91] Psalm 22:2

These days everywhere we go there is prerecorded music playing in the background. We used to call that "elevator music," because that's where we would notice the heartless renditions being played of popular songs.

Most people mentally block out background music, thinking of it only as noise. This will happen at some point, if you use prerecorded music before your church services. Because of that, I recommend your instrumentalists play for five to ten minutes before each service. Live music is much harder to ignore or consider as background music. Therefore, live music creates an anticipation for the service in a way no prerecorded music can.

Live preservice music is most effective when you have orchestral instruments, which can carry the songs' melodies. When the keyboard instruments must play the melody, it can cheapen the sound enough to lose the attention of the churchgoers.

There are two schools of thought when choosing songs to be played before the service starts. The first says you should only choose songs with a tempo appropriate for the gate. The other school declares that gate and court songs are appropriate for this time. I have done it both ways. If I want to have the instrumentalists play a faster tempo song in the preservice, I still start with a moderate tempo first when I start the service.

A faster tempo song in preservice seems to create more of an expectation about the service than a moderate tempo song. Also, even if some people enter the courtyard in the preservice time, there will still be enough stragglers to merit you starting outside the gate again once the service actually begins.

Some people simply play through the first two or three songs on their worship plan in their preservice time. Others will choose completely different music for the preservice. I have done it both ways, and both are equally effective.

PLACES

"Places" is a term used in live theater by the stage manager. Typically, it is called five minutes before the curtain goes up. When "places" is called, it means everyone must go to their place, which they are to be in when the show begins. Therefore, five minutes before every worship service, every worship team member MUST be in their place, no exceptions!

SOCIALIZATION TIMES

It is important to plan at least two events per year where your entire worship team, including the audio/visual and other support ministries, can be together socially. You will need to decide whether you will invite spouses and children to these events. Some events are more appropriate for families than others. Once in a while, I will invite the senior pastor and spouse to a social event for the worship department. Here are a few ideas for social gatherings, which you can try.

1. August or September kickoff, welcome new members party or retreat
2. Christmas party
3. February winter break party
4. May or June end-of-season cookout
5. July Independence Day or mid-summer party

At one of these social events, you may want to recognize people for their faithful service. Pins or certificates are great gifts to recognize one year, five years, ten years, etc., of service to the worship ministry. Always show your appreciation to everyone for their hard work, which makes the worship ministry of your church what it is.

REGISTRATION AND COMMITMENT

A chief musician is a pastor of the worship ministry of a church. Administration of that department is a vital part of pastoring those people. Here is a registration form for you to use when people want to get involved in the worship ministry of your church. Feel free to adapt it to your situation.

Table 25. Worship Ministry Volunteer Form

[Church name] Worship Ministry Volunteer Form

Personal Information	
Full Name:	❏ M ❏ F
Email Address:	Bday: MM/DD/YY
Cellphone:	Home Phone:
Work Phone:	❏ I can receive calls here
Street Address:	
City:	ST/Prov: Code:

Emergency Contact		
Name:	Relation:	Phone:

Vocal Experience

❏ I know what my voice range is. I am a ❏ S ❏ A ❏ T ❏ B

❏ I'm not sure what my voice range is and need to be assessed.

❏ I am not experienced as a singer but am willing to learn.

❏ I have had experience as a singer in ❏ church ❏ school ❏ other

My experience singing includes ❏ soloist ❏ small ensembles ❏ choir

❏ I have had private vocal training. Studied how long?

❏ I can vocally read music. | ❏ I can harmonize by ear. ❏ A ❏ T ❏ B

Instrumental Skill

Most proficient musical instrument:

played since:	lessons how long?	❏ I have my own.
❏ I can read music.	❏ I play by chord charts.	❏ I can play by ear.

Second-most proficient musical instrument (optional):

played since:	lessons how long?	❏ I have my own.
❏ I can read music.	❏ I play by chord charts.	❏ I can play by ear.

Worship Support Ministry

❏ Audio technician	❏ I am experienced.	❏ I need training.
❏ Lyrics projectionist	❏ I am experienced.	❏ I need training.
❏ Video production	❏ I am experienced.	❏ I need training.
❏ Stage lighting	❏ I am experienced.	❏ I need training.
❏ Worship dance	❏ I am experienced.	❏ I need training.
❏ Flags and banners	❏ I am experienced.	❏ I need training.
❏ Drama ministry	❏ I am experienced.	❏ I need training.
❏ Costumes, sets, props	❏ I am experienced.	❏ I need training.
❏ Display arts contributor	❏ I am experienced.	❏ I need training.
❏ Administration	❏ I am experienced.	❏ I need training.

It is also a good idea to give the people who join your worship ministry a list of expectations at the time they sign up so there is no chance of miscommunication or misunderstanding. Here's an example of what I am talking about. Feel free to adjust it to your situation.

[Church name] Worship Ministry Expectations

Holiness

1. I understand that participating in the worship ministry is a privilege, not a right, and that this privilege can be revoked should I do anything to biblically disqualify myself for this ministry.

Punctuality

2. I understand that I am expected to be at every rehearsal and time of ministry on time, in my place, and ready to participate.
3. If I play an instrument that must be tuned or set up, I understand I am expected to arrive early enough to take care of that.
4. If I know I will be late, I understand I am expected to text or call.

Courtesy

5. I understand I am expected to not talk during rehearsal or any time of ministry unless given permission.
6. I understand I am expected to never leave my position during rehearsal or time of ministry without seeking permission first and that should be only in the case of an emergency.

Cleanliness and Dress Code

7. I understand that I am expected to come to all times of ministry groomed, clean, and in clean clothes.
8. I understand no jeans are permitted at any time of ministry, unless told otherwise for special occasions.

9. I understand the men's dress code for ministry is black pants, black shoes and black socks, white dress shirt with no tie or suit jacket.
10. I understand the women's dress code for ministry is black skirt or pants, black shoes, and a white blouse.
11. I understand that I am expected to purchase any clothing I wear.

Ministry Commitment

12. I understand that I am expected to commit for one year at a time to the worship ministry, starting in September and going through August.
13. I understand that I am expected to communicate with the chief musician in writing no later than August 1 regarding my ongoing commitment to the worship ministry for another year or my intensions to step down to pursue a different ministry.
14. I understand that I am expected to do my best to find a replacement for myself when or if I leave the worship ministry.

Conflict Resolution

15. If I experience any relationship difficulties with anyone, especially in the worship ministry, I understand that I am expected to follow the Matthew 18 principal of going first to the person I have an issue with.
16. If this action does not bring the desired results, I understand I am expected to then go to the chief musician for help resolving the issue.
17. I promise never to speak to any person about any issue that does not concern them!
18. I understand that I am expected to not listen if someone in the worship ministry brings an issue to me that does not concern me. I also promise to redirect them to the chief musician to deal with their issue.

Attendance

19. I understand that I am expected to participate in all rehearsals and times of ministry.
20. If my work or family schedules conflict with this commitment, I understand that I am expected to seek a release from my worship team obligations as soon as I become aware of the conflict in schedules. That notice of schedule conflict must be submitted in writing no later than two weeks before the event.
21. I understand that failure to notify the chief musician before missing a rehearsal or time of ministry will result in an unexcused absence and that three unexcused absences will result in my suspension from the worship team for three months.
22. I understand that three more unexcused absences after being reinstated following a suspension will result in expulsion from the worship ministry for one year.

_____   _____

Signature of Worship Team Member   Date

_____

Print Name of Worship Team Member

RECRUITING

Always keep your eyes open to find new members for your worship choir, orchestra, and support team. If your church has a new members class, ask to perpetually address it. At those classes, go over the list of ministries available in the worship ministry of your church. Explain how everyone is on the same worship team and that promotion to a prominent place only comes from within.

If your church has a newsletter, make sure there is always an ad in it asking for people to join the worship team. Change the look of the ad every month so people don't overlook it.

If your church has a website, make sure the worship ministry is well represented on it. Copy and paste your newsletter recruitment ad onto the website each month. Do the same for all of the church's social media as well.

With all you do to recruit new members, keep in mind there is no substitute for talking to people one on one. After every service, talk to at least four people concerning them praying about being in the worship ministry.

I like to invite people to the midweek rehearsal to see what goes on. When they show up, I put them in a chair in the choir or orchestra beside a veteran member. After they visit a rehearsal, I follow up with a phone call or personal visit to ask them what their thoughts are. If the Lord leads, I will ask them to join our ministry.

PROTECT THE LEADERSHIP

Because our corporate worship gatherings are so important, our enemy is not going to sit by and let us use our sword of praise on him without trying to stop us. Satan's most effective weapon against our corporate worship is to attack the leadership. Therefore, it is every worshiper's responsibility to protect those giving leadership in the corporate worship gathering(s).

This responsibility does not just include individual prayers for the leadership prior to the worship gatherings. It also includes the realization that, no matter how spiritual you think you are, you too can be used of the devil to attack the leadership. Prior to the corporate worship gatherings, the leaders need to keep their focus on bringing God's people into God's presence and bringing God's presence to the people. Any distraction—no matter how innocent—can result in bringing the leadership's focus onto earthly or natural things and off of their mission. Here's how to avoid this:

1. Try not to speak to those giving worship leadership prior to a corporate worship gathering.
2. If that is unavoidable, only speak encouragement on a spiritual level, unless it cannot be avoided.
3. Never discuss problems with your leadership before a worship gathering.

4. Never talk about the weather or yesterday's golf game with worship leadership or anything that will diffuse their focus.

5. Never argue with leadership before a corporate gathering. Even if you're right, drop it and discuss it later.

6. Speak words of support to your worship gathering leaders. Assure them of your support.

7. Some bad news may be unavoidable on rare occasions before a worship gathering. If that is the case, be as tactful as possible while being as truthful as possible. And ALWAYS provide whatever support that leader needs to deal with that news. That may even mean releasing them from their responsibilities as a leader for that meeting, even at the last minute, for their sake and the sake of the body of worshipers.

Any of these and other things can be used to destroy the effectiveness of a corporate worship experience. Make sure you're not the one being used by the enemy to dilute the strength of a worship gathering! That can mean the difference between life and death on a spiritual level for so many people!

BIBLIOGRAPHY

"776. Erets," Bible Hub, accessed December 22, 2020, https://biblehub.com/hebrew/776.htm.

"1966. Helel," Bible Hub, accessed December 11, 2020, https://biblehub.com/hebrew/1966.htm.

"2318. Chadash," Bible Hub, accessed April 27, 2021, https://biblehub.com/hebrew/2318.htm.

"2319. Chadash," Bible Hub, accessed April 27, 2021, https://biblehub.com/hebrew/2319.htm.

"5035. Nebel," Bible Hub, accessed November 1, 2020, https://biblehub.com/hebrew/5035.htm.

"8067. Sheminith," Bible Hub, accessed November 1, 2020, https://biblehub.com/hebrew/8067.htm.

Alexandria, Clement of. *Shepherd of Eager Youth,* trans. Henry M. Dexter. Accessed April 16, 2021. https://hymnary.org/hymn/H1955/471.

St. Ambrose. *O Splendor of God's Glory Bright,* trans. Robert Seymour Bridges. Accessed April 16, 2021. https://hymnary.org/text/o_splendor_of_gods_glory_bright_o_thou.

Billington, Dave. *Awesome in This Place.* Integrity's Hosanna! Music, CCLI Song # 847554, 1992.

Browning, Dave. *Take Me In.* Curb Dayspring Music, CCLI Song # 19272, 1987.

Chisholm, Thomas Obediah and William Marion Runyan. *Great Is Thy Faithfulness.* CCLI Song # 18723, 1923.

Crouch, Andraé. *Soon and Very Soon.* Bud John Songs, Inc. and Crouch Music Corp., CCLI Song # 11249, 1971.

"Ezekiel 28:14," Bible Hub, accessed December 15, 2020, https://biblehub. com/parallel/ezekiel/28-14.htm.

Funk, Billy. *Be Glorified*. Integrity's Praise! Music, CCLI Song # 429226, 1991.

Gaither, William and Gloria Gaither. *Because He Lives*. Hanna Street Music, CCLI Song # 16880, 1971.

Hall, Mark and Matthew West. *Thrive*. Be Essential Songs, My Refuge Music, Highly Combustible Music, House of Story Music Publishing, One77 Songs, CCLI Song # 7006228, 2014.

Hooper, Matthew, Richie Fike, and Travis Ryan. *We Believe*. Integrity Worship Music, Integrity's Praise! Music, Life Worship, and Travis Ryan Music, CCLI Song # 6367165.

Kendrick, Graham. *Rejoice*. Make Way Music, CCLI song #1338, 1983.

Lockyer, Herbert. *Nelson's Illustrated Bible Dictionary*. (Nashville: Thomas Nelson Publishers, 1986).

Luther, Martin. *A Mighty Fortress Is Our God*, trans. Frederic Henry Hedge. CCLI Song # 42964, 1528. Accessed April 16, 2021. https:// en.wikipedia.org/wiki/A_Mighty_Fortress_Is_Our_God.

Millard, Bart. *I Can Only Imagine*. Simpleville Music, CCLI Song # 2978857, 2001, 2002.

Morgan, Reuben. *My Redeemer Lives*. Australia: Hillsong Music Publishing, CCLI Song # 2397964, 1998.

Mullins, Rich. *Awesome God*. Universal Music – Brentwood Benson Publishing, CCLI Song # 41099, 1988.

Perronet, Edward. *All Hail the Power of Jesus' Name*. CCLI Song # 25400, 1779. Accessed April 16, 2021. https://hymnary.org/text/all_hail_ the_power_of_jesus_name_let.

Smith III, James D. "2,000 Years, 25 Hymns," Christian History Institute, 2015, accessed April 16, 2021, https://christianhistoryinstitute.org/ magazine/article/2000-years-25-hymns.

Stone, Shamblin. *Biblical Worship* (Bloomington: Westbow Press, 2012).

Stone, Shamblin. *Portrait of a Worshiper* (Bloomington: Westbow Press, 2018).

Stone, Shamblin. *The Importance of Worshiping Together* (Bloomington: LifeRich Publishing, 2020).

Stone, Shamblin. *At Your Footstool*. Shamblin Stone Music, 2015.

Strong, J. *Strong's Exhaustive Concordance of the Bible* (Peabody: Hendrickson Publishers, 2007).

The Holy Bible, King James Version.

The Holy Bible, New International Version (Colorado Springs: Biblica, Inc.,1973, 1978, 1984, 2011).

The Holy Bible, New King James Version (Thomas Nelson, 1982).

The Holy Bible, The Passion Translation (Savage: BroadStreet Publishing Group, LLC, 2017, 2018, 2020).

The Living Bible (Carol Stream: Tyndale House Foundation, 1971).

The Holy Bible, New American Standard Bible (The Lockman Foundation, 1971, 1977, 1995).

Tomlin, Chris, Jesse Reeves, and Michael John Clement. *You Do All Things Well.* sixsteps Music, Vamos Publishing, and worshiptogether.com songs, admin. by Capitol CMG Publishing], CCLI Song # 4403605, 2004.

Tomlin, Chris, John Newton, and Louie Giglio. *My Chains Are Gone.* sixsteps Music, Vamos Publishing, worshiptogether.com songs, CCLI song #4768151, 2006.

Utterbach, Clinton. *The Name of the Lord.* Universal – Polygram International Publishing, Inc., Utterbach Music Publishing Company, admin. by Universal Music Publishing Group, CCLI Song # 265239, 1989.

Watts, Isaac and William Croft. *O God Our Help In Ages Past.* CCLI Song # 43152, 1714. Accessed April 16, 021, https://songselect.ccli.com/Songs/43152/o-god-our-help-in-ages-past-st-anne/viewlyrics.

"What Color Is Linen? The Natural Linen Color Explained," Magic Linen, accessed November 6, 2020, https://magiclinen.com/blog/what-color-is-linen.

"What Does It Mean That Saul Is Also Among the Prophets?" Got Questions Ministries, accessed April 17, 2020, https://www.gotquestions.org/Saul-also-among-the-prophets.html.

OTHER BOOKS
by Shamblin Stone

THE IMPORTANCE OF WORSHIPING TOGETHER

Why is music the most popular expression of Christian worship? Is there a biblical reason for this? In *The Importance of Worshiping Together,* author Shamblin Stone explains why it's important for Christians to worship God together with others from a biblical perspective. It explains God's reasons for unified group worship and talks about how to protect, build, and maintain human relationships so worship isn't hindered.

The Importance of Worshiping Together is the third book in a series on Christian worship. This collection of stories and Bible teachings contains how God saved Stone, transforming him from a starry-eyed performer and songwriter to a worshiper of God. It also chronicles how God taught Stone to use the power in music to bring people to Jesus, along with several extremely major miracles he has experience along his journey.

Softcover: 6x9, 188 pages, ISBN: 9781489728654
Hardcover: 6x9, 188 pages, ISBN: 9781489728647
Ebook: 188 pages, ISBN: 9781489728661

PORTRAIT OF A WORSHIPER

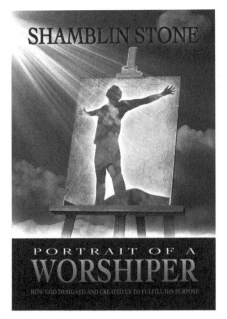

Every person who has ever lived has wrestled with the question of the purpose of human life. Stone answers that question definitively with the Word of God that mankind's purpose for existence is to be "to the praise of His/God's glory" (Ephesians 1:14). Because that is God's purpose for us, then the way God designed and created us has everything to do with us accomplishing that purpose. This book examines in detail how God made us in His likeness and image and how every part of us is necessary to accomplish God's purpose for us. The book also looks into God's redemption plan to redeem all parts of a human being so that we can fulfill the purpose for which we were created. Finally, this book explains how each part of our humanity functions when we obey God's purpose for our existence and worship Him.

Softcover: 6x9, 270 pages, ISBN: 9781973613039
Hardcover: 6x9, 270 pages, ISBN: 9781973613046
Ebook: 270 pages, ISBN: 9781973613022

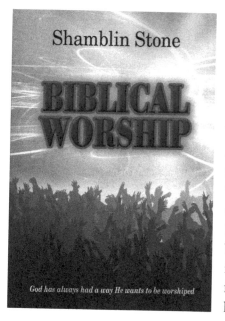

God has always had a way He wants to be worshiped. He has outlined that way for us in His written revelation—the Bible. In it, He has commanded us to worship Him with our entire being, holding nothing back. According to Jesus, this is the first and greatest commandment. The reasons God has given us for obeying His commands to worship Him are because of who He is and because of what He does. Worship is the biblically declared reason for mankind's existence. However, how and when we worship is just as important as the fact that we do worship. Also, what God means when He uses the biblical synonyms of the word "worship" is important to understand when we are trying to obtain a more complete picture of how God wants us to worship Him. *Biblical Worship* is a book for every Christian, regardless of their preferred worship style or worship traditions. The fresh, new insights contained within its pages about what type of worship God desires from us all have the potential to shock you at times. At the very least, this book will cause you to never view worship the same way again.

Softcover: 6x9, 162 pages, ISBN: 9781449737139
Hardcover: 6x9, 162 pages, ISBN: 9781449737146
Ebook: 162 pages, ISBN: 9781449737122

For More Worship Resources

go to

www.theworshipcollege.com

- FREE eight-week Bible class/Sunday School curriculum
- FREE ebook downloads
- FREE music downloads
- Books to purchase
- CDs and DVDs to purchase
- Online/video vocal training course
- The tone-deaf Challenge
- *The Worship Magazine*

9781489739919